QUICK CLICKS

2ND EDITION

Fast and Fun Behaviors to

Teach Your Dog with a Clicker

Mandy Book
Cheryl S. Smith

Dogwise™ Publishing

Wenatchee, WA

Quick Clicks, 2nd Edition
Fast and Fun Behaviors to Train Your Dog with a Clicker
Mandy Book and Cheryl S. Smith

Dogwise Publishing
A Division of Direct Book Service, Inc.
403 South Mission Street, Wenatchee, Washington 98801
509-663-9115, 1-800-776-2665
www.dogwisepublishing.com / info@dogwisepublishing.com

Graphic design: Lindsay Peternell
Cover photograph: Donn Dobkin, Just A Moment Photography
Interior photographs: Donn Dobkin, Just A Moment Photography; Cheryl Smith

ISBN 978-1-929242-76-4

Library of Congress Cataloging-in-Publication Data

Book, Mandy.

   Quick clicks : fast and fun behaviors to teach your dog with a clicker / Mandy Book and Cheryl S. Smith. -- 2nd ed.

       p. cm.

   Includes index.

   ISBN 978-1-929242-76-4

   1. Dogs--Training. 2. Clicker training (Animal training) I. Smith, Cheryl S. II. Title.

   SF431.B655 2010

   636.7'0887--dc22

                                    2010036120

Printed in the U.S.A.

DEDICATION

Many thanks to the people who participated in the completion of this book—Donn, Carol, Kay, Lena, Marjorie for the photos, and Kay and Ellen for their review of the material.

Thanks also to all the dogs who helped us fumble our way through our early stages of clicker training and brought us to this level of understanding.

TABLE OF CONTENTS

ROAD MAP

You'll notice a new format in this edition of the book. We will present the instructions in a fashion similar to our other book, *Right on Target*. You'll see two sets of instructions for most behaviors. The first set will be an outline, or streamlined, set for more experienced clicker trainers called **Speed Steps.** This is followed by a section entitled **Keep in Mind** which alerts you to training details you'll need to be aware of for the particular behavior. The **Troubleshooting** section will discuss any common (or not so common) stumbling blocks you may run into while working on the behavior. **Variations** offers some other ways to use the behavior. We'll also suggest verbal cues to use for each behavior, and sometimes visual cues.

If you need more help with breaking down the behavior, look for more detailed instructions at the end of each behavior in the **Detailed Training Plan.** The same steps are covered but with a deeper explanation to help with any difficulties you may encounter. This is especially helpful if clicker training is new for you.

Each chapter includes two types of boxes:

- **Quick Clicks** offer hints for accomplishing the behavior being trained or include important details about clicker training.

- **Slick Clicks** provide some tales of clicker training from Mandy and Cheryl, as well as some well-known names in the world of clicker training.

We'll be using a couple of abbreviations throughout the book to save space and repetition:

- "CT" stands for "click, treat" or "CT-ing" (depending on the context).

- "RF" stands for "reinforcer," which might be a treat, a toy, play or social activities.

We are no longer breaking down training into sessions, even in the Detailed Training Plan. This is because everyone will have a different training experience and people and dogs learn at different rates of speed. Just remember to keep your sessions short (one to three minutes) and to take frequent breaks. You can get a lot accomplished in three minutes!

At the back of the book you will find a Glossary of key terms bolded in the text, Resources for more information and an Index of behaviors.

Dexter (20 month old Boxer) has been clicker trained since he was 8 weeks old, is a Canine Good Citizen and preparing for a career in agility.

Chapter 1
CLICKER TRAINING BASICS

Clicker training is a simple concept—you use a sound to "mark" a desired behavior, so that you can reward it and increase the probability of it occurring again. Marking a behavior the instant it occurs allows you to deliver specific, useful information to the dog in a timely fashion. The clicker offers you the best possible timing; it actually makes it easier for the dog to learn.

You could also use a short word ("yes," "wow," "right," "bink") in place of the clicker, but our dogs hear us talk all day. The sound of the clicker is unique, something not in the dog's usual auditory environment, and the clicker doesn't carry any of the vocal shadings of our verbal communication (saying "yes" in a happy, upbeat voice versus saying "yes" through teeth clenched in frustration).

The clicker also lets you "build" a behavior by clicking and rewarding the rough beginning steps and working bit by bit toward the final, finished picture. With a clicker, you can accomplish things that would be difficult if not impossible to achieve any other way.

Because clicker training doesn't involve force, it works particularly well with fearful or insecure dogs. It can be managed by children and seniors, even with large-breed dogs. (For dogs that are fearful of the clicker, you can train using a bridge word as an alternate marker. See Chapter 5 for more information.) It's useful for breaking through problems in teaching, and for increasing attention. You can work with a dog of any age or size—eight-week-old puppy to eight-year-old adult, Italian Greyhound to Irish Wolfhound. Even deaf dogs can be clicker trained, using a light in place of a click as your marker.

But best of all, with clicker training the dog is an active partner. Instead of having training done to him or her, the dog participates actively and eagerly, and actually learns how to learn.

Slick Clicks

"I never really knew much about the finer points of dog training. I thought a bit and researched a lot, and realized that compared to electric collars and choke chains, clicker training is easier and gentler on the dog and the trainer. Once I got started on clicker training Tempo, my toy poodle, she just couldn't get enough! Tempo is sensitive and a little shy, but when I get the clicker and touch stick out now she bounces, spins, prances and wags her whole body. Working in small steps was very important to me, and I think to Tempo, too. I'm learning that if you take baby steps and listen carefully to your dog's body language you can strengthen your bond and teach her some great tricks. Tempo can touch my hand, is learning to follow the touch stick, and can 'dance' and walk on her hind legs like she's doing a cha-cha. She's not as fearful as she was before we started, either. I think this is the best method of dog training, and it is the only one I'll ever use." Mara D., age 11

The basics of CT-ing

There's nothing magic about the clicker. It's a tool, and to be effective with it, you have to learn to use it well. The three essential concepts to understand in clicker training are timing, criteria and rate of reinforcement. Any problems in your training can be traced back to problems in one of these areas. We'll take a look at each.

The basics behind clicker training are very simple. The dog does a **behavior,** you mark the behavior, you reward the behavior. Behavior that is rewarded (or reinforced) tends to increase, so you see more of the behavior. It's that simple.

First, a note about reinforcement. This is, generally speaking, a reward that the dog will work for. Clicker training tends to use a lot of treats. Treats are easy to dispense, take little time to consume (allowing you to train quickly) and are something most dogs want.

Food is a **primary reinforcer,** or RF, something the dog inherently values and desires, and will work to get or keep. Other primary RFs are water, freedom, play, sleep, and touch, though they will vary from dog to dog. Some dogs are chow hounds and others are toy nuts. The only thing that really matters is whether your dog will work for what you are offering.

The clicker is a **secondary reinforcer,** also known as a conditioned RF or a **bridge** or **marker.** It gains value by being associated with a primary RF. When you click and then treat, or smile and then pet your dog, you are "conditioning" the click or the smile to be a secondary RF. These secondary RF allow you to give the dog information about his behavior, even at a distance from the dog.

Quick Clicks: Click mix

You can make a "click mix" of treats by combining a couple of cups of your dog's usual food (if you feed a dry kibble) with some treats (the smellier the better). The treats impart some of their appeal to the kibble, and the dog never knows whether he's going to get a bit of kibble or a special treat. Don't forget to subtract the amount you use in training from the dog's daily ration.

Timing

A mis-timed click can mark a behavior entirely different from what is wanted, so **timing** is critical. We joke that our first clicker dogs needed to learn to subtract time from our very late clicks to figure out what they were actually being rewarded for. Even experienced clicker trainers can benefit from a brush-up on their timing. There's a reason that "You're late!" is the most often-heard phrase at chicken camps (See Quick Clicks: Chicken camps on next page).

The better your timing, the easier it will be for your dog to learn. Practice the following exercises without your dog, for three to five minutes at a time. Either videotape yourself for later review, or enlist a family member or a friend to give you feedback on the timing of your click.

1. Toss a tennis ball straight up, as if preparing to serve. Click when the ball is at its highest point.

2. Drop a tennis ball and click as it hits the floor. (You can actually hear if your click and the ball's "thunk" occur at the same time.)

3. Have a helper walk around, changing speed and direction often. Click each time their left heel touches the ground.

4. Watch a DVD or recorded show. Choose a behavior to "click," using your remote as the clicker to stop the action when the behavior happens. Can you still see the behavior on the screen? If not, you're too slow. Try behaviors of varying difficulty, such as looking to the right or saying a specific word.

5. Listen to the news or a talk show about the economy on the radio, and click every time anyone says a number.

The following is an exercise to work on both timing and coordination. Coordination is important because how and where you deliver each reinforcement (for example, a treat) can help or hinder your training. This exercise also helps you to practice holding still while you are clicker training—the less visual clutter, the easier it will be for your dog to grasp what you want.

Count out ten small candies or jelly beans into one hand. Put your clicker in the other hand and, deliver the candies to either a helper or into a small bowl. Set a timer for ten seconds. Start with your hands at your sides, click the clicker, and put one candy in the bowl or hand it to your helper. Put your hands at your sides again and repeat the performance. How many candies did you get rid of in ten seconds? Repeat this practice until you can deliver at least ten candies in ten seconds.

Quick Clicks: Chicken camps

Chicken camps are hands-on seminars where people learn to use clicker training to teach a variety of behaviors to chickens. Bob and Marian Bailey started the camps in Arkansas to teach trainers the art and science of clicker training. After many camps, and Marian's death, Bob retired and Terry Ryan of *Legacy Canine* took over and continues the chicken camp tradition. These camps are designed to help trainers learn the skills of good clicker training—timing, criteria setting and rate of reinforcement. (See Resources for more information on available chicken camps.)

Rate (and place) of reinforcement

While you are teaching a new behavior, every correct response (that is, every behavior meeting your **criteria,** which we discuss in the next section) will receive a click and a reward. When you are training a behavior, your **rate of reinforcement** (how many rewards the dog gets in a given time frame) has to be high. Figuring things out is hard work, and you have to make it worth your dog's effort. If you are stingy with your clicks and rewards, or don't have a clear picture of what you will be rewarding before you start, or aren't focused completely on your training, your rate of reinforcement is likely to be too low, and you will lose your dog's attention and willingness.

Where you deliver the reward can also help or hinder your efforts. Try this experiment.

Take a handful of treats and stand in the middle of a boring room (no toys or other distractions). Wait for your dog to sit (without telling him to). Each time your dog sits, drop a treat on the floor next to you. Do this for three (thirty second to one minute) sessions, one after another. What is your dog choosing to do, and where is he choosing to do it? Now toss the treat away from you each time the dog sits, to the same spot on the floor every time. Repeat this for three sessions. Now where is your dog choosing to sit? The location of your reward matters. We'll discuss this in detail with specific behaviors.

If the treat is tossed close by, the dog will sit nearby. If it's regularly tossed farther away, the dog begins to sit farther out.

Criteria

You can't train if you don't know what you want. Some behaviors are so simple you can just CT the complete behavior (a Sit). For more complex behaviors, you need to break the behavior down into a series of small steps that look increasingly like the end behavior (termed "shaping"). Being able to work in small steps is one of the major advantages of clicker training, but most people need help with breaking the behaviors down into achievable steps, and deciding when to move on to the next step.

Think of it this way. You have to climb to the top of the Empire State Building. If you take your time, rest when you have to, and don't care if the trip takes more than an hour, you'll probably make it. But if you try to sprint to the top, skipping every other stair, you'll probably collapse and give up before you get to the top. It's the same with training. Trying to take steps too big too quickly (called "lumping") will ultimately result in failure.

The other extreme will also work against you. Back at the Empire State Building, if you rested five minutes after every two steps, the observation deck would close while you were still on your way to the top. Staying too long at the same criteria can convince your dog that it's the final behavior, and make it difficult to move on to the next step. Or, you may break a behavior down into tiny steps (called "splitting"), but your dog progresses through three or four of your steps in one jump. If you don't evaluate and make changes to your plan as you proceed, you can stall out your training and confuse the dog.

Quick Clicks: Lumpers and splitters
Your authors complement each other in the criteria area. Mandy is an excellent splitter, carefully breaking behaviors down, but sometimes staying too long at one step. Cheryl is a lumper, pushing to take bigger steps and living on the edge. We tend to balance each other—a good reason to train with a partner.

A practice behavior
Therefore, learn to break down behavior (it's a valuable skill) and always start your training with a plan, but be willing to adjust that plan as you go.

Let's use the behavior Spin in a Circle for practice. You're not teaching your dog the behavior, you're practicing breaking a behavior down as a written exercise. This practice is for you.

The end behavior is the dog spins in a complete circle to the left. Where would you start? Take a moment to write down the steps you think you would take to train this.

How many steps did you decide on? Your dog might need as few as four, but you need to be prepared with more in case the process doesn't move so quickly. Ten steps is always a good minimum starting point. We'll specify the ten we came up with in a moment. First, let's look at your first step. Was it something like "take a step to the left?" That would be a typical thought, but what are you going to do if your dog just stands and stares at you? Maybe "turn head to the left" would work. But maybe not. You might have to make your steps even finer. Here is our sample ten-step plan.

1. Eye flick to the left.

2. Head turn to the left.

3. One step to the left.

4. One quarter turn to the left.

5. Halfway between one quarter turn and one half turn to the left.

6. Dog turns body halfway to the left, until he is facing in the opposite direction.

7. Halfway between one half turn and three quarter turn to the left.

8. Three quarter turn to the left.

9. Dog turns most of the way in a circle to the left.

10. Dog completes spinning in a circle to the left.

This may seem like a lot of work, but a couple of aspects of clicker training make it go quickly. First, you will CT the criteria you've decided on for a step ("eye flick to the left" for your first session) *or anything better than your criteria for that step.* You would also click a head turn to the left or a step to the left if you see that. For this session (only ten clicks and treats), you would still click an eye flick if that was all you got—you don't change your criteria in the middle of a session. But if you were getting a step to the left for the majority of repetitions, you might want to make that your step for the next session (jumping over our Step 2 of a head turn). To summarize, you click anything at that level or better for the criteria step, but re-evaluate if most of the responses are "or better."

Second, a session should take less than a minute (remember your timing practice from earlier?) and you might only need one session at a particular step. Even if you had to use all ten steps and repeat several of them because the dog was not ready to move on, that would still total less than fifteen minutes of actual training time.

Real-time training of this behavior might go something like this. You have your clicker and treats, with your dog standing in front of you. The dog stares at you for a while, but then looks away. You CT. (Deliver the treat to the side of the dog's head to help speed along the behavior.) That makes the dog stare at you some more, but then he glances away again. You CT. You repeat this ten times. Most of those repetitions (at least 80%) involve a glance away and three of the repetitions involve a definite head turn. Take a ten-second break and reload your hand with treats.

You may have to start with an eye flick away from you as your first step for "spin in a circle."

Now you're going to move to Step 2, so you won't click a glance any more, you'll wait for a head turn. (We'll discuss in a moment how to decide to move on to the next step or repeat the step you are working on.) It might be a tiny movement or a full "look to the left"—you'll click them both. CT ten times, take another ten-second break, and move on to Step 3. Take a longer break of a few minutes after three to five steps—you and your dog will both need it. When you start another session, begin at the step where you left off. It's a good idea to jot a note of where you stop, especially if you're training multiple behaviors or multiple dogs.

If in a particular session the dog never gives you the behavior you've specified for that step (never "meets criteria"), then your step was too big. Stop training, sit down, and figure out some additional steps to insert into your training plan. Trying to take steps that are too large is one of the most common reasons for problems in clicker training. Often, your dog will let you know you've asked for too much by shutting down (leaving the area or lying down) or acting silly (barking or jumping around). If you experience this a lot, practice breaking down behaviors on paper (we've done it for you throughout the book), and see the sections on crossover trainers and dogs and warm-up exercises.

One of the places beginners struggle with clicker training is when to move on to the next step in the training plan. Not to worry, though, as there is a rule of thumb to use (based on the Baileys' experience with training a variety of species). When the dog reaches your criteria 80% of the time, move to the next step. That means if the dog was clicked and treated eight out of ten attempts, you can move on. There are small variations in number depending on individual dogs and whether you are at the start or end of the behavior plan, but that 80% rule will hold up the majority of the time. But you'll need to keep track of things in order to use it!

Keep in mind that a dog may do more than 80% at each step, even though you are moving on to the next step every ten treats. This gives you important information, namely that you have broken the steps down more finely than your dog needs for that behavior. You may find that to be the case when you work with our training plans in this book, as every dog is an individual. If you're not confident about modifying the plan then just keep moving to the next step as long as the dog is working at 80% *or better*. You may progress a little more slowly than you could have, but you will still get there. It won't ultimately affect the final behavior. But don't stall out—make sure you move up to the next level when the dog is successful at least 80% of the time. You'll notice in many of the plans that we move very quickly through the first few steps, sometimes only repeating a step three times. This will happen more often as the dog (and you) gain experience in clicker training.

There can also be a tendency to skip steps because the dog does one brilliant leap forward. An example of this happened with Mandy while she was working on Sit Pretty (Sit Up). The dog she was training sat up for an extended period when she was at the start of the behavior. Does that mean she should skip the steps where the dog has to learn to pull her front end up, stay seated, and balance? Probably not. On the other hand, if the dog offered a long, steady Sit Up repeatedly during an early training session, it would definitely be Mandy's cue to stop and evaluate the training plan to see whether shaping steps could be skipped.

It's important to be clear in your definition of the behavior, both to decide how to break it apart for shaping, and to be able to recognize it in its final form. In which of the pictures on the next page is the dog walking nicely on leash? It's up to you to decide exactly what you want the behavior to look like. Think about it. Write it down. Then, be sure that you don't reward something less than what you've defined as acceptable criteria for that level of behavior. For example, if we were trying to increase the number of steps that the dog walks nicely on leash, we have to count only when the dog is where we've determined our range of "walking nicely" to be. Pulling on the leash doesn't count, obviously, but what about if the dog is a little forward of your leg? How precise are your requirements? The important thing is for you to decide, and then to *be consistent* about what you will accept as your minimum level of criteria. Do not proceed unless you have a clear idea what the next level of rewardable behavior will be. As you gain experience, you'll be able to do this rapidly, but in the beginning, refer to your step plan frequently.

Everyone would agree that Bernie is walking nicely in the first photo, but not the second. But what about the third or fourth? It's up to you to define what you want, and it's important that you decide before you start working.

Crossover dogs and crossover trainers

If you're a brand new trainer with a brand new dog, and you're starting off with clicker training, congratulations. You and your dog have a lot of fun training time ahead. However, a lot of you reading this may be crossing over from some other form of training. A person who has learned to train in a traditional way (whether that means using food to lure behaviors, or with a choke chain and a leash) and now wants to clicker train is called a crossover trainer. In general, **crossover trainers:**

- Find it difficult to let go of control of the behavior (letting the dog figure it out is a challenge for them).

- Have a tendency to fall back on what worked in the past (resorting to luring or corrections if the dog isn't figuring things out quickly enough).

- Assign motivation to the dog's behavior ("he's blowing me off").

Crossover dogs have been taught to wait for instructions by the nature of their previous training. They don't tend to offer behaviors in the absence of lures or prompts. They wait to be told what to do. You'll have to teach the dog how to learn and respond differently. Right now she's waiting for you to show her what to do because that's what she's experienced her whole life. The hardest step for her will be learning to offer behaviors. Do the Warm up exercises over and over until your dog starts doing lots of silly things when you pick up the clicker. Don't worry about actually training a behavior until you have a dog who offers behaviors freely.

Quick Clicks: Teaching a bridge word

Some crossover trainers struggle with clickers. While not as precise, you can teach your dog a bridge word by pairing treats with the word as an alternative to clicking. The word needs to be one syllable and something that you will say in more or less the same way every time. Choose a word that you don't use in normal conversation. Some ideas include, "Yes," "Right," "Yep," "Beep," or "Click." Say the word, and give the dog a treat. (You don't want to telegraph that a treat is coming or the dog won't pay attention to the word.) Repeat several times. Change locations and continue practicing in different locations over the course of several days. When the dog's eyes "pop" when he hears the word, you'll know that it has been conditioned as a secondary reinforcer for the dog. You can now use the bridge word instead of the clicker for behaviors that do not need a more precise marker. The bridge word is also a useful tool to have if you don't happen to have your clicker handy. Remember, you will not get the precision of a clicker, but for some behaviors a bridge word will do fine. In the instructions, we'll indicate that you should mark the behavior, which means to *either* click or bridge (not both).

Warm up exercises

The first thing you need to teach a dog, if you want to use clicker training, is to try different things rather than standing around waiting to be told what to do. This is especially important for crossover dogs and trainers.

Show the dog that you have a treat. Wait patiently for the dog to do something. . . anything! Impatient for the treat to be given, the dog may back up, lift a paw, stand up, or any of a dozen other actions. CT the dog for any random action.

Quick Clicks: You get what you click
Though we say to click for any action, you probably want to avoid objectionable actions, such as barking at you or jumping up on you. You should also try to avoid clicking a Down, Sit or Looking at you. If you spend too much time rewarding these stationary behaviors, you may have difficulty when you later want movement from your dog.

Now wait again, but this time CT for a *different* action. (If your dog is really stuck, and having a hard time, you could CT the same action up to three times, but try to move on as quickly as possible.) Repeat this another four or five times, CT-ing a different action each time. Take a break and repeat at a later time. Do this exercise as often as you like to keep the dog offering fresh responses when you take out the clicker.

Another fun warm-up exercise is to clicker train a silly behavior using a canvas bag. (If you don't have such a bag, use a pillow case, a blanket, a towel, whatever you have available.) Put the bag in the middle of the room. Click and treat the first ten behaviors the dog does with the bag, regardless of what they are. Take a five-minute break. Try it again—you want the dog to get the idea that "fooling around," offering different behaviors, gets rewarded. Repeat as often as you like.

Hand Touch

Now let's work a bit on training an actual behavior, to get a better idea of how some of these concepts come together. Hand Touch is called a "target" behavior because you're using your hand as a target for the dog. You'll need your dog, clicker and treats. Before you start, write down the steps you think you would need to get the dog from where he is today (no interest in your hand) to your end goal of touching the palm of your hand, or even following the hand as it's moving.

Here are the first few steps you might use:

1. CT the dog for looking at your hand.

2. CT the dog for leaning forward toward your hand.

3. CT the dog for touching anywhere on your hand.

Okay, let's begin the training, keeping in mind that you might have to add more steps if your dog needs more help. Remember that this is practice for both of you, so don't worry too much about results. Think of this exercise as a *learning experience.*

Bring your dog into a boring room. Gather five treats (in a bowl, on the counter or in a training bag on your hip or in your pocket). Hold the clicker in one hand, and put your other hand out at the dog's nose level, with your palm facing the dog, about a foot in front of his nose.

Hold the clicker in one hand and put your other hand out at nose level, palm facing the dog. (The visual cues for stay and touch look similar to the dog, that's why we favor a verbal cue in addition to a visual cue for Touch.)

CT when he looks at the hand, then put your hand behind your back. Put it again in front of the dog's nose at the same distance, CT when he looks at it, put it away. Repeat five times total (no more, or the dog may think this is all he needs to do).

Remember, you are working on your timing and learning how to shape. Try to click exactly when the dog looks at your hand. If he touches your hand before you click, you were too slow (but you'll still give the dog a treat anyway—he shouldn't suffer for your mistakes). It won't matter too much for this behavior, but it will for others later on. Practice your timing. And don't forget—don't reach for a treat until after you have clicked.

Now it's time to "up the ante," that is, move to the next step. Just looking at the hand won't work any more. The dog has to try harder to get his CT. Working in the same room, reload your treats. Now offer your hand in exactly the same place in front of the dog's nose, but don't click when he looks at it. Wait patiently until he moves his head forward a bit, then CT. Repeat up to five times, removing the target hand each time after you've clicked. Time the click with the forward movement of the dog's head. If you're slow, he might think he's supposed to be moving his head *away* from your hand.

Quick Clicks: Where to hold the clicker

Be careful where you hold the clicker. Clicking with it right next to your dog's ear can be an unpleasant experience for him. He'll hear it just fine with the clicker held at your side (and you'll be less likely to be moving and "telegraphing" your intention to click). You also don't have to aim the clicker at the dog as if it were a remote control.

Working in the same room, reload your treats. Offer your hand, but now wait for the dog to actually bump it with his nose, anywhere on the hand. CT the touch, repeating up to five times. Try to anticipate when the dog will touch, so you time your click exactly when you feel the wetness of his nose on your hand. If you can anticipate, and are *ready* to click when the dog touches, your timing should be dead on.

Congratulations! You have just clicker trained your first behavior. Take a break and evaluate how you and your dog did. Would you need additional steps for your dog (in other words, did he follow along with the book)? Could you have clicked and treated only three times at each level instead of five? Did the dog immediately touch the hand when it was offered, skipping the first two steps? Did he wander off or look at a bug on the floor because the steps were too big for him and he wasn't getting clicked very much? This is all good information, as it will help you to know how many steps your dog might need for other behaviors, and how long you might stay at each one. (If you want to complete the Nose Touch behavior, full instructions are in Chapter 6.)

Another way to get behaviors

If you attended a puppy kindergarten class, you probably taught your pup to sit by using a food treat (a "lure") held over his head to get him to look up and put his rear on the ground. This process is called **"lure training," "luring"** or **"lure and reward."** You may have found it really easy, and might be wondering why we haven't suggested it until now. We wanted you to start with a little **shaping** (breaking behaviors into small steps to reward) to experience how the dog can learn on his own. But using a lure to give the dog a clue can often help get the dog jump started on the first step of a behavior. Some clicker trainers insist that you should never use a lure to get a behavior. Practical dog owners will probably find many situations where using a lure is helpful.

There will be times when shaping will work better and other times when luring might be preferable. In generally, luring is best when you know it is unlikely the dog will start the behavior on his own, or if you are having trouble getting started on the first step. If you wanted to shape "drinking water," for example, you might have to wait a very long time for the dog to approach the water bowl. And you would probably only be able to click it once before the dog stopped doing it. But by dropping a treat in the water bowl, you can quickly get some drinking behavior, which can be clicked and treated, and repeated.

Luring is also good for shy or sensitive dogs, who tend to shut down and give up if they are not quickly successful. Some initial lure training will help to build their confidence. Keep in mind that a lure can be anything that gets the behavior, like using a treat, a toy, a target or another behavior to start your training.

But using a lure has two major disadvantages. For many behaviors, you'll want to eventually get rid of the lure. After all, you want the dog to perform the behavior whether or not you happen to be carrying any treats. Because luring is easy, people tend to hold onto lures for far too long, making the process of fading or weaning off the lure difficult. Second, using a lure will keep your dog in the mode of waiting for you to show him what you want. It will be a crutch. If you really want your dog to start thinking and participating in the training process, avoid using a lot of lures in your training in the early stages.

If you do choose to use a lure, here are some important considerations to keep in mind to make your luring effective:

- Don't tease the dog with the lure. If you use a food treat or toy to lure, the dog needs to get it when he does the behavior or step of behavior you're looking for.

- Food and toy lures should be used sparingly, usually in the beginning stages of a behavior. A good rule of thumb is to use the lure three to five times, then wait and see what the dog does without it.

- You will still be CT-ing, even if you are using a lure. The lure just gets you the behavior; you still have to mark it and reward the dog for doing that step.

- If the lure seems to be interfering with the behavior, try shaping instead.

Shaping may sometimes start more slowly than luring a behavior, but not always. Some simple behaviors, such as shaking hands, can be shaped very quickly. Even if you do find shaping slower initially, you won't have to spend time later getting rid of a lure. For a treat-focused dog easily distracted by a piece of food waving in front of him, shaping is definitely the better choice for most behaviors. And you will learn a lot more about the clicker training process through shaping without lures.

In our individual behavior instructions, we sometimes start with luring and sometimes shape from the very beginning. If shaping isn't working for you, try luring a few times. If we suggest a lure, and you find it isn't working (the lure is too distracting, or the dog seems to be dependent on it), shape the behavior instead. Remember that our instructions are just one way to get a behavior, not the only way.

Naming behaviors (cueing)

Before you can move on to a new behavior, you need to name the one you've already taught. Naming (adding a cue) teaches the dog to discriminate between different behaviors. Without the naming of behaviors, you will end up with a dog who performs an amazing array of actions, in no particular order, whenever you bring out your clicker. Cues, by the way, can be verbal or visual. When we say a behavior is "named" we mean that the dog does it when given a cue, whatever type of cue that may be.

If you continued teaching the Hand Touch, when is it ready to be named? When the dog will touch your hand most of the time, regardless of how you orient it, when it's almost as fast and sustained as you want it to be, and when you can predict that the dog will do it fairly reliably.

Slick Clicks: Advice from Bob Bailey, training guru

"Marian (my wife) and I teach the 80% rule. If you are training a behavior that will be cued, you get the behavior to the point that about 80% of the time it is given just as you want. That is when the cue goes on. Most trainers don't wait long enough (behavior too weak or imperfect) and they lose behavior, or wait too long (behavior is virtually 100% for a while) and there is a lot of extinction required, slowing down the installation of the cue. Certainly, what you don't want to do is train a behavior to the point of fluency before the cue is started. There is nothing magical about 80%. 73% is pretty good too, as is 84%. What you don't want is to be adding cues when the behavior is at 50-60% (too soon) or at 95-100% (too late)."

By the way, the Brelands came up with the 80% rule in the late '40s. Much later, the laboratory types discovered that, lo and behold, a lab rat fully trained is slower to adapt to a new signal than a less well-trained rat—surprise! Just another example of how early field work with animals was often far ahead of the much more restricted applications in the lab.

To add the cue, at your next training session, just before the dog touches your hand, say "Touch" or "Bonk" (or whatever cue tickles your fancy—remember, dogs don't know English, so the word doesn't have to mean something, but you do have to remember it). CT when he does it. Repeat the sequence of cue-behavior-click-treat about fifty to sixty times over a period of several days. Next, you will teach the dog to only do the behavior when cued. To do this, every ten touches or so, don't say "Touch" when you put your hand out, and don't click the dog if he touches. At first, the dog won't be paying much attention to what you're saying. But gradually he'll figure out that if you say something just before he touches and he does it, he gets a CT and if you don't say anything, he doesn't get anything. Your verbalization starts to become meaningful when the dog realizes that it predicts a CT if he does the behavior. Eager to get his reward, he'll do the behavior when he hears the cue. In this case, the only cue is the verbal "Touch." Holding your hand out is not relevant to whether the dog gets a treat. Holding your hand out is not a cue for the dog, although you can make it one, if you like.

Quick Clicks: Cue words

Put some thought into the words you choose as cues. "Down" can often become a problem because people use it when dogs jump up and they want the dog to stay off them, or when they want dogs to get off furniture. To keep English effective in communicating with dogs, words should have one meaning and one meaning only. If you think "Down" is likely to be misused to indicate things other than "put your body on the ground," choose another word.

When you start to see that the dog does nothing when you say nothing, but touches when you say "Touch," you'll know he's starting to understand that the cue tells him to do something specific. Now you can say the cue gradually earlier and earlier, so it's not just being said directly before you think he'll do the behavior, but far enough in advance that the dog does it because you said the cue.

At this point, you can alternate your cue "Touch" with another cue the dog knows well (such as "Sit") and with not giving any cue at all. CT only when the dog performs a behavior that matches the cue you have given. Don't click if he offers a Hand Touch or sit when you have not given the appropriate cue, or if he does something else.

The same process is used to add a visual cue to a behavior, or to combine a visual with a verbal cue.

If you're wondering why we don't just use a cue right from the start of training (as much traditional training does), there are several good reasons. First, you don't have a focused "final picture" of a behavior for the dog when you start training. Though the Hand Touch may take only a few sessions to complete, a more complicated behavior such as a retrieve could take several weeks of working step by step to get the finished behavior. We want the dog to associate the cue only with the final, perfected behavior.

Verbal and visual information is more meaningful to the dog if you have been quiet throughout the initial training. He will be naturally more inclined to pay more attention when you do say something or use a hand signal. It will be easier to associate a specific word or hand gesture with a particular behavior.

Finally, telling the dog the cue does not help him learn how to do it. Telling you "perform open heart surgery" isn't going to let you actually do it without some serious and prolonged training. And you probably consider yourself smarter than your dog.

This is yet another reason to be still when you train. If you move around a lot during your training, the dog may think that your movement is relevant to the behavior he is supposed to do. After you think you have the behavior trained, the dog may not perform it if you stand still and don't make the same movements you made during training. It will also distract his attention from the verbal cue you are trying to attach to the behavior. Have someone watch you, or tape yourself, to make sure you aren't, for example, reaching for a treat before you click, or pointing at something you want the dog to touch, without being aware of it. Such unintentional body language can interfere with the dog's learning, or even prevent him from learning an appropriate signal for the behavior. You can reach for the treat after the click—the small time delay does not generally matter.

Avoid pointing at something you want the dog to touch. Notice that Ping's focus is on the finger, not the target.

A behavior can have more than one cue—we often use a verbal cue and a visual cue (such as a hand signal). But each cue should mean only one thing. A common example of trying to use one cue to mean multiple things (usually unintentionally) is "Down." People often tell the dog "Down" when they mean "Don't jump up." Then they expect the dog to lie down the next time they say "Down." This doesn't work. For dogs, cues should mean one and only one thing, although you can have more than one cue for a behavior, such as a hand signal and a word for "Down."

Having both verbal cues and visual cues for behaviors can prove useful. There might be a time when you are in noisy surroundings and would have to shout to be heard, or you might be some distance from the dog and don't want to yell. You can use hand signals in such cases. For older dogs losing their hearing, or for deaf dogs, hand signals are invaluable, and the only option you have. But there could also be times when your arms are full of grocery bags (or otherwise occupied) but you need to direct the dog to do something. Now your verbal cue becomes really helpful. In some competitive dog events, you are restricted in whether you can use a verbal or a visual cue for the performance of a behavior.

You also need to have a cue that lets the dog know he can stop doing the behavior. You can't just leave him in a Down-Stay forever! Choose a release word. "Okay" is a common choice, but it tends to come up in conversation and can release your dog when you didn't mean to.

Quick Clicks: Release word suggestions

A release word tells the dog he is done for the moment, that he no longer has to do the behavior. Some suggestions for a release word are "Release," "All done," "Free," or "Go." ("Okay" is also commonly used, although we don't recommend it.) If a release is new to your dog, you'll have to teach him what it means. Say your release cue, then make him move—tickle him, pat your thigh, make a sound, jump around. Do something different to make the dog move each time so the word is the cue, not what you are doing. If you use your release word consistently, the dog will begin to wait for it—you're on your way to teaching a Stay!

Using punishment

Punishment is either doing something unpleasant (a yank on a choke collar, called positive punishment) or removing something pleasant (leaving when the puppy bites you too hard, called negative punishment), which *decreases a behavior.*

Shouting out the door at the dog to stop barking could actually be a reinforcement for your dog. If he craves your attention and you ignore him until he barks, he will bark more to get your attention. Punishment, like reinforcement, is based on the dog's point of view.

Punishment has side effects. You can unintentionally create a fearful or aggressive response toward a particular person or in particular circumstances. The dog may learn to discriminate, that is, cease doing a behavior only when you're around. (Consider the human behavior of driving slowly when a police car is in sight and returning to speeding once it has departed.) Punishment can result in a "shut-down" dog, one fearful of doing any behavior in case punishment may follow. This certainly isn't what you want in a clicker dog!

We are not fans of punishment, especially positive punishment, as a training methodology. It has been demonstrated to be extremely detrimental to and conflicts with what we are trying to accomplish in clicker training. The reason we bring it up is that there may be times when you need to use negative punishment (taking away something the dog likes) during training. An example might be when the dog becomes overexcited and barks instead of working, or is distracted by other things in the environment. Rather than shouting at or correcting the dog, you can simply interrupt the training session. It can be as brief as turning your back on the dog or more sophisticated by pretending to talk on the phone (thus taking your attention away from the dog and offering no chance of a reward). In our opinion, though, if this is happening often you need to reevaluate your shaping plan!

The less you use this tool, the less forceful it needs to be. Dogs who are used to being rewarded can find a momentary break from your attention (less than thirty seconds) quite upsetting, because the opportunity to get rewarded is gone. It's important to understand this because humans often let "life" interrupt their dog's training sessions. You could unintentionally be teaching the dog that you aren't fun to work with.

And please, don't ever punish your dog by doing something unpleasant to him while he is learning. Learning is tiring (and sometimes frustrating), and the dog should be able to stop and get a drink, or just lie down in the middle of a session without being punished.

Quick Clicks: Laws of learning
The acquisition of behavior for all animals (including humans) is guided by these main principles of learning, sometimes called the "Laws of Learning:"
- If a behavior is rewarded, it is likely to increase.
- If a behavior is not rewarded, it is likely to decrease.
- Once learned, if a behavior is randomly rewarded, it increases rapidly and can become obsessive.
- If a behavior is associated with a disagreeable experience, it decreases rapidly and can be extinguished.

Variations in behavior
As you become more expert on the use of the clicker, you'll probably find that you want to modify different pieces of a behavior, or even go back and fix some behaviors that don't look quite the way you want them to. How a behavior looks is called the **topography** of a behavior. For example, how high a dog reaches with his paw when he shakes, as well as how fast he moves his paw and how hard he touches with it, is part of the topography of the Shake. The **duration** of a behavior is how long the animal does it, such as how long the dog holds his nose on your hand when he touches. The **latency** or **speed of response** is how quickly the dog begins the performance after getting his cue, such as beginning the process of sitting immediately upon hearing the word "Sit."

You can change the dimensions of a behavior easily with a clicker, but there are a couple of things to keep in mind. First, change only one dimension at a time. If you want the dog to respond more quickly when you say "Sit," don't try to change how the sit looks during the same session. Think of each dimension as a corner of a rubber band stretched into a triangular shape. As you make changes to one corner, the other corners have to give a bit. When you have one piece looking the way you want, you can work on another piece. You will gradually improve all three "corners" bit by bit over several sessions.

Second, break apart any chain of behavior to work on the piece you need to fix separately. If you are trying to get the dog to sit straight in front of you, don't leave the dog, call him to you, then try to get a straight sit. Instead, work on your sit with the dog directly in front of you until it looks the way you want it to. Then, add it back into your chain bit by bit. Have the dog come to you from gradually increasing distances to a straight Sit, until you have the distance you need. Then, leave the dog, call him, and get your straight Sit.

"Twofers" are a way to introduce variability into a behavior to change a dimension of the behavior. They should only be used for a couple of sessions (ten to twenty repetitions) to avoid the dog thinking this is the next step of the behavior. If you are teaching a touch behavior, for example, CT the dog for doing two or three touches instead of clicking the initial touch. As you do this, look for the longer touches on your hand. These are the repetitions that will get clicked in the next session, to start building duration. The change in duration for this behavior is going to be in quarter-second durations, so you'll have to practice looking for these slightly longer touches. Twofers can be used to introduce variability in speed, duration, or other aspects of performance of a behavior.

Variations in behavior are a necessary part of shaping. You won't be able to go to the next level of criteria if the dog does the exact same thing every time. You can, and should, plan for variation, as it's one way to get the dimensions of speed, intensity, or duration of a behavior. Unplanned, or unanticipated, variations can throw your whole behavior in a different direction, however. Once you have a finished behavior, you don't want variation.

Adding duration (aka Bouncing Around or Bouncing Around an average)

Important: This is a key concept in successfully accomplishing your training goals. We will be using it frequently throughout the book. Be sure you understand it and know how to put it into practice.

Bouncing Around is used when you want to increase the amount of time the dog is doing the behavior (such as on a Stay) or how far he goes before each reward (such as on a Heel). Increasing distance or time (called duration) on a behavior is one of the more difficult aspects of a behavior to modify. It requires good timing, and a clear idea of what you will be clicking. You need to "Bounce Around an average" rather than simply making the behavior continually more challenging. This unpredictability will keep the dog working much better than if he sees the work always getting harder and harder for the same amount of "pay."

If you don't consciously plan what you are going to reward, you are likely to unconsciously fall into a rhythm. And if you always, however unconsciously, ask for the same duration of a behavior, you will teach the dog that that's as long as he ever needs to do it. You'll then have trouble if you want to increase duration.

While you are training a new behavior that needs to be done for an extended amount of time or distance, delay the CT for one count (a count can be one second or one step forward). After ten repetitions at a one-count delay, extend the delay to two counts. Work up a count at a time until you can delay the CT for about five counts. Now you can begin your "bouncing." Back off a couple of counts from your maximum—so if your highest count was five, your average will start at three. Now vary each time how long the dog has to maintain the behavior before you click, staying around your average of three. A session might go like this:

- Dog holds behavior for count of three, CT.
- Dog holds behavior for count of one, CT.
- Dog holds behavior for count of three, CT.
- Dog holds behavior for count of two, CT.
- Dog holds behavior for count of six, CT.
- Dog holds behavior for count of three, CT.
- Dog holds behavior for count of two, CT.
- Dog holds behavior for count of three, CT.
- Dog holds behavior for count of four, CT.
- Dog holds behavior for count of three, CT.

For ten repetitions, the dog held the count an average of three (thirty total count divided by ten). Most repetitions should be at the low end of your numbers. We encourage you to write down how long you are going to count on each repetition so you don't fall into a pattern.

As your next step, you increase the average. Your average will now be four. Figure out how many repetitions you will do (no more than ten) and what the count will be at each repetition.

If the dog stops the behavior before you get to the number you were counting to for that repetition, reset the count—don't click for less than what you planned on initially. If you find as you increase the average count that the dog is less successful (he's not getting clicked at least 80% of the time because he stops the behavior before you get to your count), just stay at a lower average for another step or two and build up your average more slowly. This is a place where the art of training comes in, figuring how much and how fast to move up so you can add time without losing the dog.

With this method, the dog never knows how long he may be asked to continue a behavior. You will find it much easier to accomplish whatever duration you may need.

When using the Bouncing Around technique, people often fall into a couple of traps that weaken this otherwise powerful tool. Often, they will use the same count over and over, or a few numbers repeatedly, rather than actually varying their counts around the average. Humans are truly creatures of habit. One helpful way to prevent this is to write a ten-click sequence in large black letters on poster board or a wipe-off message board and put it on the wall directly in front of where you are training. You can start each set at any point in the group of ten and have a fairly random pattern. Be sure to increase your average when the dog is correctly meeting criteria 80% of the time. (An easy way to do this is just to add one or two to each of your set of ten repetitions listed.) Another way to solve this is to write your numbers on a set of cards and just flip through them, or have a friend hold a new one up after every repetition. (This might be a little slower, but it will help ensure that you are being random.) Another option is to use a counter to click off the number of steps or the count each time. After ten repetitions, divide your total number by ten and you'll have the average count. You'll still need to practice a bit with the other two suggestions to be sure you are being random.

A second common error is to lower your criteria if the dog doesn't meet it. Say you're working on Sit-Stay, and, for the current repetition, you are going to count to seven, then CT if the dog is still sitting. At six, the dog breaks. Most people will then immediately lower their count to four or five. Instead, reset the dog and count again to seven. It's possible that the dog may fail to meet the criteria again. If it happens several times in a row, you should definitely stop and evaluate whether you need to lower your average. But, if you've been carefully increasing your average when the dog meets criteria 80% of the time, this usually won't be necessary. When the dog makes a mistake, he is learning from that as well, and experienced dogs won't be put off by not getting clicked every time.

Working at a distance

The clicker is an excellent tool for building behaviors at a distance from you. It allows you to mark, with precision, exactly what you want without having to be directly next to the dog to provide your reward. If you've trained a behavior in close proximity and want to build distance from the dog, shape it the way you would any other criteria. Start close to the dog and add a few steps of distance every four or five repetitions. (You can use Bouncing Around very effectively, as well.) A solid "Wait" will help the dog understand he is not to follow you as you move away. You can also work the dog on a mat or a platform to define the area he is to remain in for him. (Our other book, *Right on Target,* has instructions for this and other uses for the behavior.) Being able to have the dog catch a tossed treat will also help encourage him to stay put.

Fluency

Fluency is what makes you say "Gee, that is a *well*-trained dog!" It means that the dog performs the behavior with precision and speed, immediately upon being given the cue, and only when cued. The behavior has been added to his repertoire of behaviors. When behaviors are fluent, the dog can perform them regardless of what else is going on (they are distraction proof) and will do them with a minimum of reward (they are extinction proof) in any environment (they are generalized). It's similar to learning to speak another language. You can generally understand a fair bit of Spanish before you can speak it yourself—you're not yet fluent in it, it's not second nature. Training to fluency means the dog has mastered the behavior—he can "speak the language." The games we suggest in this section can help your dog master fluency of a behavior. Remember, when training to fluency, you can only modify one dimension of the behavior at a time. As the dog becomes more fluent, all of the different aspects of the behavior will improve.

Improving latency

Latency, you may recall, is the time it takes a dog to respond to a given cue (as opposed to the time it takes for him to complete the behavior). A dog that has a very short latency to cues is well on his way to being fluent. You can improve latency on any behavior following the directions below.

Do three repetitions of a behavior that your dog knows well, CT-ing after each repetition. Note the dog's average response time from when you give the cue to the beginning of his response to it. (This is likely to be a very short amount of time, so it might be handy to have a helper time his response for you.) Set your maximum response time to the longest of the three repetitions. This time will be your "limited hold"—which means that after this amount of time, the treat is no longer available even if the dog does respond.

Now cue the behavior ten times, but CT only the responses that are less than your limited hold time. You'll have to do this with a bit of intuition, since you won't be able to ask your helper with the timer and still click in a timely manner. (It can help to count "one-ba-na-na" as each syllable is about a quarter of a second.) Some of your clicks might be wrong, but don't worry about it. You're looking for an overall pattern of faster responses to your cue. If the dog does not respond within the maximum time allotted, turn away and eat his treat (or just pretend to) or release him with no reward. Then re-cue him. If the dog gives an unusually fast response to your cue, heap on the verbal praise and petting, as well as the treats.

Remember, you are CT-ing for starting his response to your cue, not for completing the behavior. You will probably find that the behavior itself deteriorates a bit. If you're clicking the dog for a fast response to "Down," he will be clicked when he starts to perform it, before he actually completes the Down. At other sessions, work on fast completion of the down so you don't lose the behavior (see next subsection).

Speed drills

The object of speed drills is to maintain precision while building behaviors that are completed quickly, gradually getting faster and faster with each repetition. Before you start speed drills, the behaviors you are working on should look the way you want them to and be on a random schedule of reinforcement (see Chapter 8 for more information on reinforcement schedules). In other words, you're not CT-ing every single response.

Start with one behavior. Using a manual counter (one that doesn't make noise) or having a helper count, cue the behavior over and over, noting how many times your dog does it during your set time frame (we'll start with a short amount of time, ten to fifteen seconds). Let's say you decide to work on Sit. Cue "Sit," then release, "Sit," release, for fifteen seconds. How many times did the dog Sit during that time? Write it down. This is your baseline. For the next set of trials, CT the fastest completed sits during the fifteen-second time, dropping the treat on the floor to get the dog up and reset for the next repetition. For this drill, remember we are clicking the fast *completion* of a Sit, not the response to your cue as before (although how fast the dog responds to the cue will also impact how many behaviors he does in a given time frame). In other words, you're clicking him for getting his rear on the floor quickly.

Try to increase the number of Sits for each fifteen-second session, gradually building up to the maximum number the dog is physically capable of doing. Take a break between sessions. If your dog makes an error or doesn't respond to the cue, wait a moment, and then re-cue. If this happens repeatedly, or if the behavior deteriorates, stop working speed trials and go back and solidify the behavior.

Keep track of your progress. For example, say the first time you do this, you are able to get six sits in fifteen seconds. Try for eight behaviors in the same time frame, then eleven, and so on. When you get to the maximum you think your dog can do in fifteen seconds, up the time to twenty seconds. Continue to build rapid-fire responses for longer periods of time, up to one minute.

Add another established cue, such as Down (so you'll be cueing "Sit," "Down," "Sit," "Down" in rapid succession), starting with a fifteen-second time frame and building to faster repetitions before adding more time. When you add a third cue, cue the behaviors randomly. Continue to intersperse more cues as the dog becomes speedier with his responses. Over time, your speed will build to the point that you can give rapid-fire cues that the dog completes instantly. You can maintain proficiency with very little practice—once a week or so work on speed trials just for fun. You'll have a dog who not only understands and listens for the cue, but also responds instantly and eagerly, on his way to being fluent!

Generalization

Once you have a behavior on cue, you need to generalize the behavior. **Generalization** means that skills or performance of a behavior are easily transferred from one environment to another. For example, your behavior of driving a van transfers over to driving a compact car. The skills of turning the steering wheel and applying the brake or gas pedal are consistent from vehicle to vehicle. Traditional training refers to this as "proofing for distractions." Unfortunately, this tends to encourage people to look at the dog as an adversary, a creature who is resisting training instead of participating in it. We prefer to look at it as a way to teach the dog that the behavior is done exactly the same regardless of when, where or what else changes. Keep it interesting and build in the kinds of things that might encourage your dog to go off track, such as throwing a ball and either calling him to you or sending him to get the ball. The dog doesn't know initially which behavior he will be asked to do, but he gets rewarded either way, so there is always a payoff for doing what is asked.

Dogs don't generalize very well. That's why one of the most oft-heard handler laments is "But he always does it at home!" To help your dog generalize, be aware of:

- Your body postures—practice while you are sitting, standing, crouching, and even lying down on the couch or ground.

- Your orientation (or how you are facing the dog)—try facing the wall, standing behind him, standing on the left or right side of him and every angle in between.

One of the variables in generalizing behavior is your orientation to the dog. Will he still do the behavior when your back is to him?

- The dog's orientation (or the direction the dog is facing)—change where the dog is facing in the room.

- Your location in the room—move to a different part of the room farther away from the TV, closer to the bed, next to the table, etc.

- Changing rooms—practice in different rooms and go through all of the above once you change rooms.

- Time of day—don't train at exactly the same time of day once you have the behavior if you want to generalize it.

- Other items in the environment—things that your dog finds rewarding are going to draw him into other behaviors. Use this to your advantage by offering the distraction for performance of a specific behavior you asked for (see Mother May I? in Chapter 5 for more information on doing this).

- Changing locations—take it on the road to increasingly more distracting environments. Rank the environments so you gradually increase distractions. For most dogs, the least to the most distracting would be: back yard, front yard, in front of next door neighbor's house, on the way to the park, at the edge of the park, in the park, etc. (See Quick Clicks: Level of distraction versus level of treat on page 94 and the chart on page 127 for more information on distraction levels.)

Keeping records

One of the important things chicken campers learned from Bob and Marian Bailey was to keep records. We realize that this is something not widely practiced in dog training, and you may not decide to follow through on this suggestion. But we feel obliged to tell you why record keeping is valuable. Then you can make your own choice.

When you work with multiple dogs, or are teaching multiple behaviors, it's sometimes difficult to remember what you're doing with each dog or each behavior (sometimes it's hard to remember even when you're only working with *one* dog on one behavior!). Records allow you to set a baseline of a behavior. How will you know if there's improvement if you don't know where you started? They also allow you to modify your training program, if your dog didn't follow along with the book. Records will help you break behavior into smaller bits when needed, and move ahead faster when you can. Plus, it's fun to go back and realize that you really haven't been working on a behavior all that long and be encouraged by your success!

You can make records as detailed or brief as you like, but at a minimum you should include:

- The date.
- The session number.

- The success rate of the behavior—whether the dog got to the criteria you wanted, or whether he's far enough along in the behavior to add a cue. You can simply note how many treats the dog got out of the ten you started with (did he meet 80%?). Or, another way to determine the success rate of the behavior as well as the length of the session is to count out ten treats and set your timer for one minute. During that time, you might note how many treats the dog got, which indicates how many times the behavior was repeated correctly. Or, you could time how long it took you to get rid of ten treats. If the dog is getting faster, you'll know the behavior is moving along well.

- A baseline if you're trying to change something specific about the behavior (for example, speed, duration, fluency). If the dimension you're concentrating on isn't changing, you'll know something needs to be changed in your training plan.

- How long you worked—by session or repetitions.

- What your plan is for the next session—what will your criteria change be, do you need to split the behavior finer, can you jump ahead? If you tried something different, did it work? How will you build on it?

- You might also want to include environmental information (where you are working, with who or with what), types of rewards, an overall impression of how the dog is working or the time of day. What you include is totally up to you, your needs, and your willingness to write things down. Even very minimal records will help you improve your shaping skills and work effectively with your dog.

Guidelines for shaping

- Never click without giving a treat. It makes the clicker less meaningful for the dog.

- Work in short sessions. Shorter is always better. One minute sessions are a good starting point for beginners.

- Quit training before you or your dog get tired or bored. In the beginning, ten minutes of total training time is plenty.

- Remember our story about the Empire State Building—steps can go up or down and you can rest on a step for a while if you run into problems. It's all okay—you'll be back on your way to the top in no time.

- If you hit a "learning plateau" (the dog doesn't seem to be progressing over the course of several sessions), your first line of defense is to review your shaping steps to make sure they are small enough and the dog is getting frequent clicks and treats, at least every three to five seconds. If you're waiting longer than that to click, your step is too big.

- When just starting out, work before meals, when the dog is most likely to be attentive. Once the dog has some experience with shaping, you'll be able to work any time.

- If you and your dog are new to clicker training, work on only one behavior until you have finished and named it. As you both get better at this, you can work on multiple behaviors, but only one in each session.

- Keep in mind that the dog must be physically capable of performing the behavior you want to teach. No amount of training will help a dog learn to open a jar because you need opposable thumbs for that.

- Decide before you start working what the end behavior (the "final picture") is going to look like and what the first behavior you will CT will be. Have in mind how the steps will progress for at least the first part of the behavior (or even better, plan it all, write it down, and adjust as needed).

- You may need more enticing treats in group classes or other more distracting locations.

- Realize that as your dog gets more clicker savvy, you may not stay at one step for very long before you get something better that you can click. It's best not to linger too long at any one step if the dog is doing well, or you might get stuck there.

Slick Clicks: Unsticking a dumbell

A Boxer learning to retrieve came to training class. His owner said she couldn't get the dog to pick the dumbbell up off the floor. When asked to demonstrate what the dog was doing, she put the dumbbell down and the dog promptly grabbed it and held on as if his life depended on it. . . with the dumbbell still firmly on the floor, looking as if it had been glued down. It was obviously clear in the dog's mind that he was supposed to grab the dumbbell, but he had no idea that he was supposed to be picking it up. Asked how long she had stayed at this step, the dog's owner said one week. She had clicked and treated this step so much that the dog was convinced it was the final behavior and he wasn't supposed to do anything else! The trainers solved the problem by clicking the dog only when he accidentally pushed the dumbbell forward as he grabbed it. A few steps later he was successfully picking it up off the floor.

- Remember that we humans generally want to get where we're going in an awful hurry. Clicker training works in steps. Resist "final pictureitis." If you find that your dog just isn't getting the hang of clicker training, take a close look at how much you're expecting in the initial sessions. Are you trying to teach the dog too much in too short a time? Are you trying to work on multiple behaviors at once? Are your steps small enough to ensure that the dog is successful? You should be able to break ANY behavior into a minimum of ten steps. Write them down if you have a tendency to skip ahead without waiting for the dog. Have someone observe you if you run into problems.

- Periodically review your plan to make any adjustments for the dog's progress—either faster or slower than you anticipated.

- Encourage everyone in the family to get involved. Each person should work on their own behavior. Natural inconsistencies between trainers will confuse the dog if more than one person works on the same thing. Trainers who aren't skilled with timing the clicker correctly can just practice giving the dog food for the correct behavior without clicking.

- Don't interrupt a session to do something else—answer the door or chat on the phone—while the dog is working. Most dogs will see this as punishment.

- If what you're doing isn't working, try some other shaping plan. Ask family and friends for ideas. The ideas we give you in this book have worked for the dogs trained to do these behaviors, but that doesn't mean there aren't other ways to arrive at the same place.

- Vary the time of day you train, the length of a session, and the rewards you use as the dog starts to understand how to play the game. As the behavior becomes stronger, you will also work in other locations, gradually increasing the amount of distractions for the dog.

- If you're training more than one dog, put the others in another room so you can focus on the dog you're working with. Later, as you and the dogs get used to clicker training, you can work with one dog while the others are in a Down-Stay.

Clicker training one dog while the others are in a Down-Stay. Don't forget to reward the patient dogs.

- If your dog seems to go blank and lose all sense of what you're working on, don't panic. Go back to the previous step for a few clicks and treats, then try stepping up again, or just stop the lesson, regroup your thoughts, and rethink your shaping plan. If the dog stops working completely (lies down or leaves the area), seems confused, or exhibits stress, end the lesson. Try again another day, after you've reviewed what you're doing. You don't always have to end on a good note. Sometimes it's a good idea just to end.

- Another option, if the dog is confused, is to "reset the dog" by having the dog do a well-learned behavior like Sit or Touch for a treat. That gives you a chance to stop the training without punishing the dog.

- It's okay if the dog makes a choice that doesn't get clicked. He is also learning from not being clicked. It's not uncommon to see experienced dogs test other options once they have figured out the behavior.

- But, if your dog makes the same mistake over and over, it means your shaping step was too big or you are clicking something different than what you intend. Review your shaping steps, and at the next training session, do a short review at a lower level and take smaller steps when you advance. Have someone watch you and tell you what *they* think you're clicking for.

- At the beginning of each session, go back a bit and briefly review with the dog what was learned at the end of the previous session.

- Don't try to shape two different dimensions of a behavior at the same time, or both you and your dog will get confused about what you are clicking.

- The taught behavior can be self-rewarding to the dog. Launching a tennis ball from a dog-a-polt may be more fun than eating the treat you are offering. If the dog is still working, but doesn't come to get the treat when you click, don't fret. You may get more interest in the treat at a different session or in a different environment.

- The click sound may stop the shaping temporarily as the dog comes back to you to get "paid." This is normal, and the dog will return to his task once he collects the reward. Or, you can heed the Baileys' dictum to "feed for position," and deliver your treat so it advances your training.

- Keep track of what you and your dog are learning at each session.

- Keep it fun! Remember that dogs are individuals and learn at different rate, the same as humans. Be patient. Be positive.

Slick Clicks: More advice from Bob Bailey

"I find most dog trainers to be in a great hurry all of the time. Why? Where are they going? Take your time and make sure you have what you want pretty good before you move on. One successful trial does not a behavior make! By the same token, one unsuccessful trial does not a behavior break! Don't be discouraged when things don't go exactly as planned. Keep gathering data and learning from each experience. There will be a strong and natural tendency to want to abandon the systematic approach and go with what is expedient. Memory is fickle. Memory is very short. Those that rely on memory are doomed to repeat many mistakes because they think they remember, and they don't."

Java (8 year old Boxer) has been clicker trained since he was a puppy. Here he reprises his pose ("head down") from the front cover of our first edition of Quick Clicks.

Chapter 2
Basic Good Manners

In this chapter, we'll review some easy basics that can be taught using a clicker. Because these are foundation behaviors taught in every beginning level dog training class, we're going to just offer streamlined versions of the steps.

Note: These steps are condensed for simplicity. At a minimum, you will work through each step using three to ten repetitions of click/treats. In the early steps of a behavior, you may repeat only three to five times. As the behavior progresses, you should move to the next step only if the dog is successful 80% of the time at the current step (or, in eight out of ten tries the dog has been clicked and treated.) If you CT, that means the dog has met your criteria for that step. These steps are meant to be completed over several sessions of work with the dog. Generally, you should count out ten treats for a step. After the dog has been clicked and given all (or most) of the treats, stop, record and re-evaluate your plan. This gives the dog a short break after every step. You may need to repeat the step or you may be able to move to the next step.

As a rule, young and inexperienced dogs can work about ten minutes maximum total training time, but shorter is always better. You should be able to move through several steps during that time. Set a timer if you have a tendency to train longer. You might also experiment with working for only one minute at a time for a couple of days. This has the advantage of really amping up the dog's performance and making him excited to get to work.

Slick Clicks: Mandy's training session tips
A typical training session with Mandy's dogs looks like this: All three dogs do a Down-Stay (Take a Break). One dog is called out to work on the behavior using ten treats. When the treats are gone, Mandy evaluates any changes needed to progress the behavior. After three to five sets of ten treats (thirty to fifty treats total or less than five minutes), the dog is put back into a

Down-Stay and all the dogs are given a treat for remaining in a Stay. Any information about the behavior is recorded. The next dog is pulled out. With a new behavior that doesn't require a lot of location changes, the dogs are cycled through three or four times in about forty-five minutes of training. The youngest dog starts and ends the training, so she is doing more work although still in short sessions.

Mandy also has the luxury of having a retired dog to use for experimenting with new behaviors. If things don't work out, she isn't messing up her competition dog. If she runs into difficulties, she will put up the dog and take another one out to work through the problem. But in the long run, it doesn't really matter because problems (slow performance, shaping the wrong behavior, additional behaviors the dog is combining that complicate things), if caught early in the shaping process, are easy to fix.

Even dogs without a lot of skills in their repertoires—puppies—should learn these with ease. You can work in two-minute training sessions and be amazed at how much you can accomplish quickly. If you need more help with these behaviors, find a great local clicker trainer to help you or review one of the many basic clicker tomes out there. If you have any doubts about what you're doing, go back and consult "Guidelines for shaping" in Chapter 1.

In the remainder of this chapter we will cover the following "good manners" behaviors:

- Attention.
- Take a Treat Gently.
- Sit.
- Down.
- Come.
- Walk on Leash.
- Wait (at the door or in the car).

You'll need these behaviors on cue in order to use them with other behaviors in this book. Get your equipment together and set a few minutes aside. Ready? Begin!

ATTENTION

The dog looks directly at you (the trainer) instead of at the treat in your hand. Attention is a useful behavior that you'll need if you are going to be using treats in training. This is especially good for dogs that lunge at your hand when you have food in it. It's such an easy behavior that we aren't even going to bother to write out the steps for you—that would be good practice for you, though (hint, hint!). Some trainers call this "Doggie Zen"—to get the treat you must ignore the treat! This is also the beginning of a Leave It behavior.

Suggested verbal cue: "Watch," "Look."

Put a bunch of treats in one hand and your clicker in your other hand. Hold the hand with the treats out to the side, perpendicular to your body. Your dog will probably stare at your treat hand, waiting for a CT (or maybe just waiting for the treat!). He may start drooling or pawing at you. Watch for the dog's eyes to leave your hand. Even if he looks at your knee or your foot or your elbow or the floor, CT the instant he looks away from your hand holding the treats. Repeat several times, CT-ing when the dog looks away from your hand each time. Take a break, and write down all the steps you think you will need to eventually get the dog looking up at your face. (Hint: You'll need a lot fewer steps if the first couple of glances were in that general direction than if they were at your toe!)

CT for looking at your knee (or wherever the dog first shifted his gaze) until the dog has done that three to five times. Then work up your body slowly until he is making eye contact. Once the dog looks at your face immediately instead of at the hand, you can give this behavior a cue.

Your dog has just learned that he has to *do* something to get the treat besides stare at it. He's also learned that you *are* not going to do something *to* him, like lead him around with the food.

Generalize the behavior:

- Working in different places.
- Holding your hand normally at your side or close to the dog.
- Working with other dogs around.
- Having other people practice the behavior.

 ## TAKE A TREAT GENTLY

The dog uses his tongue, not his teeth, to take a treat from an outstretched hand. This is important if you're going to use food for training. Teaching this is messy, but effective—keep that in mind as you practice! This behavior is also a building block for Leave It.

Suggested verbal cue: "Gentle," "Nice," "Easy."

You will need: Soft, sticky treats such as peanut butter, spray cheese in a can, cream cheese, or liverwurst.

Speed Steps

1. Mash a small amount of the treat into the palm of your hand and close your fist around it, leaving an opening at the thumb side big enough for the dog to get his tongue into. (Yes, we know it's disgusting. But you'll thank us in the end, when you don't have to worry about a canine version of a piranha.) Hold your hand out to the dog and let him try to get at the treat. The dog might nibble, chew, or lick to try to get the food. When he licks, click and open your hand.

Close your fist around the food, and click when the dog licks at the food.

2. Require that the dog lick several times before you click and open your hand.

3. Change to a different treat and repeat Steps 1 and 2, gradually making the dog lick longer before being clicked and allowed a big taste of the gooey food.

4. Change locations and repeat Steps 1 through 3 several times.

5. Add your verbal cue just before presenting your food-laden fist: cue "Gentle," present fist, click for licking, open fist.

6. Continue to change locations and treats while you work on adding the verbal cue.

7. Now use an interesting chewy treat such as steak, chicken, or hot dog slices. Hold it between the tips of your thumb and fingers so that the treat is covered. Say your cue and offer it to the dog. If he licks, click and give him the treat.

8. Continue to build on the number of licks before you click and release the treat. Work on Steps 8 and 9 with a variety of chewy treats.

9. Offer a hard treat such as a biscuit. Repeat with other hard treats.

Quick Clicks: Adding cues

When teaching a new behavior, you'll need to pair a cue with the behavior at least fifty to sixty times before the dog begins to make the connection between what you say or signal and what he should do. Once the dog starts to make the connection, occasionally (every tenth time or so) do not give the cue and see what the dog does. When he does the behavior when cued, but doesn't do it when he's not cued, then you'll know he understands the cue. The behavior has been "named." For more information, see Chapter 1.

Generalize the behavior:

- Changing locations frequently. Dogs feeling some stress tend to take treats more quickly and harder. If stress induces your dog to chomp rather than lick, you'll have to gradually work in more stressful environments.

- Getting the dog revved up and excited, then offering a tasty treat.

- Getting the dog revved up and excited using a toy. No matter what, the dog should not put his teeth on you!

- Having the dog take treats nicely from different people, including children. Wait until the dog is fairly reliable. If you're worried about small fingers being chomped, you can cover the child's hand with your own at first.

Keep in Mind

If the dog chomps at any time, yelp loudly (AIP!) and turn your back on him, ending that repetition. Make it sound like you've been mortally wounded! Do not, under these circumstances, let him get the treat, even if it's painful. Yelping and ending play is also an effective way to inhibit biting of all types—especially with a young puppy. Don't forget to *reward* playing nicely!

Some dogs give up very easily early in the process and may just sit back and wait for you to give them the treat. You *could* CT this—the dog is learning not to grab at treats, and that can be useful, especially if you have young children in the house. But the dog is not learning to "take treats gently." Try using a different type of food if he won't go after it eagerly, or have someone watch you to make sure you aren't accidentally using some verbal correction to stop the dog. Or, if he reacts strongly to your yelp when he makes a mistake, just turn your back if he bites.

Note: Labrador Retrievers, Doberman Pinschers and German Shepherds are often particularly difficult to train to take treats gently, so these and similar breeds may take longer to teach this behavior. Your persistence will be rewarded!

Troubleshooting

The dog paws at my treat hand rather than biting or licking at it.

- Hold your hand still and work on CT-ing for not pawing the hand as your first step. Once the dog learns pawing is not what you're looking for, he'll try other things, and you can start working on licking.

It hurts too much to work on this. The chomping is getting worse!

- Never jerk your hand away if the dog chomps. It gives the dog the idea he wasn't quick enough or forceful enough, and he'll try harder next time.

- Wear gloves. It will hurt even more as the dog gets better at lunging for treats, so you'd better start working on it now.

- Work in a very low-stress environment, with no other dogs or people around. Dogs will sometimes be less grabby in more secure surroundings.

The dog licks until he gets clicked, then grabs the treat when it is offered.

- Open your hand just slightly and be prepared to yelp if the dog makes a grab for it.

- After you click, place the treat as far into the dog's mouth as you can manage. This prevents the dog from needing to grab at it.

- Put a treat between your forefinger and thumb. Hold it in the dog's mouth far back on the tongue. Click when you feel the tongue moving instead of the teeth. (This variation is a bit rough on your fingers but the payoff is worth it.)

Variations

Could you teach your dog to leap up and grab a treat without touching your fingers? Or, do a variation on the killer whale leap to take a fish from the trainer's mouth? Don't try this if you don't like jumping dogs! If you have multiple dogs, teach each dog to take a treat only when he hears his name. This is a terrific way to prevent food problems between dogs, even if you don't have other dogs at home.

 ## SIT

The dog plants his rear on the ground in response to a verbal or visual cue (a hand signal), in any environment, on any surface. These directions are for a lured Sit rather than a purely shaped one. It's an easy behavior to use a lure with, and the lure can then become a visual cue. This behavior is used for almost everything, as either a foundation or control behavior. It's used to prevent jumping on people, working at doorways (as we'll be doing later with Wait), and is the starting position for Down as well as performed in many types of canine competition events.

Suggested verbal cue: "Sit," the traditional German cue "Sitz!" or "Park It" if you want to be clever.

Suggested visual cue: Traditionally palm up and hand moving up slightly, just like the gesture you make when you have a lure in your hand.

Speed Steps

1. Start with the dog in front of you, facing you. Hold a food treat directly over the dog's nose (palm up) and move the treat up slightly. CT when the dog tilts his head back.

2. Start at the dog's nose again, but move the treat up and back over the dog's head, keeping it low so the dog doesn't jump up. CT when the dog looks up and begins to bend his back legs.

3. Start at the dog's nose again, and move the treat farther back over the dog's head toward his rear, until he sits. Repeat until the dog puts his rear on the ground five times in a row.

4. Hold your hand as if you have food, but don't use food this time and get the dog to repeat the behavior five to six times, CT-ing each time.

Quick Clicks: Where to keep and deliver treats
Have treats in a bowl nearby, but out of the dog's reach. You won't have to have them in your hand but they need to be readily available. Try to deliver the treat quickly enough that the dog's still sitting when he gets it.

5. Gradually modify your hand motion until you are moving your hand up, but not forward over the dog. The movement of your hand a few inches up will become the dog's visual cue for this behavior.

Gradually modify your hand motion until you are moving your hand up, but not forward, over the dog.

6. Work in new locations until the dog responds reliably (80% of the time) to your visual cue in any location. This means he should get clicked 80% of the time.

7. Now it's time to add a verbal signal (also called a cue word or just cue) if you want one. Add your verbal cue just before you give your visual cue.

> ### Quick Clicks: Adding a new cue
> To add (or change) a cue for a behavior that already has a cue, just remember the alphabet "N-O." That's new cue ("Sit"), old cue (hand signal), dog sits, CT. (Review Naming Behaviors in Chapter 1 if you don't remember why the verbal cue isn't given at the same time as the hand signal.)

Generalize the behavior:

- Changing locations and surfaces, gradually adding more distractions.

- Waiting a few seconds before CT-ing the Sit, building up to a Sit-Stay.

- Practicing a Sit beside you (on either side) rather than in front.

- Practicing Sits when you are facing the dog, standing behind him or standing with your back to him.

- Improving the speed of response to your cue. To do this, CT as the dog bends his back legs (rather than when he completes the Sit), release, take a step away from the dog, and repeat. The dog may abort the Sit when he hears the click, but don't worry about it. We're clicking for a fast response time (one criteria) so the completion of the Sit (another criteria) sometimes falls apart. As the dog starts to anticipate your cue, his response will speed up, and you can work on the performance of a completed Sit.

- CT-ing only the best Sits—fastest, prettiest, whatever you like.

- Then gradually wean off the clicks and immediately treat, praise, pet or play with a toy. Remember to release the dog from the Sit!

Keep in Mind
Some dogs may back away from the handler rather than Sit in the initial steps. Sometimes just holding your hand a little higher will work. Or, you can practice in a corner so that the dog can't move backward.

If you find you have lost the dog when you eliminate the food lure, use treats on two of the five repetitions in Step 4. Make sure your hand looks the same whether or not you are using treats.

Troubleshooting
If you can't see when the dog's legs bend.

- If you have trouble seeing when the dog's back legs bend, have someone else watch and click while you treat, or try doing this while you are seated.

The dog paws at or jumps at you.

- If the dog jumps at the treat, you may be holding the treat too high. Move it just over his head, close but not touching.

- Work in a doorway with a baby gate between you and the dog. CT for calm behavior first, then work on shaping the Sit.

- Don't use a food lure. Shape the Sit instead. It may take longer, but you won't get frustrated with the dog jumping on you.

- Work on the attention exercise earlier in the chapter so the dog learns that not lunging for the treat gets him the treat.

The dog is biting at your hand as he follows the food.

- Go back and work on Take a Treat Gently earlier in this chapter.

- Offer treats on a spoon or fork.

- Switch to less exciting treats.

Variations

- Shape the Sit instead of using a lure.

- See whether you can get the dog to Sit at a Distance from you (remember our practice work in the first chapter).

- Once the dog learns Down, teach a Sit from the Down position. It uses different muscles and is great for the dog physically.

 ## DOWN

The dog puts his body flat on the ground in response to a verbal cue and/or visual cue, in any environment, on any surface. Some dogs lie on one hip or the other while some lie centered between the hips, sphinx-style. We aren't going to be picky here about which position the dog chooses BUT in some types of competition you'll need the sphinx-style Down (namely the Down on Recall in AKC obedience). The dog can get up faster from the sphinx position, which may also figure into your training. Traditionally, the Down on a Hip is considered a "relax for a while" position. Before you start, you'll want to be clear whether you prefer a specific position. (Or, you can always teach it later, with a little more work.) Down-Stays are useful for keeping the dog out from underfoot while you are performing some task. Down is used in many varieties of canine competition and is the basis for some popular tricks and other behaviors. For this behavior, we are again using a lure, but it can also be shaped. It's helpful if the dog knows the Sit, but not absolutely necessary.

Suggested verbal cue: "Down," "Plotz," "Crash," "Drop," "Take a Break," "Relax."

Suggested visual cue: Hand with palm down moving toward the floor; hand raised in the air as if you were asking a question (traditionally used in obedience competitions).

Speed Steps

1. Start in a familiar environment with few distractions. You may find it helpful to be on a slick floor surface—the kitchen often fits the bill. Draw a treat down from the dog's nose to between his front paws. CT when he drops his head to follow the treat.

2. Draw the treat down between the dog's two front paws and slightly behind them so that the dog moves his head closer to the ground. Continue increasing your criteria every three to five repetitions, until the dog reaches all the way down to the floor to get the treat and lies down.

Draw the treat down between the dog's two front paws and slightly behind them so that he moves his head closer to the ground.

3. Now eliminate the food from your hand. Use the same hand motion keeping your fingers together as if you still had a treat. CT when the dog lies down. (Remember to have your treats handy.)

4. Change locations and repeat, continuing to work without food in your signal hand.

5. Gradually modify your visual cue until you are moving your hand only partway toward the floor, until the visual cue looks the way you want it to.

6. CT the best responses only—such as when the dog is already lying down before you've finished giving your cue.

7. Working in a new location, continue until your dog is responding reliably to your cue (lying down 80% of the time when the cue is given).

8. Add a verbal cue, if desired.

Generalize the behavior:
- Continue to change locations and surfaces (carpet, linoleum, grass, dirt, cement), and gradually add more distractions.

- Work on getting the dog to lie down whether you are sitting on the floor or a chair, or standing up. You will need to change positions gradually so the dog doesn't get confused by the change in body language. If he does, back up to a previous step and make the changes more gradual.

- Delay your CT until the dog has been down for a second or two. You can build up to a Down-Stay this way. Remember to use your release word!

- Practice Downs beside or behind you rather than in front. Be sure to work on both the right and left sides.

- Improve the speed of response (latency) to your cue. To do this, CT *as* the dog starts to lie down (rather than waiting for the dog to complete the Down), release, take a step to get the dog up and repeat. When he hears the click, the dog may abort the Down—that's okay. Remember that when you're changing one criterion (asking for a speedy response to your cue), you have to relax other criteria (completion of the position in a certain way or how fast the dog completes the Down). As the dog begins to respond more quickly to your cue, you can add the other elements back in.

- CT only the best Downs—the fastest, straightest, best rolled hip or whatever you're looking for.

- Gradually wean the clicks and use praise, petting, your release word, and playing with a toy as alternates to treats. Don't reward every response.

Quick Clicks: Position game
Play the "position game" to see if the dog really understands your cues. Give your dog a cue for Sit or a cue for Down or say a nonsense word. Only reward what you've asked for. If you delay the reward does the dog change position, hoping to get a click? That's your sign that he really doesn't understand what each cue means.

Keep in Mind
If your dog doesn't Sit on cue yet, start with him standing on all fours. Hold a treat in front of his nose and move it down between his front feet. CT when he ducks his head a little. Gradually ask for more head movement, until the dog is putting his head on the ground. Eventually, the rear end should follow. Whenever it does, even if it's while you're still shaping "head on the ground," have a party!

As an alternate method, you can use the additional prop of a chair or coffee table or even your own bent leg while you're sitting on the floor. Lure the dog under with your treat, CT-ing as he puts his body on the ground. Once the dog starts to get the idea, you will need to wean him off the additional prop as a separate step in your training.

For most dogs, training using the above instructions will result in a sphinx position. If you want the dog to relax on a hip, you can train that separately once the dog is reliably going into a Down. To get the dog to roll on a hip, draw the treat slightly to the dog's shoulder once he is lying down.

To get the dog to roll on a hip, draw the treat slightly to the dog's shoulder once he is lying down.

CT when the dog rolls onto a hip. (If you want the dog to respond both ways depending on the situation, make sure you use a different cue for each.) We like to use "Take a break" for the Down rolled onto a hip, since the dog will be hanging out for a while.

We haven't addressed how the dog lies down (folding back into a Down or lying down front end first.) For some competitors, how the dog sits or lies down is important. The directions we listed usually result in a dog that lies down front end first. If you have some experience with clicker training, you can shape a speedy fold back or drop into a Down. Details to do these variations are beyond the scope of the book, but here are a couple of suggestions. Make sure you are clear in your mind exactly what kind of performance you want from the dog. Write out the steps to get from your starting point to the end behavior. Add more steps than you think you will need!

Quick Clicks: Creating speed

For safety reasons, you may want your dog to perform the Down behavior quickly. Speed can also be important in competitive events, so build that in at the outset by only rewarding performance for an acceptable speed. (You set the criteria.) You will need to set minimum levels of performance at each step. For example, the dog must get clicked and treated within a quarter of a second, or all ten treats must be delivered within thirty seconds for the step you are working at. Creating speed in a behavior is a challenge for beginning trainers. We recommend that you work on building speed into a behavior the dog already knows before incorporating it into a plan to train a brand new behavior.

Troubleshooting

The dog's rear stays up even when his head is on the ground.

- Try moving the treat down more slowly, and drawing it slightly away from the dog's nose once it's on the ground.
- Use the alternate method described in "Keep in Mind," page 45.

The dog is biting at my hand as he follows the treat.

- Teach "Take a Treat Gently" first.
- Offer treats on a spoon.
- Switch to less exciting treats.

The dog works fine at home, but won't lie down in public or in more distracting environments.

- This is usually a response to stress. The Down is a vulnerable position for a dog, so if he's unsure of himself in public, you'll have difficulty convincing him it's a good idea to lie down. Work on building his confidence by practicing things he knows.
- Stay in a safe environment and slowly add more distractions such as other people, other dogs, moving objects. Work until the dog is comfortable with all of this before moving to a new environment.
- Use really exciting treats when out in public.
- Make the Down a "default behavior"—frequently asked for and highly rewarded. Cue a Down before you let the dog do anything fun (eat, play, walk out the door).

Quick Clicks: Grandma's rule or the Premack Principle

The Premack Principle says that you can use a high probability behavior (something the dog gets a lot of RF for or intrinsically enjoys) to RF low probability behaviors (something that isn't RF often, or that the dog doesn't particularly care about). Many trainers call it "Grandma's Rule," otherwise stated as "you have to eat dinner before you get dessert." To put it in doggie terms, playing with another dog (a high probability behavior) can be used as a reward for looking at you (a lower probability behavior). You can also use this principle to add a variety of rewards to a dog's repertoire. If the dog loves food, but isn't very interested in chasing a ball, you could shape ball chasing using a clicker and treats. With enough pairings of "chase a ball, click, get a cookie," chasing a ball will increase in value for the dog because it predicts the CT. Eventually, it can become rewarding enough for the dog that you no longer have to offer a cookie for ball chasing. We call behaviors the dog likes to engage in "life rewards." As a human, you have control of a lot of the things a dog wants. Use them to get the dog to do what you want him to do and teach him to be excited about a variety of rewards!

Variations

After you have the basic Down reliably on cue, work on having the dog Down at a distance. Down is a powerful cue, and being able to drop your dog at a distance may save lives in an emergency someday. Teach the dog to Down from either a Sit or a Stand. Work the Down in a play group while other dogs are moving about. In our training group, we've played a fun game of tic-tac-toe using dogs sitting or in a Down as "markers."

Slick Clicks: The harmonica playing walrus

This comes from Kathy Sdao, former marine mammal trainer: "We used clicker training at Point Defiance Zoo & Aquarium (Tacoma, Washington) to teach one of our walruses, E.T., to inhale and exhale on cue, either through his nostrils or through his mouth. It was a "housekeeping" behavior (things useful for care of the animal), and a huge help when researchers from the University of Washington came to study E.T.'s lung capacity and other respiratory values. While we were doing the training, we hit on the idea of using a harmonica to let us know when E.T. was exhaling forcefully out of his mouth. To our surprise, he seemed to enjoy the sound he produced with the harmonica! He'd continue to blow into it without any food reward. Too bad none of his trainers had any musical talent—we could have taught him to play an actual tune!"

 ## COME

The dog comes directly to you from wherever he is and remains near enough to you for you to touch him (and snap a leash to his collar if need be), regardless of what he was doing at the time or what is going on around him. As an option, the dog can be taught to Sit directly in front of you (used in obedience competitions). The important detail is that the dog comes to you and remains there until given further instructions. Having a dog run to you but then immediately run away in a sort of "catch me if you can" game isn't very useful. This is one of your essential behaviors if you ever want the dog off leash, even in your own yard. It also figures into many dog sports. Note: Although the initial training goes quickly, training to reliability in a variety of off leash environments will take many months.

Suggested verbal cue: "Come," "Here," "Front," "Quick," your dog's name.

Suggested visual cue: Hand outstretched and drawn toward the chest with your arm parallel to the ground.

You will need: A closed container to hold kibble, a boring toy or chew bone and a safe environment where the dog cannot run off, and where he has few options other than to come to you (empty tennis courts and pool enclosures can be useful if dogs are allowed). It's helpful if the dog will already Sit on cue, but not required.

Quick Clicks: Don't deliver!
When working on Recalls, the dog should come to you to collect his treat after being clicked. Unless otherwise indicated, don't be Domino's—don't deliver the treat to your dog.

Speed Steps

1. In a boring environment with your hungry dog, show the dog you have a treat, then back one step away from him. CT if he moves toward you.

2. Move to a new place in the room and repeat. Repeat this step several times, until the dog won't let you get away from him.

3. Put a treat on the floor and while the dog is eating it, take three steps away from him. When he turns his head toward you to see where you've gone, click, *drop a treat on the floor at your feet,* and move three steps away. Repeat one to ten times.

4. Throw a treat a short distance away from you. While the dog is eating it, move a couple of steps away and turn your back on the dog. When he comes around in front of you, click, drop a treat, move away and turn your back on him again. Repeat one to ten times.

5. Change locations and repeat steps three and four until you have worked in at least five different locations. These do not have to be dramatically different (for example, they can be different rooms in your house).

6. Now, toss a treat away from you and wait for the dog to eat it. CT when he has taken three steps back toward you. If he doesn't go for the tossed treat, but instead moves toward you, CT immediately. Continue at this step, working in multiple familiar locations including your yard if you are able to (if not, we will build it in a later step) until you have practiced in at least five different locations.

7. Put your boring toy on the floor and step away from it. When the dog turns toward you, CT. Don't worry if the dog picks up the toy and brings it with him. Our only criterion at this point is that the dog turn toward you. Repeat in multiple locations.

8. Put the same toy on the floor, but now step away and turn your back to the dog. CT when he comes around in front of you. Alternate with tossing the toy and moving

quickly away from the dog. Repeat one to ten times, then change toys. Continue until you have practiced with at least five different toys of varying interest to the dog.

9. Put your closed container with treats inside down on the floor and step quickly away from it, as far as you can. The dog should have the hang of this game by now, and come running around in front of you. Alternate with tossing the container. (Note: The treats you are giving the dog MUST be more interesting than the treats in the closed container, but if the dog doesn't go for the container, use tastier treats inside.)

10. If your dog is reliably coming around in front of you when you toss the treat container—at least 80% of the time—it's time to add your verbal cue. Put a distraction on the ground and step away from it, turning your back. Immediately say, "Come" (or whatever cue you've chosen), and when the dog *turns toward you,* click and let the dog come all the way to you to get his treat. (You'll need to peek over your shoulder to know when the dog turns toward you.) Change locations and continue pairing the cue with the behavior for at least fifty repetitions over the next day or two.

11. Add collar grabs. When the dog comes around in front of you, tell him what a good boy he is, reach down and touch his collar, and CT the collar touch. DO NOT use the hand holding the clicker to touch his collar—the noise of the clicker right next to his ear might be unpleasant or startling to the dog.

12. Continue building up the amount of time you hold onto the collar and adding your release word.

Quick Clicks: Judging reliability
A good way to judge if your dog is responding reliably is to consider if you would bet money on his response. If you would lay down that bet (and be confident of winning!), it's time to add your cue.

Generalize the behavior:
- Continue to work at short distances with gradually more interesting doggie distractions. The ultimate success of your Recall will depend on many, many repetitions with a huge variety of distractions in lots of different environments.

- Continue to work at short distances in gradually more distracting environments. Don't forget to practice in places where a quick Recall may really be necessary someday, like at your front door (on leash if necessary).

- Gradually add more distance to your Recall—no more than five feet at a time. Do at least ten repetitions at each distance in different environments before increasing the distance.

- Build variety into your rewards. Some options are running away from the dog when he turns toward you (most dogs love chase games), throwing a toy after clicking, releasing him to investigate that smell he was so interested in or doing a fun activity when he comes to you. If he performs well in a difficult environment, give him a jackpot as this is a really significant achievement.

Quick Clicks: Jackpot

One of the tools some clicker trainers use is a "jackpot" (a large number of treats or especially good ones) when a dog has done particularly well or worked particularly hard to get a behavior. While there has been little research showing that this is effective in helping pet dogs learn better, we say go for it if you feel inspired. For the most part, trainers tend to be stingy with rewards, and we are all for anything that encourages them to be more generous! It can't hurt your training in any way to do it.

Keep in Mind

Be sure to *never, ever* punish the dog for coming to you, even if he has your favorite shoe in his mouth when he arrives! That includes sticking him in his crate or clipping his toenails after you call him.

Consider why the dog isn't coming—does he not know the cue (has never been taught it) or does he know it but is not reliable? If you've dabbled in the Recall, but he's not reliable in many different environments with different distractions, you might want to start fresh with a new cue word. Work on *gradually* adding more and more distractions until the dog ignores everything to come to you.

Troubleshooting

The dog comes, but he always brings the toy or treat container with him.

- Secure the toy or container so it can't be moved from its spot. Be sure to start practicing with the dog close to you and reward heavily for turning away from the item. Don't forget to change locations of the toy or treats, as well.

The dog does okay in some environments, but loses it when outside or in an area with more distractions.

- Break your distractions into even smaller pieces as you build up through them. For example, if other dogs are a distraction, work with dogs your dog already knows (and who are not exciting playmates), starting with them a great distance away and behind a fence (so that even if the dog takes off, he can't be rewarded by getting to the other dogs). Work gradually closer, then add additional dogs your dog knows, then add dogs he doesn't know (again at a great distance) and so on.

- Change your rewards. The same old treats you train with every day may not be enticing enough to compete with really interesting smells, the chance to get petted by a stranger or play with another dog. You (and your rewards) need to be more interesting than any other thing your dog may encounter.

- If your dog has had a problem with Recalls in the past, it may take a *long* time to retrain. The secret is repetition, repetition, repetition. Don't give up, even if you only seem to be making a smidgeon of progress with each work session.

- In some cases, you may be able to use a negative punisher (taking away something to decrease a behavior) to bump the dog's response to a Recall in distracting environments. This is one of the tools that clicker trainers use along with extinction and positive reinforcement. (For an excellent discussion of operant conditioning and how it applies to clicker training, see *Click for Joy* by Melissa Alexander or http:// www.clickersolutions.com/). To use a negative punishment in training Recalls, you would disappear if the dog doesn't respond to "Come." You'll need a second person as a spotter to help you out. Hide and stay hidden until the dog appears to be looking for you, then call the dog again. This is most effective with very young dogs or dogs that have a very strong bond to their owners. As a precursor, you can train the dog to look for you by playing hide and seek games in your house and yard (see Find Me in Chapter 8). Please be aware that this can increase separation anxiety in dogs (although usually these are not the dogs that take off on their owners).

- Some dogs will never be truly reliable off leash. Yours may be one of them. If so, it's a valuable piece of information to have—you will know that you will have to avoid putting the dog in situations where lack of a reliable Recall could have terrible consequences.

The dog comes, but seems stressed, is crawling, comes very slowly, or urinates as he approaches.

- Pay attention to your body language. If you are leaning forward and frowning with concentration, you might be frightening the dog. Stand up straight, breathe deeply, and smile at the dog. Try your initial repetitions while you are sitting on the floor.

- Have the dog Come to your side rather than in front—it may be less stressful for the dog. (See Touch in Chapter 6 for one behavior that can help move your dog where you want.)

- Click for faster approaches. You may have accidentally taught the dog to come slowly.

- Have you called the dog to you and then done something unpleasant, like clipping his nails and giving him a bath? Even one or two repetitions can quickly teach the dog that bad things can happen when he comes. Pay attention to what happens to the dog when he is called and make sure that it is *always* a positive experience.

Quick Clicks: Emergency recall

Because Recalls are a behavior that could be life or death for a dog, everyone should teach it. If you don't want to invest the time in having a reliable off leash Recall, at least prep the dog for an emergency Recall. To do this, use super-high value treats such as baby food, steak or liverwurst—something that the dog doesn't normally get (test first to see if he likes it!) Choose a cue word that you won't be using regularly such as "Car!" "Stop!" or "Cookies!" It's important that you say the cue in a panicky voice so that it becomes part of the stimulus for the dog. Three to four times a day, say your cue word and immediately deliver the goods. Repeat for at least a week, then on a regular basis thereafter using the most fabulous treats you can find.

Variations

Teach the dog to check in with you periodically, even if you haven't formally called him. This is a particularly good idea if you are working with a deaf or hard-of-hearing dog that you want to be able to have off leash. Teach the dog to drop into a Down in the middle of a Recall (an advanced exercise in obedience competition).

WALK ON LEASH

The dog walks without pulling forward on the leash, regardless of distractions. The dog should not pull no matter how long the leash is. This is one of the all-time, most-requested behaviors for our clients and also one of the more difficult to accomplish because, well, frankly, people get lazy about it. If you don't want to work on this behavior during a particular walk for whatever reason, we recommend using a no-pull or regular harness to prevent the dog from being rewarded for bad habits. Walking on leash is critical for socializing and exercising your dog. Walking off leash is a separate behavior addressed later in the book. In the early steps, your body language for this behavior looks similar to the body language for the Recall, above. You'll need to make sure you have added a cue to the Recall before starting this behavior.

Suggested verbal cue: "Let's go," "Walkies," "Let's walk," "Easy."

Suggested visual cue: Hold your left arm down at your side, palm facing forward, and make a short forward scooping motion.

You will need: A regular buckle collar and four to six foot leash. It will be helpful if you have already worked on Attention from Chapter 1 with your dog.

Quick Clicks: In the same hand

Hold the leash and clicker in the same hand, opposite the side you want the dog on. That leaves one hand free (on the dog's side) to deliver treats right where you want the dog to be. Keep the treats in a pocket or bait bag, or keep several in your free hand.

The leash and clicker should be in the hand opposite the dog. If you hold the leash on the same side the dog is on, you will have difficulty delivering the treat where you need to. Notice that after a couple of poor treat deliveries, Ping is hanging out more in front.

Speed Steps

1. Start in the house, with your dog on leash. Stand still and keep the leash short enough that you can reach the dog, no more than three feet. CT each time the leash goes slack. You don't need to worry about where the dog is at this point, only whether the leash is slack. Notice the slack leash in the second photo above.

2. Continue changing locations in your house until the dog is keeping the leash loose no matter where you are at least 80% of the time.

3. Put a toy on the ground out of the dog's reach. Click when the leash is slack and release the dog to get the toy. Repeat in multiple locations, sometimes delivering a treat from your hand and sometimes releasing the dog to play with the toy (about 25% of the time). Change toys and treats as necessary to keep the dog from getting bored with them.

4. Have a friend or family member sit nearby holding a boring cookie. They should not look at or say anything to the dog (choose a helper who can manage this!). Click when the leash is slack and *release* the dog to get the treat from your helper. Repeat, sometimes delivering a treat from your hand and sometimes releasing the dog to get the treat from the other person. Practice with multiple people until the dog is successful 80% of the time.

5. Repeat Steps 2 through 4 with the increased criteria that the dog must now put slack in the leash *and* look at you. By "look at you" we mean the dog is aware of where you are, not necessarily making eye contact. Change locations frequently. Jump away from the dog if he glances away (make it a fun game).

6. Continue until the dog won't look away from you. At this point, you can begin working outside in your back yard.

7. Continue to change locations, gradually adding more distracting environments, until you are able to work in your front yard at the foot of your driveway, with the dog not looking away from you no matter what goes by on your street.

Quick Clicks: Be a tree

Up to this point, you have been standing still with the leash kept about three feet long. From this point on, *whenever* you have the leash on your dog, you will "become a tree" (stop moving) any time he pulls for any reason. You move forward *only* when the leash is slack. If you need to, find some other way to exercise your dog while you're working on this behavior, so the dog doesn't learn that sometimes you let him pull.

8. Decide which side you want your dog to walk on. Begin in your front yard at the foot of your driveway. Drop a treat on the ground, and while the dog is eating it, turn and take a giant step away from your dog. Your back is now to the dog. CT when he takes a step toward you. Deliver the treat from your hand on the side you want the dog to walk on, held alongside your leg. Continue until he is successful 80% of the time at the speed you desire.

Quick Clicks: If you prefer the left

If you want the dog to walk on your left (the side used for formal obedience or Rally), have the leash in your right hand and pivot to your right each time you step away from the dog. This will keep the leash manageable and encourage the dog to come up on the correct side. Hold the leash and clicker in the left hand and pivot left to work the dog on your right side.

Mandy pivots right and feeds with her left hand to keep Ping in position on her left side.

9. Now, CT *as the dog* moves into Heel position, right next to your leg (so he has to take more than one step). Here is where delivering the treats in the correct place can really speed up your training! Change practice locations frequently. Work to 80% in each new location.

10. Can you predict that the dog will come to your side for a CT? Then it's time to add a name to this behavior. Starting in a new location, step away from the dog, say your cue, CT when he comes to your side, then step away again. Repeat this pairing of "cue, behavior, CT" at least fifty times over the next couple of days, changing locations frequently.

11. As the dog runs to your side, take a step or two so he must move with you while you are moving. CT after a couple of steps, then turn away again.

12. Gradually increase the distance you walk together before CT-ing the dog, until you can take at least five steps with the dog trotting beside you before you CT.

13. Vary the number of steps the dog is required to take before getting a CT.

Generalize the behavior:

- Continue to increase your average number of steps taken before clicking and treating, using the Bouncing Around technique. If you find you are often losing the dog at this stage, you are taking too many steps for him and your average is too high.

- Continue to add more and more distractions in your environment. Don't forget to make a big deal if the dog ignores something particularly interesting to stay with you!

- Add changes of pace such as walking faster or slower.

- Vary your rewards. Sometimes throw a ball or toy for the dog to chase (with a release first!), sometimes pet him, sometimes give him a treat and sometimes release him to sniff an interesting scent.

Keep in Mind

Walking on a leash without pulling is one of the most difficult things to teach a dog, mostly because humans don't pay attention to the dog on the end of the leash unless he is creating a problem. If you want to be successful with this behavior, from now on, any time your dog is on leash you *must* work on keeping the leash loose. If he gets even an occasional reward for pulling, such as getting to touch noses with another dog or greet a person, or get to his favorite park more quickly, he will continue to pull. Remember, variable rewards make a behavior *stronger!*

The longer the dog has been pulling on leash, the longer it will take you to teach him that it doesn't work any more. And, if you walk your dog on a retractable leash and don't want him to pull, stop using it right now. He is learning to pull every time you walk because the dog has to put pressure against the collar in order to draw the leash out.

Troubleshooting

The dog works okay until I move outside with him, then is uninterested in me and my treats.

- Stress can cause a dog to stop working in a new environment, and stress often appears as "disinterest" in a dog. If you know your dog is on the shy side, build up very slowly through new distractions, changing the environment as minimally as possible each time.

- Work before meals and use the most exciting treats you can find, delivered in his food bowl. Something about having a bowl plopped down in front of him is simply irresistible to most dogs!

The dog isn't trying to pull me forward on walks—I'm usually pulling him along.

- This can be due to fear or shyness. The good news is that this exercise works the same even if the dog isn't pulling. You are still CT-ing for coming to your side. Move more slowly through each new environment if you suspect that this fits your dog.

- Stop pulling. If you stand still and only move forward when the leash is slack, neither you nor the dog has any reason to be pulling on the leash. If you are trying to drag the dog along, he may just be putting on the brakes as an automatic reaction to the tension YOU are putting on the leash.

The dog works all right until another dog (or person, child on a bike, etc.) goes by.

- Work separately on getting attention around the particular distraction that is a problem for your dog. See the beginning of the chapter for an attention exercise for more information. Wait until you have good attention to begin your work on walking on leash around that particular distraction.

Variations
Teach your dog to touch your hand while you are moving, then use your hand as a target or lure as you walk with the dog on leash (this will result in something a little closer to formal heeling, and the dog will need to stay closer to you—not as much fun for the dog on walks, but great for crowds or crossing the street). Teach the dog to do the same "close" walking (no more that a six-foot leash away) without a leash. (See Walk Off Leash in Chapter 4 and Touch in Chapter 6.)

 ## WAIT AT THE DOOR
The dog waits at any doorway, without moving forward, until released. He does not have to remain in a particular position such as a Sit or Down, but he must not cross the threshold you have specified. This behavior is a must-have for all dogs for safety reasons. This can (and should!) be used at doorways, at street crossings, or when opening your dog's crate. Remember to practice in the car, too—hatchbacks or the large rear doors of SUVs or sliding van doors give the dog plenty of space to bolt before you can get a leash on him. This behavior is also a building block for sitting politely at the door for greetings.

Suggested verbal cue: "Wait," "Hold up," "Pause."

Suggested visual cue: Waving hand in front of dog's face.

You will need: Treats, a hungry dog, a leash, and a clicker, plus multiple obvious thresholds (doorways).

Speed Steps
1. Start at a doorway, with the dog on leash. Keep the leash short enough so that the dog is right next to you and can't step through the door. Open the door. CT when the dog stops pulling forward to get through the doorway. Repeat one to ten times.

2. Practice at multiple doorways, including in your car.

3. Start at your original doorway with the dog on leash. CT when the dog looks at you, then release the dog to go through the doorway *with you*. Work both directions through the doorway. Practice at multiple doorways. Repeat one to ten times each time you change criteria.

4. Starting with a new doorway, lengthen your leash so that the dog could step through the doorway if he chose to. Don't choose a doorway the dog is likely to want to charge out, such as the front door or the door to the back yard. Open the door. If the dog hesitates or looks at you, CT, then release and walk through the doorway with the dog. Repeat ten times.

5. Change locations to a more enticing doorway (but still not the front or back door) and repeat. Repeat in several new locations, at least ten times at each doorway.

6. Is the dog getting predictable yet (does he pause and wait for more information at the doorway)? If so, time to add your cue. (If not, continue to work at gradually more enticing doorways until he is pausing for your instructions at least 80% of the time.) Say your cue, open the door, dog pauses, you CT then release to go through the doorway. Continue changing doorways and pairing your cue with the behavior for at least fifty additional repetitions in various locations over several days.

7. Start at a doorway with the door already open. Approach the doorway with the dog on a loose leash. Just before the dog reaches the threshold, say your cue and stop moving. CT if the dog pauses. If he doesn't pause, repeat, but shorten the leash so he isn't as far ahead of you.

8. Repeat Step 7 at the back door, front door and most exciting doors you regularly encounter.

Generalize the behavior:
- Practice leaving your dog behind while you go through the doorway, then return to the dog—start with just a step in front of the dog, and gradually get farther and farther away.

- Work on the Wait at safe doors without the leash.

- Increase the time of the Wait using Bouncing Around.

- Practice Wait while you open and close the door but the dog does not go through the doorway.

- Work on the Wait at enticing doors such as your front door, without the leash. Have a back-up plan ready in case the dog leaps through unexpectedly—can you set up an exercise pen around the front steps or block the walkway?

- Have someone standing on the other side of the door waiting to come in. Vary whether people come inside or not.

- Have someone with a dog walk by your front door. Have a friend bring a dog your dog likes and stand on your porch. Sometimes they come in, sometimes they don't. Use a brief play session with the visiting dog as a reward for a good Wait.

- Have your dog do a Wait while kids are playing in your front yard.

- Practice Wait when you open the car door, at curbs before you step into the street, and when you open the dog's crate door.

Keep in Mind

If the dog doesn't seem to get it, use a less distracting doorway, such as the door to your bedroom rather than your kitchen. It can be helpful to have a second person holding the leash. This allows you to work in different places at the doorway yet still prevents the dog from crossing the threshold without being released.

Deliver all of your treats to the dog on the correct side of the doorway. You want him to have a reason to stay behind. When you get to the point that you are leaving the dog, you will toss the treat or other reward to him on the other side of the threshold.

Troubleshooting

The dog does okay while on leash, but bursts through the opening when the leash is off:

- Start with very boring doorways. Work slowly up through the progressively more interesting doorways in your house.

- Use your body to block the dog's exit—step in front of and move toward the dog to make him back away from the doorway. (Use your foot for a small dog.)

- Work on the attention exercise at the beginning of this chapter first so that the dog is more likely to check with you instead of trying to run through the door.

Variations

Have a conversation with a friend or delivery person on the front porch while your dog does a Wait with the door open. See if you can teach your dog to Wait behind a less obvious threshold such as the change from linoleum to carpet, or with no threshold at all.

BONUS BEHAVIOR: THE MOVING WAIT OR SIT AT A DISTANCE

This is a modification of an exercise taught by John Rogerson that doesn't use clickers, but is a great example of using the Premack Principle to teach a behavior.

Start with three people, a dog and a really exciting toy. The dog has to be *very interested* in catching the toy (this is critical to the success of this behavior taught this way). You won't need a third person for very long, just at the beginning.

One person holds the dog's leash so the dog can't get to the toy. The dog's owner will throw the toy to the catcher. Stand in the following triangle formation, with dog and owner about fifteen-twenty feet apart, and catcher slightly off center of the line between dog and owner.

The leash holder is on the left, the catcher in the center, and the dog's owner on the right. The dog runs to the catcher, anticipating that the ball will be thrown there.

1. Owner begins by playing with the toy to get the dog's attention, then tosses it to catcher who plays briefly with it. Repeat three times, or until the dog is tracking the thrown toy.

2. Owner tosses the toy to catcher *at the same time* that dog holder lets go of the dog. Catcher should play with the toy a bit and let the dog touch it, but don't let the dog play with it. Repeat three times, or until the dog is running to catcher when released (that is, running to the point midway between dog and owner.)

3. Now owner tosses the toy *at* the dog (at same place where catcher is) trying to stop the dog's forward movement at that same point. Repeat three times or until the dog is stopping on the same line as the catcher. Catcher can gradually fade out of the picture.

4. Now pretend to throw the toy—fast and underhand. The instant the dog stops, the toy is tossed over his head, aiming for the rear end. (Making the pretend throw look real and timing the actual toss are the most difficult parts of this exercise.) This causes the dog to stop dead in his tracks, and rock backward into a Sit to try and catch the toy. The Sit isn't mandatory, but will help get the behavior.

Throw the toy fast and underhand to get the dog to stop dead in his tracks and rock backward into a sit.

Continue generalizing with the following steps:

- Gradually add time to the dog's pause, varying how long he waits until you throw the toy.

- Add a verbal cue (Wait or Halt) to your visual cue so you can practice when the dog is facing away from you.

- Vary distance and orientation to the dog.

- Vary the practice environment.

- Vary the delivery of the toy. For example, sometimes someone hiding nearby drops a toy behind the dog, sometimes it is thrown behind the dog, sometimes you rush in behind the dog to play.

Ping (8 year old Boxer), Jenga (20 month old Boxer) and Perretta (13 year old Golden Retriever) wait for their turn. Ping is a Delta-registered Animal Assisted Therapy Dog and retired from agility. Jenga is an International Ch. in conformation, a Canine Good Citizen, and is training for agility. Perretta is retired from agility.

Chapter 3

FOR HEALTH AND WELFARE

This chapter covers some behaviors that are useful when your dog visits the veterinarian or groomer. Handlers of large (and often dangerous) animals routinely train "housekeeping" behaviors such as these to help keep their charges healthy without endangering themselves. Elephants learn to extend their back feet through the bars of a cage for a pedicure, and orangutans hold still for a blood draw.

You can accomplish the same behaviors with your dog. In this chapter you will learn the following behaviors:

- Relax for Veterinary Exams (including handling ears and mouth).
- Toenail Clipping.
- Stand Still for Bathing/Grooming.
- Offer Paw (for a blood draw, to check feet or for toenail clipping).
- Freeze (don't move a muscle).

Both the Speed Steps and the Detailed Training Plan are included for each behavior. Use whichever suits your level of expertise with clicker training. If you are using the Speed Steps and find yourself having difficulty, take a look at the Detailed Training Plan, particularly the Quick Clicks—they may have just the tip you need. Remember to keep sessions short and to take a significant break after every one to three steps, depending on how many repetitions you've had to make at each step.

RELAX FOR VETERINARY EXAMS

The dog lies quietly on his side, without struggling, while you handle his feet, tail, ears, and teeth. Other people, such as his veterinarian, can examine him with equal ease. This is terrific training to make general care of your dog less stressful, and can be a good building block for toenail clipping. If you have a large or rambunctious dog, this can help settle him for social interactions with other people by teaching him to be calm when he is touched.

Suggested verbal cue: "Settle," "Hold Still," "Relax" (draw out the "a" for a nice soothing sound).

Suggested visual cue: Hold your palm flat toward your dog and make a slow massage circle in the air.

You will need: A sleepy, relaxed dog who already knows Down.

Speed Steps

1. With the dog in a relaxed Down, touch the dog's side for a second, CT. Touch his chest, CT. Touch a front leg, CT. Touch each part of the dog's body once, for a second, followed by a CT.

2. Touch the dog all over again, with slightly more pressure.

3. Touch all over again, holding the touch for longer, one to five seconds.

4. Repeat Step 3 several times in different locations.

5. Now when you touch, actually encircle smaller areas such as legs and ears, and pull a little on the skin over the back and sides.

Gently grab smaller areas such as legs and ears, and pull a little on the skin over the back and sides.

6. Repeat, progressing to more enthusiastic grabbing.

7. Add your cue.

8. Hold and/or move two body parts before CT.

9. Increase the number of body parts touched.

10. Check each body part carefuly as you handle it—spread toes, look in ears, check teeth, touch toenails.

11. Massage the dog's shoulder and hip. Keep it short. CT and release.

12. Change to a new floor surface and repeat Step 11.

13. Continue changing locations and surfaces. Don't forget to practice outside.

14. Have other people touch the dog while you CT. Start with people he knows and likes and move to people he doesn't know.

Quick Clicks: Why not 80%?

It's okay if you work each step to more than 80% success for many of the behaviors in this chapter—in fact, it's better if you strive for 100% success before moving on. It is really not a problem even if you repeat many times at each step. Since the goal in most husbandry behaviors is a relaxed dog, rather than changing criteria to get to a final behavior, the 80% rule doesn't really apply. We'll indicate in the Detailed Training Plan if it's important not to stall out at a particular step (such as on the Offer Paw behavior).

Keep in Mind

Some dogs are very stressed by being touched, and you want to reward calm, relaxed behavior. If you have to, start by holding your hand over an area without touching (as close as you can get without stressing the dog), keep it there until the dog is still, then CT and stop. The dog's reward for not pulling away or otherwise reacting is that you stop and leave him alone. This is likely a much more powerful reward than a treat at this point. Wait at least ten minutes before you repeat. Try to get about an inch closer to the dog each time, until he is able to be calm while you touch him in one place. Follow the Detailed Training Plan on page 68, taking extra time at each step.

You can also teach the dog to initiate a touch by teaching Offer Paw (later in this chapter).

If you can touch certain parts of your dog (shoulder, side, under the chin), but not others (feet, tail, head), start with the easy parts. Work on them until you can get a ten-second touch without the dog pulling away. Then, move to the next least stressful area (see the photo for the general body sensitivity areas of dogs) and repeat. Add a third area, then a fourth. Proceed with the training plan.

In the photo above, 1 is the least stressful, progressing to 6, which is generally the most stressful area for dogs.

Quick Clicks: You are in charge

Remember, it's your dog, and you have the right to direct how things are done with him. Discuss things with your veterinarian in advance if you have any concerns. Mandy had a vet (not her regular one) that poo-pooed the need for treats with a fourteen-week-old lab puppy she was training. Mandy was vindicated ten minutes later when the vet complimented her while the dog held absolutely still on the table for a painful catheter procedure because she was clicked and fed the entire time.

Troubleshooting

My dog won't take the treat after I click.

- Your dog is probably stressed. You are moving too fast for him. Don't be in a hurry with this. You want to be able to reward calm behavior. Take your time, use better treats and work before meals.

My dog just doesn't seem relaxed.

- Sit on the floor rather than in a chair. Play soft, relaxing music (this is really to help you). Make sure you are breathing deeply and regularly, not holding your breath or gasping. Your own anxiety transfers readily to your dog. (See Keep in Mind above for a suggestion for an extra slow start.)

The dog goes along well for a while and then seems to suddenly regress.

- You moved too fast and spooked the dog. Start over from Step 1 and move extra slowly when you get to the point where the dog regressed.

- Something else spooked the dog—maybe something in the environment that you weren't even aware of. Back up a few steps and progress more slowly through the steps.

Variations

In preparation for toenail clipping or foot bandaging, concentrate on the dog's feet, squeezing out each toenail, tapping toenails and holding the leg firmly. Press on the end of the toenail (you might have to put styptic powder on to stop a bleeding toenail).

Concentrate on the dog's mouth, opening it and looking at all the teeth, in preparation for teeth brushing or if you are going to show your dog. Practice wrapping your leash around the dog's mouth in case you have to do a makeshift muzzle some day. Hold the dog's mouth firmly, but gently and take a good look at his eyes, lifting each lid, and checking his nose.

Lift the dog, CT-ing if he's not wiggling. Start with just a second or two of lifting and build up to carrying the dog for some distance. An injured dog may have to be carried, or lifted into a car. Be careful of your back with a large dog! (This will test your dexterity with your clicker, or you can substitute a bridge word—see Chapter 5.)

Practice Relax with the dog on an elevated surface, such as a picnic table, to simulate a vet exam table.

Take the dog to your veterinarian's office to get treats from the people in the waiting area and from your veterinarian, get clicked and treated for being on the scale, and get clicked and treated going into an exam room. Repeat many times before the dog actually needs to have a procedure done so the dog thinks your veterinarian's office is cookie heaven instead of doggie hell.

Have your vet practice a mock examination of the dog while you CT. You may have to pay for an extra office visit to practice this, but it will be well worth the money in the long run. If your veterinarian understands what you are doing, he or she should be all in favor of it. This training may make your dog the darling of the practice.

Teach your dog to happily wear costumes, backpacks, hats, goggles, bandages and boots.

Detailed Training Plan

1. Play some calm, relaxing music (this is more for you than the dog). Sit in a chair if you have a large dog, and on the floor if you have a small dog. Put the clicker in your non-dominant hand and a bowl of treats out of reach of the dog, but where you can get them easily. Allow the dog to be in whatever position he's comfortable with—sitting, standing or lying down. Using your dominant hand, touch the dog's side for one second, click (with your non-dominant hand), and treat (using the hand you touched the dog with). (The only job of your non-dominant hand is to click—it's good practice for you to be ambi-clicks-terous!) Touch the dog's chest, CT, touch a front leg, CT. Continue until you have touched the dog on every part of his body for one count, working to the back legs, tail (base and out to the end), up along his back, the ears and teeth, in that order. Pay attention if the dog seems stressed (changes position, pulls away, moves the limb or turns abruptly toward you) about any part of his body so that you can work on this separately. (See Keep in Mind for help on this.) Do not move on to Step 2 until you can touch every part of the dog's body, even if only for a second.

2. Touch each part of the dog's body again, putting more pressure on your touch, and holding it about two seconds before CT-ing. You want to click while your hand is still in physical contact with the dog, not pulling away. Once you click, you can remove your hand *and* grab a treat for the dog.

3. Repeat Step 2, holding for three seconds.

4. Change treats, and touch each part of the dog's body again, going from least to more stressful as described in Step 1. Vary each touch from one to five seconds, CT-ing the dog for quiet, relaxed behavior—i.e., not struggling, wiggling, or moving away from your touch; relaxed body; lying down; yawning; or stretching.

Quick Clicks: Why change now?

We're changing treats here because after twenty to thirty repetitions, the dog may be getting bored with the same treat, and because we are upping the stress level in this step.

5. Change locations and repeat Step 4.

6. Change locations and treats, and repeat Step 4. Try to work in a location with a different floor surface from where you started originally.

7. Change locations. Now, rather than just resting your hand on the dog, you are going to encircle the smaller parts like legs and ears, and pull a little on the skin over the back and sides. Don't grab or pinch. Be gentle about it initially, then gradually be a little more assertive as the dog gets comfortable with it. Vary the amount of time you maintain each hold from one to five counts, but always CT when the dog is relaxed, not pulling away or resisting.

Quick Clicks: Stress

If at any point the dog seems stressed (panting, resisting, moving away or stiffening, etc.) you should end the session. Start the next session at a previous step (where the dog wasn't stressed) and build up more slowly from that point, breaking your steps even smaller than indicated here. Remember to breathe deeply yourself! Your own relaxation will definitely help.

8. Continue to change locations and repeat Step 7 until the dog seems totally bored with the whole process.

9. At this point you can add the cue, remembering to CT for calm, relaxed behavior only; so it's cue, hold dog, dog relaxes, CT. Repeat the "cue, behavior, CT" pairing at least fifty times over the course of several days.

10. In a new location, hold and move at least two parts of the dog's body (lift an ear, move the tail, lift the lip, etc.), clicking for calm behavior.

11. Repeat Step 10 over the course of several days, changing locations each time, and adding one or two new body parts at each session.

12. Now gently massage each body part as you move around the dog's body, clicking for relaxed behavior. If the dog seems to be enjoying it at this point, you can dispense with the clicker, and talk calmly to the dog while you massage/examine him. This may be a matter of weeks for puppies or dogs that resist physical contact, or a matter of days for a quiet older dog. Remember to reward *relaxed and quiet* behavior with treats and/or release from restraint. Use low, drawn out praise while you are touching the dog. Breathe!

13. As you move around the dog's body, check each part to make sure it's healthy—spread toes, look in the ears, check teeth, touch toenails, check the belly, look at the

skin, etc. Remember, you're rewarding with treats for being still while you examine each part of the dog.

14. If your dog already knows how to Play Dead, have him do it, then massage his hips and shoulders, go briefly down the legs, and then back to hips and shoulders. Keep this step short—the whole process should take less than ten seconds. CT when you get back to the hip/shoulder area. Repeat ten times, having the dog Play Dead, Hold Still, massage, CT. If you haven't already taught Play Dead, have the dog lie down, then massage the hips and shoulders on one side. Most dogs like it enough that they will roll onto their side to get more, but if your dog doesn't, don't force him. You'll undo all your hard work up to this point! Instead, teach the Play Dead and reinforce often and well for that behavior, then come back to this step. (See our other book, *Right on Target*, for detailed instructions on teaching Play Dead and the Quick Clicks below for brief instructions.)

Quick Clicks: Play dead

In case you need help, here are some quick steps for teaching Play dead. Put your dog in a Down. Use a treat to lure the dog onto one hip—hold the treat in front of the dog's nose and move it toward the dog's shoulder. If the dog's head follows, the dog should automatically roll onto one hip. Once the dog is relaxed on one hip, use your lure to turn his head so it is at a ninety degree angle to his body, and move the treat up so he will put his nose up. As his nose goes up, he should start to roll back onto his shoulder. You will, of course, click each step as you go. (See page 46 in Chapter 2 for the starting point for Play Dead and page 71 for the final position.)

The final position for Play Dead.

Generalize the behavior:

- Continue changing locations and floor surfaces. Don't forget to practice outside—you never know when you will need to check an injury at a park or some other outdoor venue.

- Include other people in your handling practice as the dog gets more comfortable with it. You can CT while another person touches the dog gently. Remember to click for the touch, not the removal of the touch.

Slick Clicks: The speed of training from Mandy Book

I took my Boxer, Twister, to the veterinarian because she seemed to be having some kind of urinary problem. A standard procedure is to get a free catch urine sample to check for problems in the lower part of the urinary tract. The vet tech who followed me outside had a little contraption to collect the urine—a long metal pole with a plastic cup on the end. I told Twister to "Hurry Up." The tech stood ready, following her as she moved around. Twister was a little unsure about this stranger following her with a stick, but she finally squatted and peed. The tech quickly stuck the cup between Twister's legs, banging it against one of them in the process. She unfortunately missed the catch, and that was quite enough for Twister, who wouldn't let the lady get near her again, with or without the stick. I told her I would try it at home and bring back a sample. How hard could it be? After all, they teach whales to pee in a cup using clicker training, so I ought to be able to do it relatively quickly with a dog. Once I got home, I made a device similar to the urine-catcher with a hanger and a plastic cup. During the course of the next two hours I shaped Twister to allow me to put the "catcher" between her back legs and hold it there, without her moving away from it. This took about ten sessions, lasting about one minute each. I even added a step where I banged the cup against her legs, just in case. And I gave her water. When I felt like she was comfortable with the process, I took her outside and told her to "Hurry Up." When she squatted, I angled the cup between her legs. She filled it, not minding in the slightest, and got a cookie to boot! The morals of the story? 1) You never know what you'll need to teach or how fast you'll need to teach it! Twister's quick acceptance of the cup was possible because of the power of clicker training. 2) If I had thought to spend ten minutes using the clicker at the vet's office before they tried to get the sample, I wouldn't have had to devote ten sessions to it at home and then drive all the way back to the vet!

Troubleshooting

My dog really does not like to be touched, so will this work for him?

- For the dog who dislikes physical contact, removing your hand is doubly rewarding because the touching stops when he is still. Keep the sessions brief, progress slowly (work at the same step for several sessions), and spread sessions out throughout the day to help a dog learn to enjoy the contact.

TOENAIL CLIPPING

The dog allows you to clip his toenails without fighting, biting, or other unpleasantness. If zookeepers can do this with elephants, you can do it with your dog! Even if you plan on having the vet or groomer clip your dog's nails, teaching this will make life easier for everyone, including the dog. You may need to check a paw for thorns or burns, or bandage a foot sometime.

Suggested verbal cue: "Hold Still," "Toesies," "Tootsies," "Foot."

Suggested visual cue: Hold up the clippers.

You will need: Toenail clippers. It will help to teach Relax for veterinary exam first. You could also use Offer Paw as a starting point.

Speed Steps

1. With the dog standing, touch a front leg, click, and treat.

2. Grab and hold firmly, high up on the dog's leg, for one second. CT for relaxation. Alternate front legs.

3. Grasp the front leg at the elbow for one to five seconds. Alternate front legs.

4. Gradually work down the front leg until you reach the foot and can hold it firmly.

5. Repeat these steps with the back legs.

6. Lean over the dog and grab his front foot, bending the leg at the elbow and gently squeezing one toe. Repeat, alternating feet and holding for a count varying from one to eight, up to twenty times.

7. Tap a toenail with the clippers, CT. Repeat with each toenail.

8. Lift a foot and clip one nail. Just take off a tip so you're sure you won't cut the quick and cause pain. Repeat with each foot, CT-ing each clip.

Quick Clicks: Using life rewards

This is a really good behavior to pair with a life reward. After a session working on toenail clipping, take your dog out into the yard to chase a ball. Run out with him! Make it exciting. Or, grab a tug toy and have a rousing game. This is the Premack Principle at work.

Keep in Mind

Take your time working through the steps. You want the dog to be very relaxed at each step, and ultimately with the whole nail clipping procedure. The better foundation you create for being relaxed, the easier a lifetime of toenail clipping will be.

With a nervous dog, or one who already dislikes having his feet touched, teaching Offer Paw (later in this chapter) is a good way to start. Teach Offer Paw with both feet first, then proceed with the training plan.

Troubleshooting

The dog pulls away as soon as I touch his elbow.

- Make sure you are clicking relaxed behavior—not when the dog is pulling away or resisting, but rather is loose and wobbly in your hand. Have someone watch you to check. Start with your hand just hovering near the elbow if you have to. Stay at this step for an extra fifty repetitions.

The dog is fine until I get out the clippers, then he freaks.

- He's already had a bad experience. Change his mind about the clippers by making them fun. Remember the warm-up exercise with the bag from Chapter 1? You're going to do the same thing with the clippers. Put them on the floor and CT the dog for pawing them, touching them, picking them up. You can also work on Steps 1 through 7 while you're doing this. When the dog gets excited about the clippers and is thrilled to see them, start from Step 1, using playing with the clippers as part of his reward.

- Have someone feed the dog continuously while you do all the steps through clipping a nail. Use super scrumptious treats. Spread the sessions out over several days. Ask the feeder to let you know if the dog starts getting grabby or forceful about taking the treat—it indicates his stress level is rising.

Variations

Lift each foot and press against the end of the nail. You'll need to do this if you cut a nail too short and have to apply styptic powder.

Introduce the dog to a nail grinder. Some people (and dogs) find grinding less intimidating than clipping. If your dog is a show dog, you'll need the more professional look anyway. Hint: You'll have to get the dog used to the sound and the vibration first.

Teach the dog to lie comfortably on his side while you clip to make the job easier on your back.

You could also teach your dog to file his nails, using a large board covered with sand paper. For more information, check out http://www.shirleychong.com/keepers/nail-file.html.

Detailed Training Plan

1. Start with the dog standing. If you haven't taught Relax for veterinary exam, you might want to do that first. It will make the rest of the process easier. Otherwise, just stand the dog, touch the front leg, CT. Repeat five times.

2. With the dog standing, touch the other front leg, CT. Repeat five times.

3. Now hold one front leg firmly (high up on the leg) for one second, CT if the dog does not resist. Make sure the timing of your click is at a relaxation point for the dog. The dog then gets doubly rewarded—he gets a food treat and he gets relief from physical restraint. (If you encounter resistance, go back and review the Relax for Veterinary Exam earlier in the chapter until the dog really likes having you touch him.)

4. Alternate between front legs, grasping and holding the upper part of the leg for one to three counts each time. Repeat ten times.

5. Grasp the front leg at the elbow for a count varying between one and five, CT when the dog is relaxed. Alternate with the other leg, repeating ten times on each leg.

6. Continue working down the front legs, grasping successively closer to the foot, and holding firmly for one to five counts, until you have reached the foot and can hold it firmly without the dog struggling or trying to pull away. Stay at each place on the leg for a minimum of five repetitions. Remember to breathe deeply!

Quick Clicks: Keep balanced

Hold the leg close to the dog's body rather than pulling it away from the body. It's more comfortable and allows the dog to balance. He'll be less likely to resist. It may also help to have the dog lying on his side, particularly if he is relaxed in that position. Mandy has her dogs lie across her knees. (See photo on page 76.) This allows her older dogs to easily balance when a leg is picked up.

7. Repeat Steps 1 through 6 with the back legs.

8. Change locations and repeat Steps 1 through 7. (We recommend that you include outdoor locations and consider doing actual toenail clipping outside. That way, if you accidentally cut the quick and make the toe bleed, you don't have to worry about cleaning up little spots of blood all over the house.)

9. Change locations again and repeat Steps 1 through 7.

10. Stand the dog, and lean over him to grab his front foot, bending his leg at the elbow, and squeezing one toe gently. Hold for a count of one to five seconds each time, and repeat at least ten times (more if the dog had difficulty at the beginning). Breathe deeply while you do this (humans have a tendency to hold their breath during toenail clipping, signaling to the dog they should be stressed). Repeat with all the dog's toes.

Bend the leg at the elbow to get the dog used to the position his foot will be in for clipping. Notice that the clicker and foot are held in the same hand here.

11. Repeat Step 10 but hold for a count of one to eight, CT. Repeat, alternating feet, up to twenty times.

12. Change locations and repeat Step 11. Add your cue here if you like, by saying the cue, holding the dog's foot and gently squeezing, then CT-ing relaxed behavior.

13. Bring out the nail clippers and repeat Step 10, holding the clippers in the hand you would use to clip with, but not actually cutting a toenail. Either have someone else click at the right time, use your bridge word instead of the clicker (see Chapter 5), or hold the clippers in one hand and the dog's foot and the clicker in the other.

Hold the clipper (or grinder) in one hand and the dog's foot and the clicker in the other. Notice the treats are within easy reach.

14. Tap a toenail with the clippers, CT. Repeat with every toenail. Move on to the next step when the dog is relaxed every time, and does not pull away.

15. The big moment! Lift the front foot, *breathe,* clip one nail, CT. Repeat five times with the front foot, clipping a different nail each time (four times if your dog's dew-claws have been removed). It's not important if you actually get a lot of clipping done, just take the tip of the nail off for now. You'll get better as you get more practice. The goal at this point is to get the *dog* comfortable with the whole procedure.

16. Repeat Step 15 with each foot.

Generalize the behavior:

- Have someone else the dog knows clip his nails.

- Have someone the dog doesn't know hold his feet and work up to Step 11. If someone else will be clipping your dog's nails, make sure he gets practice having lots of strangers touch his feet. They don't have to clip, and they probably shouldn't if they don't really know what they're doing, but they should handle his feet.

- Practice up to Step 12 regularly with the dog, without clipping a single nail. This makes the actual clipping less stressful.

- Practice on a raised surface such as a grooming table.

- Clip nails while the dog is standing, sitting, and lying down.

 ## STAND STILL FOR BATHING/GROOMING

The dog stands without fussing or struggling while you bathe or groom him. This doesn't mean he'll freeze in place (that's the last behavior in this chapter), just that he'll remain reasonably still so you can accomplish whatever you need to do. You might use this for veterinary exams or toenail clipping in addition to bathing and brushing. You might choose to have the dog lying down for some of these things. That's okay. You can teach the dog to lie flat in the same way. This behavior can also be useful for pet therapy work if patients want to pet your dog, and for formal obedience that includes a Stand for Exam exercise.

Suggested verbal cue: "Stand," "Stay," "Hold Still."

Suggested visual cue: Hold your hand flat, palm facing the dog, like a traffic cop telling you to stop.

You will need: A bathtub and whatever tools you use to groom. Teach Relax for veterinary exam and Touch (Chapter 6) first.

Speed Steps

1. Start with your dog sitting in front of you, facing to your left or right. Present your hand far enough in front of him that he has to stand to touch it, without taking a step. Cue Touch. After you CT, put him back into a Sit and repeat.

2. Start with the dog in a down in front of you and do the same thing.

3. Starting with the dog in a Sit, vary whether he has to touch one, two, or three times before you CT.

4. Repeat Step 3 starting with the dog in a Down.

5. Repeat Step 3 but after the dog stands, quickly drop your hand, CT, then release the dog. Gradually increase duration until the dog will stand for up to one minute without moving.

6. Add your cue.

7. Build up duration, until the dog will stand for several minutes.

8. Stand the dog and pick up a foot. Vary how long you gently hold the foot.

9. Repeat with each foot.

10. Stand the dog and lift his tail or an ear. Vary how many body parts you touch or move before clicking, treating and releasing the dog.

11. Work in a bathtub or shower or on a grooming table. Be sure the dog has secure footing.

12. Gradually add water to the bathtub.

13. Practice toweling the dog off while he stands.

14. Practice brushing the dog while he stands.

15. If your dog's coat will be clipped or shaved, introduce the clippers.

Keep in Mind

Experiment with where to hold your hand target to best get your dog into a stand and keep him there.

If your dog will be professionally groomed, bring him to the groomer and CT for getting on the table and into the tub. Do this for several visits *before* the dog has to be groomed—things will go much more smoothly for the dog when he actually goes to be groomed. If you'll be bathing him, but at a pet wash rather than your home, socialize him to the pet wash as a separate step as well.

Troubleshooting

The dog moves when I take my hand away from in front of his nose.

- You were too slow bringing your hand back. At first, keep it away for the briefest of moments. Be sure to break your steps down, adding time the hand is away in tiny increments.

The dog moves when I start touching him.

- The dog may dislike having you touch him. Review the Relax for Veterinary Exam behavior until the dog is 100% comfortable with being touched all over.

Detailed Training Plan

1. Start with the dog sitting in front of you, facing to your left or right side. (Experiment with the Hand Touch and clicking to see which direction is most comfortable for you. When you've mastered that side, change sides so the dog will stand facing both ways!) Hold your hand out far enough that he has to Stand Up on all fours to touch but not so far away that he takes a step forward once he is standing. Cue a Hand Touch, and CT when he stands up and touches your hand. Put him back into a Sit. Repeat ten times.

2. Start with the dog in a Down in front of you. Hold your hand out far enough that he has to stand up on all fours to touch it, cue the Touch, then CT when he stands up and touches your hand. Your hand will be slightly above his head and in front rather than directly in front of him. Put him back into a Down. Repeat ten times.

Hold your hand out far enough that your dog has to stand up on all fours to touch it. The clicker and treats are behind your back.

3. Start with the dog in a Sit. Put your hand in front of him and cue Touch. *Do not* click the first time he touches. The dog will probably look at you, wondering why you didn't click him. Wait for him to touch your hand a second time, then CT. Repeat ten times, starting from a Sit every time, varying whether the dog has to touch your hand one, two, or three times before getting clicked and treated. This step helps build duration into the behavior, and will allow us to eliminate the hand target.

4. Start with the dog in a Down and repeat Step 3.

5. Now stand the dog using your Hand Touch cue. Quickly drop your hand, count one-one-thousand, and CT if the dog hasn't moved. Release the dog and make him

move. Repeat ten times, varying how long your hand disappears from view, and CT-ing the dog for remaining in a stand during that time, then releasing the dog. (If you need help with this step, please see Bouncing Around in Chapter 1.)

6. Continue adding duration until the dog will remain standing still for up to one minute.

7. Can you predict that the dog will wait patiently, with your hand away from his nose, until you click? Then it's time to add your new Stand cue. Remember, the order is new cue ("Stand"), then old cue ("Touch"). Say the Stand cue first, then signal and cue Touch, drop your hand, and when the dog is still for the amount of time you decide, CT and release the dog. Repeat the pairing of your cue with the behavior at least fifty times, changing locations every ten times. When the dog starts to anticipate the cue for Touch by standing immediately, you can drop the Touch cue and hand signal.

8. Once the dog is starting to understand the cue, you will occasionally not say the Stand cue (about 10% of the time). The dog should remain in whatever position he is in and not Stand Up. If he stands without being cued, you need to continue working on adding the cue. (See Chapter 1 for more help on adding cues.)

9. Slowly build up the amount of time the dog remains standing still, until the dog will remain still for up to five minutes. Use the Bouncing Around technique.

10. Repeat Step 9 in a new location.

11. Stand the dog. Pick up a front foot, CT if the dog doesn't move, and release the dog. Be aware of how you hold the foot—don't clamp down on it like a vise. Simply lift it and support it. Repeat ten times, alternating front feet and varying how long you hold the foot up by a few seconds each time.

12. Stand the dog, then pick up a back foot, CT if the dog doesn't move, and release the dog. Repeat ten times, alternating between the back feet and varying how long you hold the foot up by a few seconds.

13. Stand the dog, touch his tail, lift an ear, CT when the dog doesn't move, and release the dog. Repeat ten times, touching one, two, or three different body parts each time, and holding for varying amounts of time.

Generalize the behavior:

- Work the Stand in a bathtub or shower. Make sure the surface the dog is on is very secure so the dog doesn't slip or fall. Practice first with no water in the tub, then with a small amount already in the tub, but no running water, then with running water and the dog outside the tub. When the dog is comfortable with each step, you can move closer to an actual bath experience. For a Labrador, this might take one afternoon. For a dog who already hates baths, plan on a lot more sessions!

- Practice the Stand on a raised surface. You will want to start with the surface very low (and make sure it is secure!) and gradually increase it to full height. Be careful not to let dogs jump off a high surface, as they could be injured.

- Practice toweling the dog dry while he Stands. Dry for a short amount of time (a few seconds) initially, gradually building up to more time while the dog stands still.

- Practice brushing the dog while he stands still. Introduce the dog to the brush first, then incorporate the Stand, brushing just one part and clicking, treating and releasing the dog, then building up to more and more complete brushing.

- If your dog is clipped, introduce the dog to the noise of clippers, holding them in your hand and picking up body parts while he is standing still, then gradually touching the dog with the clippers, then using them on the dog.

OFFER PAW

The dog lifts a paw and allows it to be held without struggling or pulling away. If you wanted to use this as a trick, the directions would be for Shake, but if you had the dog reach higher, you could cue "Wave" or "High Five." You could also combine this with the previous Stand behavior as a starting point for a "Limp."

Suggested verbal cue: "Shake," "Gimme Five," "Paw," "Say Hi."

Suggested visual cue: Hold your hand out flat, palm up, as a surface for your dog to place his foot on.

Quick Clicks: Is your dog right or left pawed?

Have you ever determined whether your dog is right or left sided? It will help make it a little easier when teaching some new behaviors if you know. If you've never thought about it, here are some ways to find out:

- While the dog is moving directly away from you (have someone else crouch down and clap or whistle to get the dog started toward them, if need be), call the dog. Does your dog turn to the left or right to head toward you? Try it three times—two out of three or better to the left indicates that your dog is left-sided.

- Is it easier to get your dog to turn in one direction than in the other? The easier direction of turn indicates the dog's favored side.

- Use a treat to lure your dog around in a tight circle in front of you. Most dogs will follow the treat much more readily in one direction than in the other. Going clockwise well indicates a right-sided dog, while good counterclockwise movement means a left-sided dog.

- If you don't get clear results, maybe your dog is ambi-paw-trous!

Speed Steps

1. Put your dog in a Sit. CT a small front foot movement.

2. Wait for a higher foot lift.

3. Continue to require a slightly higher foot lift, staying at each height for three to five repetitions.

4. When the dog raises his foot to between his chest and nose level, put your hand under it and support it there for a second.

5. Gradually change from supporting the foot to holding the foot. Vary how long you hold the foot.

6. Add your cue.

Generalize the behavior:

- Squeeze a toenail or pinch some skin on the foreleg (simulating toenail clipping or a blood draw).
- Have someone the dog knows hold his foot.
- Put the dog on a grooming table or other raised surface.
- Have someone the dog doesn't know hold his foot.
- Intersperse your cue for Offer Paw with cues for other behaviors the dog knows.
- Teach the dog to Offer Paw to someone while facing away from you, so it really looks like he's shaking hands.

Keep in Mind

Some dogs don't tend to offer a lot of foot movement. Try shifting your weight as you stand facing your seated dog. Sometimes the dog will mirror you and shift his weight in response.

You could teach a Paw Target first (See Chapter 6).

Some dogs will shift their weight as they stand up or sit down, so try alternating these behaviors to get a clickable movement.

Troubleshooting

The dog lifts a paw a little bit but never raises it any higher.

- Is there a physical problem? Check with your veterinarian if you suspect there may be something wrong. Or, your timing may be off. Are you clicking as the dog's foot is moving up, at its highest point, or on the way back down? Highest point is the best, but better to be early (on the way up) rather than late, or the dog may think all you're after is picking the foot up and putting it back down again.

The dog sits up (balancing on his haunches).

- You may be trying to do too much too quickly. Be sure you are clicking for one foot moving and the other foot staying on the floor.

Variations

Teach the dog to offer either front foot. Signal with the hand closer to the foot.

Ask for a higher lift and call it Wave, or get a higher lift and then hold out your palm to connect for a High Five. Teach the dog to put both paws up for a Put'em Up behavior.

Detailed Training Plan

1. Cue your dog to Sit. Stand or sit facing the dog and wait for him to move one front foot. CT when he does. If you've been teaching the behaviors in this book, your dog should be offering all sorts of movements, and being in a Sit will mean that it's easiest for him to move his front legs (and his head, but you'll ignore head movements). Your dog will favor one foot over the other, so once you start seeing movement, concentrate on that foot. Repeat three to five times.

Quick Clicks: The critical point
The initial movement is the most critical part of getting this behavior. You'll need to watch very carefully for even a weight shift (to the opposite side of the paw that will lift) if the dog is relatively new to clicker training. It will be easier to see if you are sitting in front of the dog rather than standing. Savvy dogs will be dancing on their front feet if you aren't precise with your timing. (Come to think of it, that would be a fun behavior to teach, too!)

2. Wait for a slightly higher foot lift, maybe one to two inches off the ground. CT. Repeat three times.

3. Again, wait for the dog to lift the foot slightly higher. Remember not to change criteria in the middle of a step—so if the dog suddenly gives you one beautiful high foot lift, don't wait for him to do that again before clicking. CT whatever you have decided meets your criteria for this step. Repeat three times.

Quick Clicks: Use a measuring tape
It can be helpful to tape a measuring tape onto your wall to judge the height of the foot lift as you raise your criteria at each step. You can also eyeball it using something else as your reference point (a piece of the pattern in your wallpaper, etc.).

4. In a new location, continue to require a slightly higher lift for a CT, repeating at each height three times. End this session when you have worked for approximately five minutes.

5. When the dog raises his foot to between his chest level and nose level, put your hand under it and support it there for a second. Do not grab the foot, just put your hand beneath it so the foot can rest on it. Repeat ten times. Sensitive dogs may startle at your touch, so you may need to CT at this step for more repetitions.

6. Gradually change from supporting the foot to holding the foot. Don't use a death grip, but do wrap your hand around the foot. Continue at this step until the dog does not pull away.

7. Vary how long you hold the foot before CT-ing. Increase the amount of time the foot is held up to one to ten seconds. (You can Bounce Around or just increase it gradually, since the amount of time is short.) Remember to breathe calmly while you hold the dog's paw.

8. Change to a new location and repeat Step 7.

9. When you are willing to bet your dog will offer his paw and let you hold it (and he does it at least 80% of the time), add your cue. Remember to say the cue before you make any movement. Associate the cue with the behavior at least fifty times, changing locations every ten repetitions. When you think the dog is starting to understand the cue, you can say it earlier and earlier. The next step in the dog acquiring the cue is to not say it every once in a while. Does the dog offer the paw only when requested? Then your behavior is named! The last step is to intersperse other behaviors with the Offer Paw.

Generalize the behavior:

- While you hold the foot, squeeze a toe, tap a toenail or gently pinch some skin on the foreleg (simulating toenail clipping or a blood draw). CT for relaxed behavior. Keep the dog's leg close to his body while you do this, so you don't pull the dog off balance.

- Have someone the dog knows hold his foot while you CT.

- Put the dog on a grooming table or other raised surface and practice.

- Have someone the dog doesn't know hold his foot while you CT.

- Intersperse your cue for Offer Paw with cues for other behaviors the dog knows.

- Teach the dog to Offer Paw to someone while facing away from you, so it really looks like he's shaking hands.

- Teach the dog to Offer Both Paws.

Quick Clicks: An alternative to petting

This behavior is useful if you have a dog who doesn't like being touched by strangers. Teach the dog to Sit and Offer Paw to new people. It allows the dog to be a bit farther away from the person, and in our experience, most people will forget about petting the dog since they've been officially "introduced." If the dog won't Sit and Shake, that's a clue for you that the dog is already too nervous, and you probably shouldn't press this interaction.

FREEZE

The dog freezes in a position, not moving any body parts until you release him. Some dogs will get so intense about this that they won't even move their eyes. This behavior builds on the Relax for Exam from the beginning of the chapter. The essential difference is here we want the dog to freeze in position, not moving a muscle.

Once your dog has this cue in his repertoire, you can ask him to Freeze in the midst of other things, resulting in positions that might otherwise be difficult to train. If you perform in Freestyle (dancing with your dog), this offers some great possibilities for routines. (Of course, you won't ask your dog to Freeze in positions he can't maintain, such as with front feet off the ground in a hop.) This behavior is particularly useful at the vet (for x-rays, for example) or if you have a dog who dislikes being touched or has a problem with a particular body part.

Suggested verbal cue: "Freeze," "Vogue," "Pose."

Suggested visual cue: "Jazz hands"—hands with fingers spread, palms facing the dog, about chest height.

Speed Steps

1. Touch the dog's shoulder for one second, CT while the dog is absolutely still.

2. Hold the touch a little longer, varying the length of time up to five seconds.

3. Vary the parts of the body touched.

4. Decrease the pressure of your touch so you are barely in contact with the dog.

5. Put your hand near the dog without actually touching. CT for stillness, varying how long the dog must remain still. Remember to release each time you click.

6. Gradually increase duration until the dog will be still for up to fifteen seconds.

7. Add your cue and fade the hand signal.

8. Intersperse your Freeze cue with other cues the dog already knows.

Keep in Mind

Start in locations where the dog is relaxed, so he doesn't feel the need to look around. Try not to have a lot of other activity going on. If you have multiple dogs, put the others in a different room while you work on this.

If you find it hard to watch every piece of the dog at once, start by looking for major body parts such as legs and head to be still, then refine by looking for ears and tail to be still.

Troubleshooting

My dog is never still!

- It only seems that way. Try capturing the behavior. Does your dog stand like a statue when there's something on the counter that he wants? Or, when he suddenly sees a squirrel? If you have your clicker ready, you can click while he's still, immediately release him (to chase the squirrel, if it's safe), and give him a treat when he comes back to you (or give him the object of his desire from the counter, if that's feasible).

- Ask for only a microsecond and concentrate on only gross movements at first. You might start with all his feet being rooted in place, then add his head not turning, and so on. Add duration in tiny increments.

My dog will hold still for a couple of seconds, but then starts looking around or wanders away.

- You didn't work on duration well enough. Remember to Bounce Around an average and to increase the average gradually, so that the dog still gets a lot of short repetitions mixed in with a few longer ones. If the dog considers your training too much work for too little reward, you'll lose him.

- Don't just use food. Use some really great life rewards like chasing a toy or playing with another dog.

- Be sure you're keeping your sessions short. Work only for a minute or two before taking a break.

Variations

For a dog who dislikes being handled, this behavior is a great starting point to dealing with handling of a problem area. Say, for example, your dog does not like having his feet touched. You could teach Freeze, starting at a shoulder, and incrementally working down the leg to the foot. It's best to start far away from the problem area and work gradually toward it. Working on it with this behavior will pay off for you down the road if the dog ever has to have something done medically.

You can use "Freeze" as an emergency cue—if your dog is about to walk through broken glass, or is off leash on trail and about to jump into a river that will sweep him away. (This would have come in handy for Cheryl years ago when her super-dedicated retriever saw a stick float past in a raging river and jumped in after it. Luckily she was okay!)

Teach the dog to freeze in position, like a statue, when you've moved a leg or his head (or even his tail!). This is a fun and impressive trick.

Teach the dog to Freeze while in motion as part of a dance routine.

Detailed Training Plan

1. Touch the dog's shoulder for a second and CT when the dog is absolutely still. Repeat three times, then touch a different body part. If you are going to use this cue for handling issues or at the vet, you will want to touch the dog all over. If not, you can just use a variety of easy-to-reach places without worrying about including the feet or tail.

2. Starting back at the shoulder, hold the touch a little longer, only clicking if the dog remains still. Vary from one to three seconds. If you find that you are not clicking the dog very often, back off on how long you're expecting the dog to be still. Make sure that you click while your hand is on the dog and the dog is still. You'll be able to feel the muscle movement, particularly in the shoulder.

Quick Clicks: Hold your breath
Many dogs will freeze briefly when you touch them, especially if *you* hold your breath or inhale sharply on the touch. Be ready to try this the first few times and it will speed the behavior along.

3. When the dog will remain still for up to three seconds reliably (80% of the time), practice Step 2 with other body parts. (Work the body parts in the same order each time as you go through the steps.)

4. Change to a different location and repeat steps two and three.

5. Return to the shoulder touch, and build up to five seconds where the dog will hold still, adding just one second at a time to your count. Add another second when the dog is 80% successful. Repeat with other body parts.

6. To use Freeze as a remote cue (with the dog away from you), gradually decrease the pressure of your touch so you are barely in contact with the dog (remember that each change in pressure is a separate step, and should be worked to 80% success before moving on). Continue to vary, between one and five seconds, how long the dog stays still before you CT, with most repetitions on the shorter side.

7. Put your hand near the dog but not actually touching. CT for stillness. Continue to vary how long the dog has to remain still, but making most repetitions on the shorter side.

8. Change locations and repeat Step 7.

9. Gradually increase duration by Bouncing around an average, until the dog will be still for up to fifteen seconds (or longer if you desire). Always build on success when you are building duration.

Quick Clicks: Error-free training

Do not be in a hurry to increase the duration of a behavior. The ideal training is as error-free as possible, so you want the dog to be successful the vast majority of the time. If you find that your dog is not meeting criteria at least 50% of the time, you have not broken your steps down finely enough. This is especially important for young and inexperienced dogs. Go back and review your training plan and repeat previous or add new steps where you are having difficulties.

10. Does your dog successfully Freeze at least 80% of the time? Time to add your cue. Be sure to say it *before* you make any movement. Remember that dogs innately pay more attention to body motion than to language, so your voice needs to be the only information he is getting in order for it to have importance.

11. After about fifty repetitions of your cue, fade out your movement so that your verbal cue becomes the only signal to the dog to do the behavior.

12. Change locations multiple times. This behavior will need a lot of work around increasingly difficult distractions. The dog will have a much greater tendency to want to move when lots of stuff is happening around him. Try to set up your sessions so that they become more distracting in small increments.

Generalize the behavior:

- Teach the dog to hold his head still when you hold it so that you can put in eye drops, ear drops or allow the vet to examine him without anesthesia. You can also do this with feet and tail, in anticipation of medical procedures that might require those body parts to be still.

- Teach the dog to Freeze on his side so that you can have x-rays done without using anesthesia.

- Intersperse your Freeze cue with other cues the dog knows, so the command is used when he isn't already expecting it.

Fia (4 year old Boxer) has been clicker trained since she was a puppy. She competes in agility, and is a Canine Good Citizen and has her Rally Novice title.

Chapter 4
FOR OUTINGS

We want your outings with your dog to be enjoyable for both of you rather than a battle of wills between you. Dogs generally enjoy the freedom of running off leash (where it's safe and permitted), but you should have some ways of controlling what your dog does and doesn't do. This chapter will cover:

- Walk Off Leash/Check In.
- Leave It.
- Sit-Stay For Greeting.
- Go Play/Play's Over.
- Untangle Yourself.

Remember to keep your sessions short and take frequent breaks—training works better this way and keeps the stress levels low for both you and your dog.

WALK OFF LEASH/CHECK IN

The dog walks along beside you, near enough to be touched, until released. This is great for trail walking in areas that allow dogs off leash, but where you don't want the dog running ahead into the great unknown (and possibly over a cliff). This behavior is also good if your dog is off leash and you suddenly encounter other hikers, bicyclists, or equestrians, and need the dog beside you for a while. (These instructions are a modification of Dawn Jecs' "Choose to Heel" program. If you are interested in competition-level heeling, her book of the same name is an excellent resource that is easily adapted to clicker training.) The instructions are for a dog walking on your left side (the traditional Heel position). If you prefer, just modify them to have the dog work on your right—so for example, you will start in Step 1 by walking in a clockwise circle.

Suggested verbal cues: "Close," "Side," "By Me," "With Me," "Heel," "Check In."

You will need: A distraction-free room, and, as you train, a series of distractions.

Make a list of all the things that distract your dog, ranked from low to high. For example:

- Nylabones, rawhide, latex toys, tennis ball, squeaky plush toy, rattling treats packaging, people, other dogs, squirrels.

Now make a list of your dog's favorite food treats, ranking them from low to high. For example:

- Kibble, hard treats (biscuits), cat food, soft treats, string cheese, hot dogs, steak, garlic chicken.

Speed Steps

1. Walk counterclockwise around the room. Click when the dog looks at you, and drop a low-level treat on the floor at your feet. Move away.

2. CT when the dog takes one step toward you as you move away from the dropped treat.

3. CT gradually more steps toward you.

4. Place three similar distractions from the low-interest end of your list on the floor and change to a higher level treat. Start walking around the room again, and CT when the dog takes a step toward you, whether he picks up one of the distractions and brings it with him or not. *Do not* take the distraction from the dog.

5. Add more steps until the dog is following you around the room, ignoring the distractions.

6. Add three similar items from the next level on your distraction list to those already on the floor. Continue until the dog ignores everything on the floor and is taking several steps beside you before being CT.

7. Work your way up through the distraction list. Change treats to a higher value reward each time you add a distraction.

8. Repeat the entire sequence moving in a clockwise direction with the dog still on the same side (the left).

9. Add a cue if you like.

Generalize the behavior:

- Repeat the whole sequence in at least ten different locations, both indoors and out.
- Gradually introduce other people, dogs and other real-world distractions.

- The Hot Toy Variation—Go back to your original training location. Put a variety of toys on the floor. When the dog comes to you, click and pick up the nearest toy and play with the dog. Drop the toy and move away, repeating with another toy. The dog will learn to drop what he has and follow you, to see if you've found something better.

- Carry a high-value toy on walks. If your dog ignores a distraction and turns toward you, whip out the toy and play with the dog.

Keep in Mind

Be creative when looking for a training space if you don't have indoor space. Ask a dog training facility if you can borrow or rent their space. If you must work outside from the start due to space limitations, give the dog permission to play and sniff a few minutes in the area after a brief training session so it will become less interesting as you train. (See Go Play/Play's Over at the end of the chapter.) If using open areas, be sure the dog is on a long line so you don't have to worry about him running off before he's trained! Or you could be creative in finding fenced outdoor areas, such as tennis courts, when they are not being used.

Troubleshooting

The dog only walks a certain number of steps before wandering off.

- Build up your Bouncing Around more carefully. Have someone watch you to make sure you aren't going the same number of steps every time before clicking—humans are real creatures of habit, and this is a common problem.

- Use really great treats so the dog is motivated to work hard for them. Change treats between steps to keep the dog interested.

The dog won't look at me if there are any distractions.

- Choose distractions that are in the dog's environment all the time (tennis balls, if you leave them scattered around), and use a high value treat.

- Use your treat to lure the dog away from the distracting item the first few times you work with him.

- Change treats frequently to keep the dog's interest high.

- Work on Attention first (See Chapter 2).

The dog is aggressive or possessive around toys or treats.

- Don't move toward him after he has picked up something, move away instead.

- Start with something the dog won't want to pick up (such as metal items).

- Don't remove items from the dog's mouth—drop the treat on the floor and move away. Let him figure out he can go back to the item; it won't disappear because he lets go of it.

- Work on Possession Problems (see Chapter 5).

Variations

Teach the dog to come to both sides, using a different cue for each. This is an easy one if you've already taught a solid Hand Touch (See Chapter 6).

Train your dog to go only for the toy you indicate. This variation is great for shy dogs in your household who are nervous about playing with toys when other dogs are around, for possessive dogs (they have their own toy that no one else will get), and at competitive events (someone is always squeaking something inside or outside the ring).

Detailed Training Plan

1. Start in a distraction-free environment such as a large empty room. Begin moving in a big counterclockwise circle with the dog on the inside, and CT when the dog looks at you. Drop the treat on the floor by your left foot so the dog has to come to get it. Meanwhile, you move off, continuing in your counterclockwise circle. Repeat ten times.

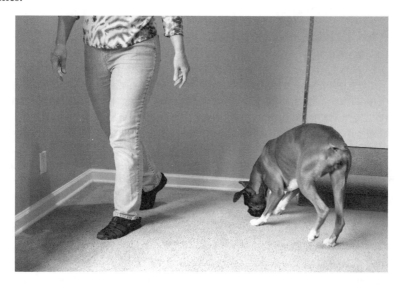

Drop the treat on the floor by your left foot so the dog has to come to get it, and keep walking forward.

2. Begin moving in a counterclockwise circle again and CT the dog for taking one step toward you. Drop the treat on the floor and continue walking after each click. Repeat ten times.

Quick Clicks: Practice without the dog

With any behavior (but especially if you're moving), it's a good idea to practice clicking and delivering the treat *without* the dog first. This will make your training progress more graceful, and help prevent you from flinging treats all over the place.

3. In the same location, continue walking in a counterclockwise circle and CT for one to three steps toward you, varying the number of steps the dog has to take each time to get clicked. Repeat five times. By now the dog should be following you around the room, trying to catch you as you move away. If not, repeat until the dog runs to catch up and takes a few steps with you at least 80% of the time.

4. Place three similar distractions from the low-interest end of your list on the floor. CT when the dog takes a step toward you, whether he picks up one of the distractions and brings it with him or not. DO NOT take the distraction from the dog. Drop the treat on the floor and move away. (Note: Here we have decreased our criteria to a step toward you again. This is because we've added complexity to the behavior by putting out the distractions.) Continue at this step until the dog is readily moving toward you as soon as you move away.

5. Repeat Steps 2 and 3 with the distractions down until the dog is following you around the room for one to five steps at a time before getting CT, and completely ignoring the toys on the floor.

Quick Clicks: Level of distraction versus level of treat

If the dog won't drop a toy to eat the treat, immediately increase the value of treats from your treat list by at least two levels. This is usually the most difficult step with easily distracted dogs. It may take from one to five minutes for the dog to leave a distraction to move toward you the first few times. After one minute, if the dog doesn't appear at all interested in leaving the distraction, lower your criteria and CT if the dog just looks at you, and toss the treat on the floor near his head without approaching the dog. Repeat five times. Then CT a look at you, dropping the treat next to you so the dog has to move to get it. Up the criteria again so the dog has to get up if he is lying down, or take a step toward you if he is standing up, to get CT. If you are still having trouble, leave the room. Have someone else pick up the distractions. Start at Step 3 again, *decreasing* the level of distraction and *increasing* the level of treat. Repeat the first three steps daily until the dog is responding within a few moments at Step 3 with low-level distractions on the floor. Then you can move on.

6. Add three similar items from the next level up on your distraction list to those already on the floor. Continue as in Step 5 until the dog ignores everything on the floor and will stay beside you for a few steps (varying between one and five) at least 80% of the time.

7. Work your way up through the distraction list, adding three items from each new level to the items already on the floor. If your dog is doing well, you might add several levels of distractions at one time. If progress is slower, you might add one new level of distractions per training session or every other training session. (Remember that

the definition of "doing well" is that the dog will stay beside you for a predetermined number of steps at least 80% of the time.) Change treats to a higher value reward each time you add new distractions.

8. Gradually add more steps beside you, using Bouncing Around the average from Chapter 1. Repeat until the dog is following you around the room ignoring the distractions, periodically getting a CT for staying with you.

Quick Clicks: Go random

As you build on the distance, you are going to CT a random number of steps, using Bouncing Around to increase the number of steps with the dog next to you. You can hand the dog the treat or drop it on the floor. In either case, the dog should immediately get into position next to you in anticipation of the next CT. If he gets his treat and goes to play with a toy, you should stop the session and re-evaluate. Do you need to back up a few steps in your training plan? Have you been working too long? Did you move to a distraction that was too high for the dog? Are your rewards too low value for the dog? Something needs to change in your training plan if the dog wants to play in between working with you.

9. Repeat the entire sequence moving clockwise. The dog is still on your left, but now he is on the "outside" of your circle, which is a tiny bit more difficult.

10. You can now build up how many steps the dog takes alongside you if you want to use this to walk the dog off leash. Use Bouncing Around an average to increase the number of steps without a CT until you are satisfied with how far the dog will go without a reward. In each new location in Step 11, you will decrease the requirement a bit so that the dog initially gets more frequent rewards.

11. Repeat the whole sequence in at least ten different locations, both indoors and out, of varying size. (If you don't have a secure outdoor area to work in, have the dog drag a long twenty foot leash for safety.) Dogs do not generalize well, and need to be shown that the same rules apply to different locations.

12. If you can predict the dog will come to your side 80% of the time as soon as you start moving, it's time to add your cue. Say the cue, the dog comes to your side and stays there for a varying number of steps, CT. Repeat for at least fifty additional pairings. Every five repetitions, change your location, direction (straight forward, counterclockwise circle, clockwise circle) or the number of steps the dog has to take.

Generalize the behavior:

- Gradually introduce other people, dogs and other real-world distractions. Remember to temporarily drop your criteria for the number of steps beside you as you add complexity to the behavior.

- Call the dog away from play with another person or dog to walk beside you for a few steps, click and release the dog to return to play.

Variations

- Practice having the dog come to your Side while you are standing still, then begin moving with the dog.

- Change directions, walk straight, make turns or stand still, all while CT-ing the dog for staying next to you.

- Vary the type of rewards, using rewards that might be available on a walk, such as the opportunity to sniff, swim, or run after you.

- The "Hot Toy" Variation—this is a great variation for doggie thieves who want to grab things around the house and is also useful for teaching the dog to play with *you* with a toy. Go back to your original training location. Put a variety of toys on the floor. Start walking around the room. When the dog comes to you, click and pick up the nearest toy. Hold onto the toy and encourage the dog to play with you for up to a minute, then let go of the toy and move away. *Do not* throw the toy for the dog to play with. We are trying to teach the dog to work *with* you, not *away* from you. When the dog moves toward you (whether or not he's carrying the previous toy), click and pick up the toy nearest you and have a rousing game with it. Then let go of the toy and move away. The dog will begin to spit out toys and run toward you each time you move away. *Do not* click and pick up a new toy until the dog has made some effort to seek you out (whether or not he is carrying the old toy). The dog is learning that the only toys that are fun (the "hot toy") are the ones you have in your hand. Everything else is boring! Note: This might be a difficult step if your dog has regular access to free play with toys without you. His desire to work with you will be low, as he has been entertaining himself.

- Now you can use the "hot toy" concept to reward the dog on a walk. Carry a high-value toy on walks. If your dog ignores a distraction and turns toward you, whip out the toy and play with the dog. You could also use something interesting found on the trail such as a stick or a feather, to play a short game with the dog.

LEAVE IT/DON'T TOUCH

The dog stops before touching an object (easy), leaves the object to check in with you (harder), or removes his nose/teeth/paws from whatever they are touching (hardest). It's your choice exactly how you want the final behavior to look. Make sure you define it for yourself before you start working with the dog. We give instructions here for "stop before touching" and "turn away." It may help save your hands if you teach Take a Treat Gently first (see Chapter 2).

Suggested verbal cue: "Leave It," "Don't Touch," "Off."

Speed Steps

1. Hold a piece of kibble in your closed hand, where the dog can reach it. CT as soon as the dog stops touching your hand.

2. Change to a better treat and repeat Step 1. Work through several levels of treats.

3. Count to two with the dog not touching your hand before you CT. Build up to a count of four.

4. Use the Bouncing Around technique to gradually build up to ten seconds without the dog touching your hand.

5. Add your cue.

6. Hold your hand out flat with a treat on your palm. Cue and CT for not touching, Bouncing Around an average ten count.

7. *Place* a treat on the floor. Cue and CT for not touching, Bouncing Around a ten count.

8. *Drop* a treat on the floor. If the dog looks at you rather than diving for the treat, CT. If the dog goes for the treat, say your cue and CT for the dog not touching.

9. To have the dog actually turn away from the treat/object/person, make sure that the dog has to turn 180 degrees to collect his treat from you after getting clicked. That means he doesn't get the treat or item on the floor any longer.

10. To have the dog spit something out, you'll need to start with something of low value and build up to higher value items or things found on the street. (See Possession Problems in Chapter 5 for some helpful ideas.)

11. Repeat the exercise with a variety of toys.

12. Repeat the exercise with other dogs or other animals as the Don't Touch object.

13. Repeat with different people offering treats or toys to the dog.

Keep in Mind

If you haven't worked on Take a Treat Gently, your dog may paw, lick or bite at your hand for a long time before giving up. Be ready to wait him out. Wait for him to stop for just the briefest moment to CT. You'll build up from this starting point.

Troubleshooting

I'm not making any progress. If I count to more than two, the dog starts grabbing at the treat.

- Have patience! Wait him out. If he doesn't get rewarded for trying to get the treat out of your hand (*never* let him be successful), he'll eventually stop trying.

If you give up and let the dog have the treat after a two count, you'll teach him this is as long as he'll ever have to wait.

- You may have stayed too long at that count before moving to the next step.

- You may be trying to increase your bounce average in too large a step. Start your Bouncing Around at a low count and gradually build up again. If a count of two is as far as you can get, give a few clicks at one, a click at two, then a click at three, then back to one again for a few more clicks. Have more counts on the low side of the average in the initial stages. Don't shoot for a count to five or six right off the bat.

My dog never paws at or mouths my hand or tries to touch it.

- Consider yourself lucky! Introduce the cue earlier, and proceed with the lesson.

- Offer the treat in your open hand or drop it on the floor. Gentle or shy dogs may be hesitant to grab something out of your hand, but may be willing if it's on the floor.

Variations
Can you cue the dog "Leave It" and seem to take your attention away from the treat, talking to friends or facing in another direction, without the dog going for it? Could you leave the room without the dog touching the food? If you're going to try this, you might want to put the treat in a container at first, so your dog can't self-reward if he does choose to go for it. Pour on the praise and treats if your dog succeeds at this level. This requires a huge amount of canine self-restraint.

Quick Clicks: You might be able to skip ahead
You'll be able to skip several steps in the detailed training plan below if you've successfully worked on Take a Treat Gently. Start at Step 11 and introduce the cue for Leave It at the outset, reminding the dog to take it gently after he is clicked. If the dog seems to be struggling, go back to an earlier step and work up.

Detailed Training Plan
1. Hold a piece of kibble in your closed fist. The dog may lick or paw at your hand. CT (using the kibble in your hand) *as soon as* the dog stops touching your hand. Repeat ten times.

2. Change to a more interesting treat and repeat Step 1.

3. Change to an even more interesting treat and repeat Step 1.

4. Repeating with the same treat, count to two with the dog not touching before CT-ing the dog. If the dog touches your hand before you get to two, restart the count. Repeat five times.

5. Count to three, then CT. Repeat five times.

6. Start in a new location. Count to three, then CT. Repeat five times.

7. Count to four, then CT. Repeat five times.

8. Count to five, then CT. Repeat five times.

9. Use the Bouncing Around technique to gradually build up to ten seconds with the dog not touching your hand. Start with an average of two to three seconds maximum. For example, count to two and CT, then four CT, one CT, one CT. Repeat ten times at each new average count.

10. Go to a new location and repeat Step 9.

11. Will the dog stay away from your hand during the entire count at least 80% of the time? Then it's time to add your cue. Say your cue, hold the treat in front of his nose in your fist, wait until the dog doesn't touch for the count you have decided in advance, CT. Continue to pair your cue with the behavior for at least fifty more repetitions. Change treats, locations or the hand you are using after every five to ten repetitions.

12. Put the treat on the flat of your hand and say your cue as you hold your hand in front of the dog. CT if the dog doesn't touch it after the amount of time you've decided in advance. Repeat ten times, Bouncing Around an average ten count. Close your hand if the dog tries to grab the treat and go back and repeat Step 11. *Do not* jerk your hand away—it may encourage the dog to try harder to grab it next time.

Put the treat on the flat of your hand and hold your hand in front of the dog.

13. Change treats and repeat Step 12.

14. Change locations and repeat Step 12.

15. Place a treat on the floor. Keep your foot poised over it in case the dog tries to grab it. CT if he doesn't touch it. If he tries to grab it, cover it with your foot and wait until he backs away, then CT. We recommend that you hand the treat to the dog, whether you pick up the one off the floor or use another one, rather than letting him grab it off the ground, as a good habit-builder (and also if you want to eventually have the dog turn away from the treat to you). Repeat ten times and change locations if the dog was successful 80% of the time. Try this in several locations.

16. Put a treat on the floor and CT if the dog looks at you. Reward with a treat from your hand. Repeat ten times each in several different locations, changing to a new location when the dog is successful 80% of the time.

17. Drop a treat on the floor unexpectedly. CT when the dog looks at you. Reward from your hand. Repeat, changing locations with 80% success.

18. To have the dog actually turn away from the treat/object/person rather than just staring at it and not touching, make sure that the dog has to turn 180 degrees to collect his treat from you after getting clicked. You can start this by standing behind the dog and dropping the treat in front of him, then CT when he avoids it. He will turn to you to collect his treat. Be sure that you don't let him self-reward with the treat on the floor. (A helper might be needed for a while.) Continue to reward the 180 degree turn as you practice additional variations and generalizations with the behavior.

19. To have the dog spit something out, you'll need to start with something of low value (like a large chew bone or boring toy) and build up to higher value items or things found on the street. (See Possession Problems in Chapter 5 for some helpful ideas.)

Generalize the behavior:

- Spill the dog's food bowl on the floor, but start with just a few kibbles in it so he doesn't get a huge reward if he's not ready for this step.

- Work the same exercise with a toy or different objects.

- Have different people holding food or a toy.

- Work this behavior using other dogs or other animals as the Don't Touch object.

- Work out in public at a street fair. You'll have lots of things on the ground that you don't want the dog to touch!

SIT-STAY FOR GREETING

The dog sits while you let someone into your house, while being petted, while you are talking to someone on the street or when another dog approaches, until released for a doggie greeting. Sit-Stay is useful for any behavior that requires you to leave the dog behind while you do something else. It is a part of the Canine Good Citizen test that often proves problematic and is a very handy behavior for a well-behaved pet—your friends will thank you.

Suggested verbal cue: "Sit," "Sit/Stay."

Suggested visual cue: Briefly show the flat of your palm facing the dog's nose.

The Stay cue looks very similar to the early stages of the Touch cue to the dog. Briefly show the dog the flat of your palm then remove your hand.

Speed Steps

1. Cue the dog to Sit on your left side. Alternate rapid CTs with one short pause, varying number of CTs both before and after the pause.

2. Add another pause to your sequence. Continue to vary the number of CTs before and after the pause.

3. Repeat with the dog on your right side.

4. Repeat in several different locations.

5. Add some minor distractions such as old toys, building up to more interesting distractions.

6. Add major distractions such as a thrown toy or a person moving around and making noise.

7. Move to your front yard and repeat.

8. Move to a new outdoor location with more distractions.

9. Go back indoors. Have someone your dog doesn't find too exciting come and start talking to you while you CT the dog for sitting beside you.

Generalize the behavior:

- Work with a variety of people of varying interest to your dog.

- Have each person greet you, then pet your dog while you CT your dog for remaining in the Sit.

- Move outdoors and repeat with a variety of people the dog knows.

- Repeat with strangers.

- Have friends with dogs walk their dogs past you while you CT your dog for remaining in a Sit.

- Have friends with dogs walk up, Sit their dog, and have a conversation with you. Release the dogs to interact if you wish (See Go Play/Play's Over at the end of the chapter).

- Work in a variety of environments with a variety of people and dogs.

Keep in Mind

If you have not worked on maintaining a Sit, allow yourself several weeks to get a solid Sit in different environments before adding a lot of distractions. Build up the amount of time the dog must Sit before being released.

If you have already worked on maintaining your Sit, this behavior should start very quickly and you can speed through the early steps.

It's up to you to decide whether you want your dog to greet other people or dogs. If you decide you want to do that, we recommend a cue different from Release which means your dog can go and interact with that person or dog. We both use Go Say Hi after we check that the other dog will be okay with it.

Troubleshooting

The dog works all right in the early steps, but gets up when the distractions get higher.

- Fine tune your list of distractions. Break it down as much as you can and work up through it very slowly.

- Use your best super scrumptious variety of treats and change often.

- Work with a hungry dog.

The dog is fine until the distraction is a person, then he loses it.

- Teach Four on the Floor for Greeting as a separate exercise. CT if all four feet stay on the ground and drop one or more rewards on the ground. If the dog jumps up, the person turns away and ignores the dog until all four feet are on the ground again. Practice with a variety of gradually more interesting people.

I can't build up time—the dog keeps getting up.

- Work in a very low-distraction environment.

- Start with a low number of CT before the release, until the dog can be successful. Add more CTs and pauses very slowly until you have built up a substantial history of success.

- Have someone watch you or videotape yourself to be sure that you are delivering treats quickly enough, before the dog has a chance to get up.

- Practice your treat delivery speed without your dog if necessary.

Variations

Work on being able to be some distance from your dog while he remains in a Sit. When you have put in a couple of pauses in your CT sequence, start taking a step away from your dog during the pause. Gradually build up the distance and then the time you are away from the dog. Could you have someone come and pet your sitting dog while you are some distance away, pretending to be busy with something else?

After you have gained some distance from your dog, cue him to do other behaviors while staying in the same place.

Work through all the steps with your dog off leash (in safe areas, of course).

Detailed Training Plan

1. In a low-distraction environment, cue the dog to Sit on your left side next to your leg. Rapidly CT three times, pause briefly ("one-one-thousand"), CT, release the dog. Make sure the dog gets up when you release (review Chapter 2 if you don't remember what a release is). Repeat ten times, each time changing the number of CTs before and after the pause, with a maximum of five CTs on either side of the pause. A single repetition might look like this: CT, CT, pause, CT, CT, CT, CT, release.

Quick Clicks: Click doesn't end behavior

This is a working demonstration that a click doesn't necessarily end a behavior (something you may hear about clicker training). If you click and deliver the treat quickly to the dog, the dog should remain sitting. You can also use the Bouncing Around technique to extend duration. Decide on an average number of seconds the dog must remain in the Sit, starting low, and Bounce Around that average. Then gradually raise the average.

2. Add two additional CTs, so your maximum is seven CTs on either side of the pause. Repeat five times, varying the number of CTs each time.

3. Raise the maximum CTs to ten and repeat five times.

4. Add another pause to your sequence. Keep varying the number of CTs before and after your pauses. Repeat until the dog is successfully remaining in a Sit 80% of the time.

5. Continue to add pauses until the dog is remaining in a Sit beside you for up to two minutes while you deliver no more than ten CTs total. Always remember to say your release cue at the end of each sequence of clicks, treats and pauses.

6. In the same location, put the dog on your right side and have him Sit. Repeat steps one to five.

7. If you want to use a Stay cue, now is the time to introduce it. It's not necessary for the dog—he should continue doing a behavior until you either cue him to do something different or release him. But humans sure like to use "Stay!" To add the Stay cue, cue Sit then cue Stay (either verbally or physically or both), do your sequence of clicks/treats/pauses, then cue release. There are no more CTs once the dog is released—all the treats come while he remains in the Sit. The lesson for the dog is that getting up doesn't pay well!

8. In a new location, add some minor distractions. (A minor distraction for most dogs would be old toys or bones they've seen a zillion times. Your distraction list from Walk Off Leash will come in handy here.) Repeat Steps 1-5 first with your dog on your left, then with your dog on your right.

Quick Clicks: On your off side
Practice delivering treats on your off side (the one more difficult for you) *without* your dog. Remember that training works best with minimal body motion, so you don't want to be twisting around like a crazy person trying to deliver treats to your off side. You might actually encourage your dog to get up without meaning to.

9. Change locations and add a more interesting distraction. Repeat Step 5. Continue to add distractions, one or two at a time, working to 80% success at each step. The distractions should be mid-level distractions.

10. Change locations and add a major distraction, such as a thrown toy or a person moving around and making noise. Repeat Step 5.

11. Move to your front yard and repeat Steps 1-5 with the dog on your left, then on your right, then with the dog in front of you or behind you.

12. Move to a new outdoor location and repeat Step 11.

13. Go back indoors, in a low-distraction environment. Have someone the dog doesn't find too exciting come up and start talking to you while you CT the dog for sitting beside you. Vary the click/treat/pause sequence, aiming to keep the dog in a Sit from one to three minutes. (It's important to vary how long the dog does the Stay each time, as well.) When you release the dog, let him greet your friend if you like, then call him back to you to get a treat. This ends the greeting and patterns the dog to check in with you each time.

Quick Clicks: Ignore him

If the dog gets excited and jumps up when released, both you and your friend should ignore the dog until he has all four feet back on the ground. Even better, your friend can immediately exit through the front door if the dog jumps up. *Ignore* means you don't look at, talk to, or touch the dog. Lesson for the dog is that jumping up ends all fun interaction.

14. Continue to practice with other friends, until your dog has remained sitting while at least five different people talked to you.

15. Now have one of your friends greet you, then reach down and pet the dog on the head. Rapid-fire CT while the dog is being petted and release when the petting stops. Ignore the dog once he is released. Repeat with each of your friends.

Quick Clicks: Greeting people

Petting and clicking/treating while the dog is in a Sit, then ignoring him once he is released, teaches the dog that all good things happen only when he is sitting in one place. Also, it's important that the dog doesn't greet the other person every time. In some cases, he won't be able to greet the other person, and secondarily, it tends to make the greetings more "exuberant."

Generalize the behavior:

- Move outdoors and repeat Step 14 with all the people the dog knows.

- Practice having strangers come up and talk to you while you work on your dog maintaining a Sit. Stand in front of a neighborhood store and plenty of people will want to come and see your well-behaved pet. (See the Quick Clicks box below *before* you initiate this step.)

Quick Clicks: Dogs and strangers

How does your dog feel about strangers and about being touched? Some dogs are not relaxed around strangers. Don't jeopardize your dog and the public by putting him in situations he can't handle. If your dog seems okay with being touched by strangers, we recommend two strategies as extra insurance that things go well. First, teach your dog a Hand Touch (See Chapter 6) and CT him for touching many different hands held above his head. This will make a hand coming over his head mean good things. Second, protect your dog from being frightened by well-meaning strangers by abiding by the rule that a person *always* must ask before trying to touch your dog. This lets you nicely educate people that there are good reasons they should always ask first. Asking to pet a dog is especially important for children, who can suffer a face bite if they run up to pet the wrong dog.

- Have friends with dogs walk by your dog while he is sitting next to you.

- Have friends with dogs walk up to you, Sit their dog, and have a conversation. Release both dogs to greet each other, if you wish, but don't do this every time.

Quick Clicks: Greeting dogs

Do not require your dog to remain in a Sit when an unleashed dog comes up to him for a sniff. This impedes the natural canine greeting body language and could make greetings unintentionally tense. The directions here are intended for greeting a dog you know will get along with your dog. If you don't know the dog, teaching your dog to Sit first gives you time to assess the approaching dog's intentions or ask the other owner if he's friendly. But be sure to release your dog if you can't stop the greeting.

GO PLAY/PLAY'S OVER

This behavior is an extension of the Sit/Stay used for greetings above. It's a great idea to teach your dog he should only interact when given permission, and that he has to stop when you say. It's easiest to teach these two behaviors together. Go Play is a variation of your release word. "Release" means "Break position, but stay tuned," while "Go Play" means "Go have fun!" To prevent the dog from being punished by play ending, Mandy teaches a Play's Over cue also, using the clicker. Another variation would be to teach "Go Say Hi," which means to approach the other person or dog and interact with them politely (See *Right on Target* for details on teaching this behavior).

You'll use Go Play at the dog park or a friend's house, or when you want the dog to run around on his own a bit. "Play's Over" means drop all your toys, stop your games and come back to me. Remember that for some dogs, the end of play can be punishing, so we need to plan for a lot of rewards while training this behavior. This also eliminates the need to call the dog when play is over, keeping your Recall from becoming something negative for the dog.

Suggested verbal cues: "Go Play," "Go Crazy," "Get Wild," "Run!," "Play's Over," "All Done," "Time's Up."

You will need: A range of toys and a secure area to train. It's also helpful if you have a well-trained doggie buddy you can work with.

Quick Clicks: Play as a reward

We are not using the clicker for Go Play. It has a built in reward, so the clicker is really superfluous. It also means we can add our verbal cue at the very beginning. We will use the clicker for Play's Over, so the cue is added later for that piece of the behavior sequence.

Speed Steps

1. Start on leash. Say your cue for Go Play and throw a toy. Run after the dog, let the dog chase you, or let the other dog loose for about fifteen seconds.

2. Stop moving or call the other dog. When your dog stops, click, drop a treat at your feet and cue Go Play again.

3. Gradually increase the amount of time playing, until the dog can play for up to one minute, but will stop when you stop.

4. Repeat Steps 1-3 off leash.

5. Add the cue for Play's Over.

Generalize the behavior:

- Add dropping a toy as part of the end of play.

- Increase the distance the dog has to go before getting treats. You can also alternate with a water break in the house or a short Down-Stay.

- Cue "Play's Over" while the other dog is still allowed to play.

Treats are delivered in multiple places (at each gate) after the dog is told Play's Over. Then the dog is released to Go Play again.

Keep in Mind

It's important that the dog get released to Go Play again often, especially in the beginning stages of the behavior. Otherwise, the payoff of a treat won't be enough to stop his play session.

Troubleshooting

The dog won't play once he gets the first treat, or is distracted by the treats I'm holding.

- Use a toy as a reward instead of treats.
- Get a more engaging playmate.

Detailed Training Plan

1. Start with the dog on leash. Say your cue for play ("Go Play") and throw a toy. Run after the dog, let the dog chase you, or let another dog loose for about fifteen seconds. You may need to have the toy on a string to prevent the dog from playing "keep away" with you. It's important that the dog engage in play in some form after you cue Go Play. With a young or shy dog, Mandy will say "Go Play" then take off, running away from the dog and inviting a game of chase. You can also use the string to drag the toy along the ground.

2. Stop moving, or call or Down the other dog. When your dog stops (even for a split second), click, drop a treat at your feet, count to five and cue Go Play again. This brief break helps make the cue to Go Play more salient for the dog and prevents the dog from escalating into craziness. Repeat steps one and two ten times. Remember that the dog is on leash while you work this step.

> ### Quick Clicks: Try freezing
> If you can't get the dog to stop playing, try freezing in position. It might also help to shorten the amount of time you let the dog play, especially if he gets out of control easily. It's important if you're using another dog as a play partner that the partner be absolutely reliable on stopping play. Otherwise, you'll have two out of control dogs on your hands!

3. Gradually increase the amount of time the dog is allowed to Go Play, one to ten seconds at a time. Stay at each additional amount of time for at least ten repetitions. Continue until the dog can play for up to one minute, but will stop immediately when you stop.

4. Repeat steps one to three off leash.

5. Is the dog responding to your lack of movement by halting play at least 80% of the time while he's off leash? Great, then it's time to add the cue for Play's Over. To do this, say "Play's Over," stop moving, click and let the dog come to you for a treat. Repeat at least fifty times in several different locations over the course of several days. When the dog stops when you say Play's Over, you won't need to stop yourself any longer. You can also eliminate the brief break before restarting play.

Generalize the behavior:

- Add dropping a toy as part of the end of play. You will need to start close to the dog, and may need to lead the dog away from the toy with the treat after clicking, delivering the treat a short distance away from the toy.

- Increase the distance the dog has to go before getting treats. Build up from directly in front of you to moving toward the door to the house in one to two foot increments. Remember to use your Bouncing Around to increase the distance. You might want to give the dog a water break in the house or feed a small amount of dinner, then have him Go Play again. You can also have the dog do a short Down-Stay, then Go Play. Be creative about what happens at the end of play to keep the dog's motivation to end it high.

- Cue Play's Over while the other dog (or dogs) is still allowed to play.

Quick Clicks: Keep playing
Remember to restart play often for this behavior! We don't want Play's Over to become a punishment for the dog.

UNTANGLE YOURSELF
The dog will not walk on the wrong side of an obstacle, or untangles himself when cued to do so. This is a very handy behavior while out walking with your dog.

Some dogs seem to figure this out on their own and rarely wrap their leash around something. Others make a habit of constantly walking on the wrong side of telephone poles, garbage cans, benches or whatever else you encounter on your walks. For the latter type, this is a neat behavior to save you some frustration.

Suggested verbal cue: "Unwrap," "Tangled."

You will need: Your clicker and treats any time you go for a walk with your dog on leash, and a variety of planned routes with varying obstacles.

Quick Clicks: Walk on the wrong side
If you're going to train this, you probably have a dog who passes on the wrong side of obstacles on a fairly regular basis, so you'll have plenty of opportunity to work on it without having to set up situations. Plan for your walks to take longer, as you'll be incorporating training into every outing.

Speed Steps
1. When the dog walks on the opposite side of an obstacle, stop walking and wait for the dog to turn back to look at you. Click and deliver the treat so the dog will untangle the leash as he comes to get the treat. Repeat with at least five obstacles.

2. Wait for him to move at least one of his front feet in your direction.

3. Wait until he takes two steps toward you before you CT.

4. Click while the dog is walking toward you and immediately start walking in the opposite direction. Treat as soon as the dog is next to you.

5. Work with a variety of obvious obstacles.

6. Work with a variety of less obvious obstacles, such as sign posts.

7. Add your cue. Stop moving and cue it as soon as the dog puts his head on the wrong side of an obstacle. Repeat with a variety of obstacles.

8. Say your cue and slow down, but don't stop. Build to a normal pace.

Keep in Mind

The longer your dog has relied you to untangle the leash, the longer you may have to work to have *him* do it. Be ready to break your steps down more. You might have to start with just an eye slide or an ear twitch in your direction and build up from there.

You will be more likely to have successful repetitions if your dog has to look *behind* the obstacle to see you. If he can see you in front of the obstacle he's more likely to keep trying to circle around in front of the obstacle to reach you.

If he can see you in front of the obstacle he's more likely to keep trying to circle around in front of the obstacle to reach you.

Try to include segments of your route that have no obstacles so you can both take a break and just enjoy the walk.

Troubleshooting

I can wait forever and my dog just keeps pulling forward.

- Are you sure you're not missing any subtle turns of attention toward you? An ear flick, the head moving up and back? See if you can arrange to have someone walk with you and observe.

- If you're really stuck, use a lure. Walk hand over hand up the leash, trying to keep the same tension on it, until you can use a treat or toy to lure the dog back toward you. Click as soon as the dog makes any move in your direction. After three repetitions with the lure, try waiting again.

- Try stopping a little short of the obstacle, so the dog doesn't have a chance to get too far forward of the obstacle, but is beside it while you are a bit behind it.

We do okay with large, really obvious obstacles, but the dog can't seem to figure it out when the obstacles aren't as obvious. (Here are some examples of obstacles that are obvious, less obvious and downright subtle: trash can, telephone pole, sign post, guy wire.)

- Work with each level of obstacle until the dog is quickly turning to come back to you.

- Be sure you start over at Step 1 and work back up through the steps each time you change to a less obvious obstacle.

- Add your cue before making the change to really difficult obstacles. Then, saying the cue should alert your dog to look back at you and, perhaps, to realize there is an obstacle.

My dog never walks on the wrong side of anything.

- Congratulations! Consider yourself lucky and choose some other behavior to work on.

Variations

Work on speed, so that you could jog and still keep the dog on the correct side of any obstacles.

Take your training to the bike! All good dog-bike attachment systems have an emergency breakaway just for the circumstance of the dog passing on the wrong side of an obstacle, but you can avoid that by using your Untangle cue.

Teach the dog to Untangle his legs from the leash. Hint: Start by having the dog Sit and Shake each time the leash goes under a leg.

Detailed Training Plan

1. Plan a route that passes substantial obstacles that your dog might wrap the leash around. When he does, stop walking and just hold onto the leash. Wait for the dog to look back at you. As soon as you see any sign of shifting attention to you, click. Hold

your treat out so the dog can see it, and encourage him to come back to you so that the leash disengages from the obstacle. Backtrack your path a little and approach the obstacle again. If the dog tangles again, repeat the step at the current obstacle. If he stays with you, walk on to your next potential obstacle. Continue until you have Untangled at least once from five different obstacles (these can be five different telephone poles or a variety of obvious obstacles).

Quick Clicks: Watch for signs

Be alert for any sign that the dog is checking in with you rather than just continuing to try to pull past the obstacle. You might see an ear flick, a slight head turn, a little rock back in the haunches. Click anything you get at first. It will be helpful if you can stop quickly enough once the dog starts to tangle so that the dog has to turn his head to see you by looking behind the obstacle rather than looking around it.

2. Walk the same route with the same obstacles. When the dog tangles, wait for a more definite response from him before you click. If you got a decided head turn in Step 1, now wait for a foot movement in your direction. If you only got an eye flick, wait for a head turn. Repeat at each obstacle at least five times. Do this step with at least five obstacles.

3. Walk the same route. When the dog tangles the leash, stop and wait for him to take two steps toward you. (If you need more steps to get to this point, add them here. If you've only gotten a head turn in the previous step, now you want a foot movement in your direction, then one step, then two.) Do five repetitions with each of five obstacles.

4. Walk the same route again. This time once the dog tangles, click while he is moving toward you and immediately start walking again, in a different direction, to get the dog back beside you. Give him the treat when he rejoins you. Repeat until the dog is untangling and moving toward you at least 80% of the time.

5. Select a different route, with different obstacles of about the same bulk. Repeat steps one to four.

Quick Clicks: Retractable leads

If you walk your dog on a retractable lead, lock the leash at a reasonable length (six to eight feet should work) while you are training this. You don't want the dog to be able to walk ten feet past the obstacle before you react. It might be even easier to change temporarily to a standard six-foot leash while you are training this.

6. Change your route again, this time so that some of the potential obstacles are less obvious—so maybe a mailbox post instead of a telephone pole. Repeat Steps 2-4 (1-4 if necessary, but your dog should be starting to get the idea by this point). Continue

at this step until the dog is responding by untangling and moving toward you when he encounters an obstacle at least 80% of the time.

7. Change routes again, to another option with obstacles of similar bulk. Repeat Step 6.

8. Is your dog initiating movement toward you most of the time when you stop moving forward and the leash tightens? Time to add your cue. Say the cue as soon as the dog puts his head on the wrong side of an obstacle. Stop moving, click when the dog changes direction, turn away from the dog and treat at your side.

9. Repeat at least fifty times with a variety of obstacles over a number of sessions. Repeat until he backtracks toward you when you give the cue.

Generalize the behavior:

- Say your cue as soon as the dog puts his head on the wrong side of an obstacle and keep walking slowly, but try not to stop. Click when the dog starts to step back around the obstacle and treat when he rejoins you.

- Change to a different route with less easily visible obstacles, maybe the guy wire for a light post or metal fence posts.

- Occasionally say your cue when there are no obstacles. The dog should turn toward you and come to your side. This will be important if it's an obstacle that isn't visible to the dog.

- Continue using your cue. Sometimes reward just with praise, sometimes with a treat, sometimes by running with your dog for a brief sprint, or by letting the dog lead you to where he wants to go.

Kahve (8 month old Boxer) has been clicker trained since he was 8 weeks old. He competes in Rally, has his Canine Good Citizen certificate, and is training for agility.

Chapter 5

FOR EXCITABLE DOGS

In this chapter we'll look at excitable dogs, noisy dogs, and pushy dogs, and see what you can do about them. Modifying these behaviors is an excellent way to put your clicker to work, and just might be the most valuable training you'll ever do.

This chapter is geared to dogs who are basically just obnoxious. The good news is that clicker training can often have a significant and positive impact on problem behaviors, with the worst side effect being no change at all in the behavior. It is, however, worth reminding you that you should proceed cautiously if you suspect your dog has a serious fear or aggression-related problem. Trying to push the dog beyond what he's comfortable with can quickly make your problem much worse. Dogs are carnivores, and capable of inflicting damage, and you have to have respect for that. If you think you are over your head with your dog's problem, then working with a private trainer will be a sound investment for you and your dog. Choose a trainer who uses reward-based training methods to deal with doggie issues. *Always* consult with an experienced trainer who can work individually with you and your dog if you don't see improvement within two to four weeks of daily work on these problems, as problems that you ignore generally get worse.

The good news is that early intervention, particularly on fear-based problems, can often have a significant impact. The younger the dog, and the sooner you start, the better the prognosis. Each new thing the dog encounters in a positive way gives him a history to draw from. If all new things are fun and result in treats, then it makes it easier to accept the next new thing. Dogs who approach life as a puzzle to solve are more resistant to developing fear problems. This is one of the many benefits to clicker training, in our opinion. Additionally, the more desirable behaviors you teach and reward, the more behaviors your dog has in his repertoire, and the less likely he will be to engage in undesirable behaviors to get attention.

Whole books have been written on solutions to deal with specific fears in dogs, including some terrific ones that use clicker training. You can find suggestions for further reading in the resources section at the end of the book. We are going to touch here on one helpful behavior you can teach your dog to help him work through his fears, the idea that toys are fun to play with. Believe it or not, some dogs don't find play very rewarding. This behavior is important because we want to have a large variety of rewards available to use with our dogs. Secondarily, teaching the dog that toys are fun, and that anything can be a toy, can be very helpful when dealing with fear issues.

We're adding a section to our behaviors in this chapter: What's in it for the dog? These are some suggestions for how the behavior might have some built-in rewards you'll need to be paying attention to. Remember that a main principle of clicker training is that what is rewarding gets repeated. These behaviors that you find obnoxious are somehow paying off for the dog. (For example, the scary person leaves when your dog barks or growls at the door.) A key to solving behavior problems is understanding how the behavior is rewarding for the dog. You are going to need to change the reward for the dog, and substitute a behavior you like that will still be rewarding for the dog.

Take a look at what your dog gets out of the behavior. It can even be helpful to have someone else who is not emotionally invested in the problem watch the dog. Ask yourself these questions: When does the behavior start? What is the trigger and how close does it have to be before my dog reacts? How specific is the trigger (i.e., is it someone walking by the house, or just when the doorbell rings)? What does my dog do exactly? Be more specific than "he's aggressive" or "he's afraid"—describe the behavior. Is the dog barking, lunging, growling, snapping, hiding behind you? Has the dog bitten? How hard was the bite? If your dog has already attempted a bite, whether that was a "nip" or a "snap" (no teeth touched, but an "air bite") or a puncture, you need to work with someone who is a professional to solve this problem. Remember that practice makes perfect. The more "nips" your dog gets in, the better he will get at it. It usually doesn't end well for the dog.

Then ask yourself: Do I yell at or grab the dog or otherwise pay attention to the behavior?

What stops the behavior? Does the person move away or leave? (This can be a clue to what is rewarding for the dog.)

Finally, what do you *want* the dog to do? Phrase it in terms of what you would like the dog to *do*, not stop doing. For example, "Instead of barking at the window when people walk by, I want my dog to come to me and sit quietly." This is different from "I want the dog to stop barking at the window." The first sentence identifies behavior that can be rewarded, the second does not.

We will use the Premack Principle for much of the behavior in this chapter. If you don't understand it, go back and review Chapter 2 to refresh your memory. You can also search the web for it to get lots more information.

If you think any of these behaviors might help, get out your clicker and work through this chapter. Take a deep breath and try to relax. You already know this stuff works, so have faith, take your time, and you will find yourself and your dog a whole lot happier with each other. Remember, if you feel like you're in over your head, consult with someone who can help you and your dog.

We will cover:

- Problem Barking.
- Focus, Focus, Focus or Mother May I?
- Possession Problems—What's Mine is Mine, What's Yours is Mine.
- Bonus behavior—step away from the food bowl.
- Creating an interest in toys and using them effectively in training.
- Matching rewards to behaviors.

PROBLEM BARKING

We'll start with barking at the window or door, since it is a common problem. Other barking issues can be resolved using the same basic training plan. For this behavior, we want the dog to quietly come check in with you when someone walks by the front window. You can train just a Come, or Come with a Sit. Allowing your dog to bark uncontrolled at the window at passersby is not just an annoying and noisy problem, but can actually increase or create aggression toward people and dogs. Walk Off Leash/Check In from Chapter 3 and Come from Chapter 2 are good foundation behaviors for the dog to have before you teach this, but are not required.

Quick Clicks: Sometimes barks are OK
Note: While we don't allow our dogs to bark at passersby, we do allow them to bark when someone rings the doorbell or knocks on the door. Then they have to be quiet when we tell them, or the door doesn't open. (Friends understand this, and will wait on the porch, but sometimes we miss signing for UPS deliveries!) During your training, you can put a sign on the door that says "Hang on, I'm training my dog" if you don't want to miss any deliveries. (If you need help with teaching the dog to Sit when the door opens, check out Sit-Stay while Greeting in Chapter 4.) You could also train the dog to be quiet when someone knocks on the door or rings the doorbell, although this is a significantly harder variation.

Suggested Cue: No cue is necessary as the dog is automatically responding to a person crossing your property.

You will need: *Super* treats (we're talking garlic flavored chicken, steak, cheese tortellini, hot dogs, liverwurst, cheese, salmon paté). Don't feed the dog at least eight to twelve hours prior to a session for the first two weeks of working on this behavior. Keep the dog away from any area where he could bark at people passing by until you have control of this behavior (remember, practice makes perfect!).

What's in it for the dog?

Barking at the window is fun. You come to check it out and interact with the dog (yelling is interaction, don't forget!). You may have rewarded it earlier by praising the dog (only now it's out of control) or cooing at him ("it's okay, don't be worried"). Those scary people run away when the dog barks (especially delivery people—remember the dog doesn't know they only planned to be there for a short time anyway!). Movement-oriented breeds such as herding dogs (Border Collies, Shelties), and protection breeds (Rottweilers, Boxers, German Shepherds) may react because of a genetic component to their behavior.

Speed Steps

1. Each time someone appears at the edge of your property, drop a treat on the floor (no click necessary at this point). Give the dog a second and even a third treat if he stays right there.

2. Give the dog multiple treats while a person walks by. Feed treats rapidly while the person is visible. As soon as the person disappears, the opportunity to get treats is gone.

3. Wait longer between the delivery of treats. Remain at this step until the dog comes to you as soon as someone appears and remains with you until they are gone.

4. If it takes an average of ten seconds for someone to walk across your property, offer treats rapid-fire for the first nine seconds, pause, then CT.

5. Reduce the continuous feeding by one second, and CT one additional second of quiet. Gradually build up the quiet time and continue to reduce the continuous feeding.

6. At five seconds of rapid-fire feeding followed by five seconds of quiet, CT quiet behavior (varying for a count of one, two, or three before the click). Continue to reduce the amount of continuous feeding and add time to the quiet.

7. Reduce the number of CT the dog gets for being quiet by gradually upping your count before clicking (using Bouncing Around).

8. The dog might bark initially, then be quiet for the remainder of the time. If you don't want this, you'll need another step. For this step, only the quiet time preceded by *no* barking is clicked and treated. If the dog barks, cheerfully say "Ooops, too bad!" and leave the room, taking the treats with you.

9. Teach the dog to come find you to collect his treat. Continue adding distance until you are in the room you spend most of your time in.

10. Add the Sit if you want to.

11. Pay attention when the dog comes to you and sits so you can be sure and reward the behavior (with treats, petting and games) as often as possible.

Keep in Mind

If you can't get the dog to eat a treat no matter what you do because he is so agitated, try working as your first step in a room where he can hear people go by but not see them. If you are still not getting any response, you need to talk to a behaviorist for help with this problem.

Troubleshooting

My canine genius figured out running to me in my office is a good way to get treats from me, even though no one is walking by the house!

- Reward only during times of day when you know people are likely to be walking by. Behavior that is randomly rewarded like this—not every repetition gets a reward—will still be maintained. Have someone walk back and forth during a time that you specify, so you will know the dog's behavior should be rewarded.

- Periodically sit in the same room and reward quiet attention on you when people walk by, and ignore the dog when no one is there.

Variations

Have the dog be quiet when someone actually knocks on the door or rings the doorbell by enlisting a friend to do it over and over, following the steps outlined above. Add different people as the dog begins to get the idea. Use the same training plan to reward the dog for being quiet while you are on the phone, while you're driving or any time the dog wants your attention.

Detailed Training Plan

1. Pick a time when you know there will be some activity going by your window. Summer evenings are good, when there are likely to be a lot of people out walking. Or, enlist a friend to walk back and forth in front of your window, if you need to. Get comfortable in a chair away from the window—you're going to be there for a while. Each time someone appears at the edge of your property, drop a treat on the floor (no click necessary at this point). What does the dog do? If he notices the treat immediately and goes to eat it while the person is walking by, perfect! Give him a second and even a third treat while he's right there next to you. If he doesn't come to get it until after they've left, that's okay too, but he only gets the one treat in that case. If he never notices it because he's so agitated, put him on leash, tie the leash to something *sturdy* close by you, and drop the treat right in front of his nose. Make the

treat more enticing if you need to. Your timing of the treat is important, even if the dog doesn't notice at first. You want it to coincide with the appearance of a person at the edge of your property. Don't try to stop the barking or control the dog (that's why you're not holding on to the leash). Stop the session when the dog has received thirty treats. Repeat at this step until the dog looks for a treat while the person is still visible in front of your property, whether the dog barks or not.

Quick Clicks: Ask for less at first

While working on this behavior we start with (and reward) a behavior that's a lot less than we want at the end because we are allowing the dog to bark initially. That's one of the great advantages of clicker training. It won't matter as long as we stay focused on our end goal and keep working step by step to get there.

2. Sit in a different part of the room. Now you are going to give the dog multiple treats from your hand while a person walks by. Make the treats unavailable (keep them in a container) until a person appears, then offer them to the dog one at a time during the entire time the person is walking by. As soon as the person disappears, the opportunity to get treats is gone and the container is closed. This is what will impact the barking later on. If the dog doesn't notice you are offering a treat, don't say anything to the dog, just quietly put the treat back in the container. If this happens a couple of times in a row, you need to go back to Step 1 for a while. Feed treats rapidly (at least one treat per second) while the person is visible and the dog is near you. The dog may interrupt his barking and start to come for the treats earlier and earlier, or may get his treat, bark at the window, then come and get another treat. Repeat until the dog has received fifty treats total, and end the session. Repeat this step several times over the course of a few days.

3. Begin to wait longer between the delivery of treats (i.e., one treat every two seconds, then one treat every three seconds). Remain at this step until the dog comes to you as soon as someone appears and remains with you until they are gone, with at least three seconds between each treat delivered. The dog may still be barking while he is eating treats. Don't worry about that now as long as he remains close to you.

4. We will now shorten the amount of time the treats are available for the dog. This, combined with clicking for quiet, will eliminate the barking, because the treats will only be available for a limited amount of time. The dog won't be able to bark and get treats. Time how long it takes someone to walk from one side of your property to the other. If it takes an average of ten seconds for someone to walk across your property, you are going to offer treats rapid-fire for the first nine seconds, pause, then CT the last second only if there is *no* barking during that last second. (If it takes longer or shorter for someone to cross your property, adjust accordingly so the dog gets treats for the first 90% of the time the person is crossing your property.) The treats are available rapid-fire for the first nine seconds only. If the dog doesn't immediately come

to you, there is less time for him to be continuously fed. The dog will learn best if it takes a long time for a person to cross your property, so if you can corral someone into helping you with this step, use them! Repeat the entire process five times, and move to the next step.

5. "Open the bar" for one second less, and CT one additional second of quiet. In our example of ten seconds, you would now be feeding for eight seconds, then waiting two seconds, CT-ing if there is no barking during the last two seconds. Repeat five times, then reduce the amount of continuous feeding by one second and add one second to the clicked and treated quiet time. Continue to gradually reduce the rapid-fire feeding and increase the quiet time, repeating at least five times at each level. Continue to the next step when you have an "open bar" for half the time and a quiet dog for the remainder of the time.

Quick Clicks: Limited hold
The "open bar" concept is also called a limited hold. It means that the opportunity to earn treats is only available for a certain amount of time. It tends to speed the dog's response time. After the time elapses (i.e., the person disappears), "the bar is closed" even if the dog still does the behavior.

6. Begin to click the quiet behavior multiple times, varying for a count of one, two or three when you CT. Our example would look like this: rapid-fire feeding (at least one treat per second) for five seconds, then one second of quiet, CT, three seconds of quiet, CT, one second quiet, CT. You will randomly determine how long the dog has to be quiet to be clicked, ranging from one to three counts. Restart your count if the dog barks before he gets clicked. End the session when the dog has received twenty treats. Repeat this step several times over a couple of days.

7. Continue to reduce the amount of continuous feeding and add time to the quiet, one second at a time. CT randomly every one, two or three seconds during the quiet time. End the session when the dog has received twenty treats. Continue at this step until the dog is quiet during the time the person crosses your property, even if he barked initially.

8. Now reduce the number of CTs the dog gets for being quiet by gradually upping your count before clicking (using Bouncing Around as described in Chapter 1). If he was getting an average of five CTs initially, gradually reduce it so that he gets fewer CTs randomly spaced during the ten seconds it takes a person to cross your property. Continue at this step until the dog comes to you in anticipation of getting a treat when someone appears and remains quietly with you, with only two or three CTs.

9. The dog might bark initially, then be quiet for the remainder of the time. If you don't want him to bark at all, you'll need this optional step. For this step, only the quiet time preceded by no barking is clicked and treated. If the dog barks, cheerfully say "ooops, too bad!" and leave the room, taking the treats with you. If the dog follows

you, great! Just ignore him. Return to the room when the person passing is gone. The dog gets another chance the next time a person walks by. *Immediately* CT the appearance of a person so that the dog doesn't have time to bark, then click at least two other points during the property crossing, varying how long you wait for the second and third click. Your timing must be impeccable for this step. If you waited too long to click and the dog barks, leave the room. If you continue to have problems, try timing your click just before the person appears (the dog knows they are there anyway). Repeat until twenty treats are delivered. Continue at this step until the dog is quiet at least 80% of the time when someone appears in front of the window.

10. Now we'll teach the dog to come find you to collect his treat. Stand at the far edge of the room you started working in. The dog at this point should assume that the appearance of a person means you'll be delivering treats, and come to you in anticipation (if not, go back to Step 8 until he does or start closer to the window area). As soon as he reaches you, CT, then CT at least two other times while he's with you (varying how long between each click) until the person is gone, ending the session. Go two feet farther away. Repeat until you deliver twenty treats. Continue building distance until you are in the room you spend most of your time in (for us, that's the home office down the hall).

11. Add the Sit if you want to. When the dog comes to find you, cue him to Sit, then give him a treat and release him. He gets a couple of extra treats if he remains with you after he gets released from the Sit. Continue at this step until the Sit is automatic. You don't need the clicker any longer at this point, by the way.

12. Pay attention when the dog comes to you and sits so you can be sure and reward the behavior (with treats, petting and games) as often as possible. You may not know that someone has crossed in front of the window since you might not be in a position to see any more. We always assume the dog has made the correct choice if he comes running without being called, and he gets rewarded for it. It's a good idea to occasionally do tune ups when there is activity in front of the window and you are in the room to CT quiet behavior. It's also a good idea to change rooms periodically so the behavior holds no matter where you happen to be.

Variations

While you're on the phone. Using the same basic directions, you will pick up the phone and pretend to have a conversation. Initially, you are going to put your hand on the phone, and feed the dog rapid fire with the other hand to start the training process. Proceed as above, moving through steps such as picking up the phone, putting it to your ear, talking into the phone (saying hello is usually sufficient), having someone actually call you (or using your cell phone to make your phone ring), and so on.

While you're in the car. Start with the car in the garage or driveway. It can be helpful to have the dog on a leash so he can't move around a lot. Progress to starting the car, backing out of the driveway, pulling into the street, and so on. It can be really helpful to have an assistant who can reward the dog appropriately or drive the car while you work with the dog. This is also a safe way to work on the behavior. Be sure to gradually work up to quiet behavior while you are driving by yourself—you can work on this in an empty parking lot for safety.

When your dog wants your attention. Any time the dog is a problem barker, you can design a step by step plan for eliminating the barking. Just be sure to make the early steps easy for dog to be successful and remember that paying attention to the dog in any way is often a reward for him.

Slick Clicks: Mandy's excited puppy

Mandy's Golden Retriever, Perretta, got so excited about meals when she was a puppy that she started barking while the bowl was being prepared. Mandy solved this by freezing when the dog barked and only progressing when she was quiet. It only took a couple of weeks to solve the problem, in this case using primarily negative punishment (stopping movement and restarting when the dog was quiet) rather than positive reinforcement (giving a reward for quiet behavior).

Cheryl's Border Collie mix, Nestle, has a floor-to-ceiling window right next to the front door, and having people walk past the driveway down the country road is a rare occurrence. Rather than stop the alert barking entirely, Cheryl taught Nestle that "Thank you" means that's enough barking. She can sit in her office (which happens to share the same view) and cue the barking to stop. Nestle usually comes and hangs out in the office for a while, because he knows that's where the rewards are!

 ## Focus, Focus, Focus or Mother May I?

Whenever the dog wants something, he looks to you first for permission, and does a "default behavior" such as Sit, Down, Nose Touch, Paw Touch or an easy trick. The more intense the distraction, the more intense his focus will be on you. Sometimes he gets what he wants (the distraction), sometimes he doesn't. This is great for a dog that likes to chase or is sidetracked or distressed by the world. If you've taught Walk Off Leash/Check In from Chapter 3 or Attention from Chapter 2, it'll make this exercise go quickly, but it's not required. For this behavior, we'll indicate specifically when you should offer a treat (as opposed to some other reward) after marking the behavior.

You will need: A variety of doggie rewards, a list of doggie distractions (see page 127 for an example), and a default behavior. Decide what your default behavior will be and train that first, with *no* distractions. The longer your dog has been doing that behavior (and the more rewards he has received), the better your success will be. For our example, we'll use a Hand Touch. (See Chapters 2, 3 and 4 for other focus-related behaviors.)

Quick Clicks: Bridge words

We'll discuss the use of another behavior marker called a bridge word. Although it's not as precise as using a clicker, it's a handy tool to have for your training. You can use a clicker, or substitute a bridge word where click is indicated, to mark the correct criteria for many behaviors.

Suggested verbal cue: "Look," "Watch," "Attention," "Say Please," or you can just wait for the dog to look at you.

What's in it for the dog?

Some dogs are highly movement oriented—you'll know this is your dog because he's been chasing anything that moves since he was a small puppy. This exercise will have an impact, although it may be limited. Other dogs may be reacting from fear that something can hurt them. Excitability and hyperactivity can be signs of a stressed dog. Focusing on something to do and removing all punitive corrections from the situation is very successful with these dogs. Or, the behavior may be a combination of both reasons. Believe it or not, active dogs are the easiest dogs to do this behavior with; they quickly learn to focus on what they need to do to get what they want.

Speed Steps

1. Choose a default behavior. Practice multiple times over the course of several days until the dog is offering the behavior quickly and reliably.

2. Teach your dog a bridge word.

3. Create your list of doggie distractions.

4. Cue your default behavior (in our example, a Hand Touch) before anything the dog wants to do. Mark (click or bridge) when the dog touches, then immediately allow him to get what he wants.

5. Cue Attention (or wait for it). When the dog looks at you, cue the dog to Touch. When the dog touches, CT. Continue at this Step with a variety of real-life rewards until the dog anticipates that he has to look at you to get a chance to Touch.

6. Vary how many times the dog has to Touch before you click and let him get the reward.

7. Get out your doggie distraction list. Starting with the lowest level distraction, present the distraction, cue (or wait for) Attention, cue Touch, CT with a low-level reward. Alternate with another strong behavior, such as Sit, in a varying pattern. CT *only* the nose Touch behavior paired with Attention. Continue until you have worked with every distraction at Level 1.

8. Work through all ten distractions in the next level. Stay at this step until you have worked through to Level 6 distractions. Change your rewards frequently.

9. Now give your dog the opportunity to do whatever is distracting him as a reward for giving you Attention and touching your hand. Some repetitions will involve some other type of reward and some will be an opportunity to get at the distraction. Continue until you have worked through all the distractions at all ten levels.

Generalize the behavior:

- Experiment with changing the topography of the Touch so the dog must focus more on his job, working in a distraction-free environment to begin with. Gradually add in distractions by level.

- Add other behaviors such as Down, Wait or Come as precursors to the Attention-Touch combo.

- Vary how many behaviors you ask for before giving the dog an opportunity to Touch.

- Vary how long the dog has to look at you before getting the opportunity to Touch.

Keep in Mind

Fearful dogs sometimes don't have a lot of real-life rewards that interest them. If that's the case with your dog, you could substitute a super treat (see Problem Barking in Chapter 5 for suggestions) as a reward for the default behavior. Use whatever you can and in the meantime build up the idea in your dog's mind that life is exciting. (See Creating an Interest in Toys later in this chapter.)

Use a trick the dog loves to do, one with audience appeal. Both you and the dog will be calmer if you have something to do that has built-in rewards for both of you. Reward heavily early on, even if it's not perfect to start with.

Troubleshooting

I can't get the dog to pay attention no matter how low the distraction is.

- Spend a great amount of time having the dog look at you and perform his default behavior before he can do anything—go through a doorway, play with a toy, get his food bowl, drink water, etc.

- Have someone else give you a list of things that would be boring, Level 1 distractions for your dog that you could start with.

- Work with a private trainer to make sure your timing, reward and distractions are appropriate and at a level that will ensure early success.

Variations

Experiment with clicking and rewarding "calm behavior." What does it look like in your dog? Don't forget you'll need to start at a low level and shape calmer behavior. For example, if your dog is bouncing off the ceiling, the first step might be clicking a less enthusiastic bounce, *gradually* building up to four feet on the floor, attention on you, or being on his side sleeping.

Teach the dog to give you the default behavior when he's stressed, as an indicator to *you* that he's stressed. Pay attention if the dog tries to Touch in a situation where you haven't asked for it. He may be trying to tell you something.

Detailed Training Plan

1. Decide on a default behavior such as Sit, Down, Shake or a nose Touch. Practice multiple times over the course of several days until the dog is offering the behavior quickly and reliably. That is, the dog responds close to 100% of the time when the behavior is cued in most environments.

2. Teach your dog a bridge word.

Quick Clicks: Teaching a bridge word

Teach your dog a bridge word by pairing treats with the word. The word needs to be one syllable and something that you will say in more or less the same way every time. Choose a word that you don't use in normal conversation. Some ideas include, "Yes," "Right," "Yep," "Beep," or "Click." Say the word, and give the dog a treat. (You don't want to telegraph that a treat is coming or the dog won't pay attention to the word.) Repeat several times. Change locations and continue practicing in different locations over the course of several days. When the dog's eyes "pop" when he hears the word, you'll know that it has been conditioned as a secondary reinforcer for the dog. You can now use the bridge word instead of the clicker for behaviors that do not need a more precise marker. The bridge word is also a useful tool to have if you don't happen to have your clicker handy. With the behavior that we are working on here, you do not necessarily need the precision of a clicker and the bridge word will do fine. In the instructions, we'll indicate that you should mark the behavior, which means to either click or bridge (not both).

3. Create a list of doggie distractions. Below is a list of at least ten items at each of ten different levels that distract your dog, ranked from lowest distraction to highest. Some examples have been filled in, but you need to complete it for *your* dog. For example, a Level 1 distraction might be a leaf on the ground and so on. List distractions until you have ten full lines of ten different levels of distraction. A Level 10 might be a stranger coming toward you with an unknown dog. Each dog's distraction list will be individual. While you're working on this behavior, don't let your dog have access to any of these distractions, if possible.

1	2	3	4	5	6	7	8	9	10
leaf on ground	bug crawling	leaf blowing	old toy on floor	other dog in sight	hand in bait open bag	horse droppings	bicyclist	on-leash dog	off leash dog
plane	flag flapping	car door closing	doorbell ringing on TV	someone missing from pack	crowds of spectators	crowds	cat running past	person playing with cat toy	squirrel chattering
clean spoon on floor	waves crashing	wind blowing through trees		rustling paper		young girls playing nearby		young boys playing nearby	person sitting eating hot dog

And so on—you would continue until you had ten full lines of ten levels of distraction.

4. Start by cueing a default behavior such as Sit, Down or Touch. The dog must do this behavior before he is allowed to do or get something he wants. (In our example for these directions, we will use a Hand Touch as the default behavior.) Some examples of activities a dog wants to do include going outside, coming inside, getting his leash put on for a walk, getting the leash taken off, getting into the car, getting out of the car, getting out of a kennel, getting his dish put down, getting his water bowl put down, greeting a person, greeting a dog, or getting a toy thrown. Think of as many examples as you can, and use the Hand Touch throughout the day as often as possible. Mark (bridge or click) when the dog touches, then immediately allow him to do what he wanted or get what he wanted. The dog will start to anticipate that you will ask for the Hand Touch before anything he wants. When the dog touches immediately (80% reliable) when cued, regardless of how exciting the distraction is, go to the next step.

Quick Clicks: Remember to sub

If you haven't practiced substituting other fun real-life rewards for food, you may initially need to say your release word in addition to your click or bridge word. Your timing for giving the reward to the dog needs to be as immediate as it would be with a treat. Be sure that your *dog* thinks what you're offering is a reward! (If your dog doesn't like to leave the house, going for a walk is *not* a reward just because you think it should be.) Real-life rewards can be even more powerful than food with a dog who is highly distracted.

5. Now add Attention to your default behavior. To do this, set up a situation where you have something the dog wants that you can quickly give him. For example, you are standing at the door with the dog ready and eager to go outside (don't do this if your dog isn't yet housetrained—it's not fair to make a puppy wait for that!) Cue Attention (or just wait for it if you are not going to put it on cue). As soon as the dog looks at you, cue the nose Touch. When the dog touches, mark and open the door. Continue at this step with a variety of real-life rewards until the dog starts to anticipate that he has to look at you first in order to get a chance to Touch, which then gets him what he wants. In other words, he looks at you before you tell him to about 80% of the time.

Quick Clicks: Premack again
Offering the opportunity to do another behavior (which is then rewarded) on completion of a first behavior is another example of the Premack Principle at work. The first behavior will benefit from the chain as the dog learns to respond quicker to the first behavior so he can perform the second behavior and get a treat.

6. Now, vary how many times the dog has to Touch before you mark the behavior and let him get the reward. Start with one or two touches. Add another touch after every five repetitions until the dog will reliably touch up to five times before getting marked and rewarded. You should vary the number of touches required, gradually increasing the amount using Bouncing Around from Chapter 1. This might look like: Rep one—dog looks at you, Touch, Touch, bridge, reward; Rep two—dog looks at you, Touch, bridge, reward; Rep three—dog looks at you, Touch, Touch, Touch, bridge, reward.

7. Get out your doggie distraction table. You'll also need a selection of portable rewards such as the opportunity to go for a walk, a variety of treats or a variety of toys that the dog likes. Starting with a Level 1 distraction, present the distraction, cue (or wait for) Attention, cue Touch when he looks at you, then mark and reward with a low-level reward.

8. Alternate with another solid behavior, such as Sit, using praise or a pat to reward the dog for the Sit. Sometimes cue Sit and sometimes cue Attention-Touch in a varying pattern. Mark and reward only the Attention-Touch. Repeat until the dog has been marked and rewarded at least five times for the Attention-Touch combination.

Quick Clicks: Pair Attention with Touch
The reason for adding another behavior such as Sit is that you'll need other behaviors out in public besides Attention and Touch. Because we want the Attention-Touch pairing to be very strong for the dog, only that combination will get a mark/reward.

9. Choose another Level 1 distraction and repeat Step 8. Continue until you have worked with every distraction at Level 1, changing the reward every time but using the lowest level rewards that you can. You may be able to do this in one training session, or you may need to work over several sessions and days to complete one level of distractions.

10. When you are ready to move to the next level of distractions, review with one or two distractions at the previous level. Then work through all ten distractions in the next level. Repeat until you have worked through to Level 6 distractions (so a total of sixty different distractions over multiple days). Change your rewards frequently, using play or privileges in addition to a variety of treats and toys.

11. When you get to Level 6 on your distraction list, you have available to you a whole different level of reward—yes, reward. Anything that your dog considers to be a distraction can also be used as a reward for him. Now we're going to give him the opportunity to do whatever is distracting him as a reward for giving you Attention and touching your hand. You'll need that distraction to be something he could actually have at this stage, like a new squeaky toy. We will use that as our example. Put the new toy on the ground and walk toward it with your dog. At the point your dog notices it, stop moving and wait for the dog to look at you or cue it, then cue Touch, mark and release the dog to get the new toy. Have a rousing game with the toy, and repeat the whole process at least five times. Out of those five repetitions, three will involve interaction in some way with the distraction (the toy in this case), and two will involve some other type of reward that's *just as interesting* for the dog, say another new squeaky pulled out of your pocket that he didn't know you had. Do five repetitions with each distraction in Level 6, and go on to the next step.

12. Repeat a few Level 6 distractions, then move on to Level 7 distractions and continue at this step until you have worked through all the remaining distractions on your list. Get creative with how the distractions at Levels 7-10 on your list can be used as a reward for the dog for the behavior you want—play with another dog that you know, the opportunity to sniff or roll in something unmentionable, etc. Don't reward with the distraction every time (every third or fourth time is sufficient) but try to offer a reward that's consistent with ignoring the distraction, i.e., you can run and chase *me* if you pay attention to me when something you want to chase is around.

Slick Clicks: Mandy's bird dog

On Mandy's list of Level 7 distractions for one of her dogs would be birds. The dog loves to chase them, but she also knows she can't really catch them (as does Mandy). The opportunity to chase would be a *huge* reward for her, but the downside to letting a dog chase birds is that you could be creating a stronger desire to chase all animals. In some cities, letting your dog (or encouraging them) to chase wildlife of any kind can be illegal. Finally, you might just encounter a bird who is wounded and can't fly, and what will you do if the dog *does* catch it? These are things you need to be considering as you decide how to reward your dog.

Generalize the behavior:

- Experiment with changing the speed of the Touch (rewarding only the fastest or slowest), getting Touch when the dog starts a distance away from you, having the dog keep his nose on your hand for an extended period, or having the dog Touch multiple times. Each time you change one of the variables, work in a distraction-free environment and gradually add in distractions by level. Changing how the dog performs the Touch forces the dog to think about completing the task, which means less focus on the distraction.

- Add other behaviors such as Down, Wait or Come as precursors to the Attention-Touch combo.

- Vary how many behaviors you ask for before giving the dog an opportunity to Touch.

- Vary how long the dog has to look at you before getting the opportunity to Touch. Work with low-level distractions while you're building up time.

POSSESSION PROBLEMS OR WHAT'S MINE IS MINE AND WHAT'S YOURS IS MINE

The dog happily gives up anything he has, whether that's a bone or your underwear. Being able to take *anything* away from your dog is a core behavior that all dogs should have. We'll offer instructions for two variations—taking something away from the dog, and making the dog back away from what he has (more appropriate for food bowl issues).

Suggested verbal cue: "Give," "Drop," "Thank you," "Yuck," "Mine," "Let Me See."

You will need: A variety of treats and a variety of items the dog might be interested in keeping. Keep items off the floor, trash cans covered and doors closed while you're working on this behavior. Even better, put the dog on a light leash (like a cat leash) that he can drag around the house. Bring him with you as you move from room to room. We don't want him to get any stealing practice sessions in while you're trying to solve this problem!

What's in it for the dog?

You will usually see Possession Problems begin when the dog is very young. This is a common problem for dogs, but is easy to solve if you address it quickly. Otherwise, at some point, you may find yourself competing against your dog for something that might be dangerous for him. The typical scenario starts with a puppy who is exploring his environment and checking out everything—with his mouth. Concerned owners take things away, justifiably worried that they might be harmful. Now it becomes a game for the dog, to either hold on to it or eat it as quickly as possible so you can't take it away. A game of chase while you try to capture the puppy adds a huge reward for him. Stop chasing the dog, and don't punish the dog for having forbidden items. This is the worst thing you can teach your dog. It not only creates problems with possession, it also creates problems with Recalls.

Possession aggression pays off for the dog in terms of attention from you, or because it successfully prevents someone else from getting what he has (either you, or another dog). High possession-instinct dogs (like retrievers) can be particularly bad with this problem, especially if you add punishment to the mix. Some dogs are just more protective of their possessions from the very beginning. A dog who eats non-food items may also be suffering from a physical problem or food imbalance. Try changing foods or discussing it with your veterinarian.

Note: Because you are working close to the dog with this behavior, there is the potential for a bite. If you see *any* signs of problems, please consult with a knowledgeable trainer. If you are working with an older dog who's been practicing possession for a while, or with a dog whose history you don't know, proceed carefully. Look for signs of stress—panting, tucked tail, head turned away, stiffened body, grabbing forcefully at the offered treat—along with more obvious signs of a problem such as growling. Do not punish growling by yelling at or striking the dog. Growling is an indicator that you have pushed the dog too far—you do not want to make it go away or you will no longer have a red flag that tells you the dog is about to bite.

Slick Clicks: A game of chase

On one occasion, clients dropped their terrier at Mandy's house for boarding during spring time. They said to be careful, because he liked to eat snails. Mandy told them not to worry, she didn't set out bait, so eating snails would at worst lead to a minor parasitic infection. The first time he went outside, he instantly grabbed a snail, then turned and looked at Mandy. She looked at him but said nothing, and didn't move from the doorway. He held it in his mouth for a moment, then promptly spit it out. He didn't really like snails, he liked the chase game that ensued when he picked them up! Since she wasn't playing, he didn't bother. He didn't eat a single snail while at the house, although he checked a few times to see if anyone might play his game.

Speed Steps

1. Offer the dog an item that he would consider low in value while holding on to it. Offer a treat. When he removes his mouth from the object, bridge and treat. Offer the object again. Repeat, changing items and treats occasionally.

2. Using the same items from Step 1, give the dog the item. CT when the dog takes his mouth off the object. Repeat, changing items and treats as needed.

3. Wait for a slightly longer pause off the item before CT.

4. Start the next session with three new items and one old one from the previous session. Continue at this step until the dog immediately drops what you give him and waits for up to ten seconds before you CT.

5. Put the treats on a counter nearby. Give the dog a slightly more interesting object and wait for him to drop it. Vary how long he has to wait before you CT dropping the item. Change treats and items frequently. Continue at this step until the dog immediately drops what you give him and waits for a CT, regardless of what he's been given.

6. Pick ten items that vary in interest for the dog. Give a low value item to the dog and leave the room for thirty seconds. Come back and approach the dog with your hand out. When the dog drops the item, click, drop a treat at your feet and leave the room again.

7. Continue to get closer to the dog, until you can put your hand on the item. Change to a higher value item and repeat, until you have completed this step with multiple items.

8. Repeat with additional items of higher value until your entry into the room causes the dog to spit out the item, or until he lets go immediately when you put your hand on it.

9. Add the cue.

Generalize the behavior:

- Pull the object toward you, look at it briefly and return it to the dog.
- Gradually increase distance.
- Practice saying "Give me that!" or "What have you got!" in a mock serious tone of voice.
- Play Tug with a tug toy and cue the dog to let go of the item.
- Lean over the dog when he has something and take it from him to examine it. Gradually practice more threatening body postures.
- Have other people practice taking things from your dog.
- Tie the dog to a doorknob and practice taking things away (the behavior is different when the dog is restricted in movement!).

Keep in Mind

If the dog won't take his mouth off the item, it means the value of your object is too high and the value of the treats is too low. Adjust both accordingly. Bridge and treat the jaw relaxing as the first step if the dog won't let go. You'll feel his jaw slacken on the item as you're holding on to it. Be sure to give a yummy treat!

If your dog has already growled at you for taking things away, or has been punished in the past for "stealing," you need to work with a trainer who is experienced with this problem. You (or someone you know) are at very high risk for a bite.

Troubleshooting

The dog runs away with the item when I let go of it in Step 2.

- Lower the value of the item (use something even more boring).
- Put the dog on leash and step on the leash.
- Sit on the floor to ensure you're not leaning over the dog.

The dog gets something dangerous while we're working on this behavior and I can't get it away from him.

- Ring the doorbell, knock on the door, pick up the leash, call the kitty or jingle your keys. Whatever you do, *don't chase the dog!*

The dog looks for items to bring to me, so he can get a treat.

- Cover trash cans or close doors so he can't get items he shouldn't.
- Stop rewarding with treats, use lower value rewards only occasionally.
- Don't reward the dog if he brings an item to you, only when you ask him to drop it. (Use your clicker to refine what you expect from the dog.)

Variations

Have the dog bring the item to you to get his treat. That way you know what the dog is getting into.

Teach the dog to pick up items dropped around the house and help you keep it clean.

If you have multiple dogs, teach each dog to take a toy or treat from you only on his name. You can also teach each dog to play with their designated toy.

Detailed Training Plan

1. Offer the dog an item that he would consider low in value—such as a plastic chew bone or toy that he has free and regular access to. You are going to hold onto the item when you offer it—do *not* let him have it. (Once the dog has possession, the rules change!) Show him a treat (more interesting than what he's giving up, but also fairly low value.) When he removes his mouth from the object (even if it's just to reposition his bite!) say your bridge word and give him the treat. Offer the object again *as soon as* he has eaten the treat. It's very important that the dog learn that the item won't disappear if he takes his teeth off of it. Repeat ten times, then change items and treats. Repeat with two more item changes (you've now traded for four different items).

Hold onto the item, and show her a treat that is more interesting than what she's giving up.

2. Put a treat in one hand and the clicker in the other. Using the same four items from Step 1, give the dog an item (you will no longer hold onto it). CT when the dog takes his mouth off the object, even for a split second. Do not lean over the dog to give the treat, just open your hand and let him take it once you click. Repeat ten times for each item. Each time you change to another item, change to a more enticing treat. End the session after you have practiced with four items.

Quick Clicks: Don't lean over
Most dogs feel very threatened by people leaning over them. You want to make your behavior non-threatening at this point to avoid stressing the dog and possibly inviting a bite, or encouraging him to swallow the item or run away with it.

3. Wait for a slightly longer pause from the dog (with his mouth off the item) before CT. Gradually build up to a ten second pause. Build up your time by using the Bouncing Around technique from Chapter 1.

4. Start the next session with three new items and one old one from the previous session. Continue at this step until the dog immediately drops what you give him and waits for up to ten seconds before you CT.

5. Put the treats on a counter nearby. Give the dog a slightly more interesting object (like a toy he hasn't seen before) and wait. When the dog drops the object, CT. Repeat ten times, varying how long he has to wait before you CT each time.

6. Repeat Step 5 with three other slightly interesting objects. After you have practiced with four items, end the session. (You can usually work through about four different items in one session.)

7. At the next session, pick four objects that are higher in value than the previous session's objects. Change treats frequently and continue increasing the value of the treats. Continue at this step until the dog immediately drops the item and waits for a CT, regardless of what he's given. This may take a week or longer, depending on the dog. Don't forget to practice with things the dog commonly picks up such as socks, underwear and tissues!

Quick Clicks: Getting control

Don't worry if you later want to teach the dog to hold onto an item (say for a retrieve). We're going to give this behavior a name, thereby giving you control over it. Any behavior you have practiced enough to name is "on cue"—you can ask for it when you want it.

8. Pick ten items that vary in interest for the dog (but would be safe for him if he chose to eat them), including some that are very high value such as tissue, and some that are really low value, such as an old bone. Give a low value item to the dog and immediately leave the room for thirty seconds. Come back into the room and approach the dog with your hand out (as if you were going to reach for the item). Stop far enough away that the dog could not bite if he decided to, and wait with your arm held out. When the dog drops the item, click, drop a treat at your feet for the dog to come get, and leave the room again. Repeat three times at the same distance, and then go one step closer to the dog when you return. Repeat three times. Continue to build one step closer, staying at each distance at least three repetitions. End the session when the dog has had thirty treats.

Quick Clicks: Warning signs

Watch your dog carefully during this step. Does he freeze or stiffen, stare at you, stop chewing on the item, but remain near it, pick it up and move it farther away, cover the item with his body, or give you any other indications that he's worried about your approach such as turn away with the item, or growl or snap at you? If so, discontinue work by yourself and seek the advice of a trainer. If he gets up from the item and comes over to you, that's a good sign you're making progress. In our group classes, we use pig's ears in Step 1 to test the dog's reaction to giving up something for a treat, before starting to let go of the item. This can give you an indication of how serious a problem you are starting with. Many people are surprised at the dog's reaction when they try to take away a pig's ear.

9. Start at the previous distance and continue to get closer, until you can put your hand on the item whether the dog still has it or not. Do not pick it up, but touch it, click, drop your treat and leave.

10. Change to a higher value item and repeat the whole process, until you have completed this step with each of the ten items. Each time you will CT when you touch the

item. Don't take it away from the dog just yet. You may find that the dog quickly spits out the item and comes running to you in anticipation of getting a better treat (Yay!). He may also bring it to you and drop it at your feet. Either one of these responses is cause for joy. You will still CT for touching the item.

11. Can you predict that the dog will drop the item (either as soon as you enter the room, or when you put your hand on it)? Time to add a cue. Give the dog a new object, say your cue *as you* reach for the object, CT when he lets go of it. Pick it up, look at it, and give it back to the dog. Repeat fifty to sixty times, using different objects and working in different places, including outside. Be sure to practice with very high value items such as pig's ears, stuffed Kongs and rawhide, as well as low value items such as an old tennis ball.

Generalize the behavior:

- Pull the object toward you slowly along the floor, CT, look at it briefly, and return it to the dog. Change objects and repeat the entire sequence. Continue with various objects until you can take any object from the dog, CT, look at it, and return it to the dog. Note: Dragging the object slowly toward you can sometimes increase the dog's interest in it. This is a tool you can use to get your dog to play with toys, by the way.

- Gradually increase the distance the dog will come away from something he has. If the dog brings the item with him, that's okay too. Don't immediately take the item from the dog, but pet and make a fuss over him, then trade him for something better.

- Practice saying "Give me that!" or "What have you got!" in a mock serious tone of voice before you give your cue to drop the item. It never hurts to practice how the real world is—someone might react just this way before they try to snatch something from your dog.

- Play Tug with the item and have the dog let go of it. To get the dog to let go initially, you may need to freeze as soon as you cue the behavior—you become a statue so the dog doesn't get rewarded for continuing to tug by having you tug back.

- Lean over the dog when he has something and take it from him to examine it. Gradually practice more threatening body posture, such as crouching over the dog or touching his body while you pick up the item.

- Have other people practice taking things from your dog. Be very careful with this step, as your dog may not react the same with them as he does with you. Work through from Step 1 with another person if you have any doubts.

- Tie the dog to a doorknob and practice taking things away (the behavior is different when the dog is restricted in movement!).

Quick Clicks: Rules for Tug
1. Don't leave tug toys around.
2. The dog can only tug when you give the cue.
3. The dog has to stop when you say to.
4. The game ends immediately if the dog puts his teeth on you.

Be clear what you expect from the dog, and play by the rules, and you can play Tug safely with most dogs. (We know you're doing it anyway, so you might as well set up some rules!)

BONUS BEHAVIOR—BACK AWAY FROM THE BOWL

This is a variation of the previous behavior, where you are teaching the dog to actually back away from something instead of just letting go of an item. Back Away from the Bowl is an appropriate variation if you are an experienced dog handler with a young-ish dog or if the problem is not severe. Because we are teaching the dog to Back Away from the Bowl as part of the process, the trainer is less liable to be bitten, but is still at risk. As always, get someone who can help you if you feel over your head, the behavior is getting worse, or there is no change after a couple of weeks of working on it. We will provide fairly abbreviated steps, since this is not a behavior a beginner should be working on. This behavior can also be very effectively combined with Wait/Release.

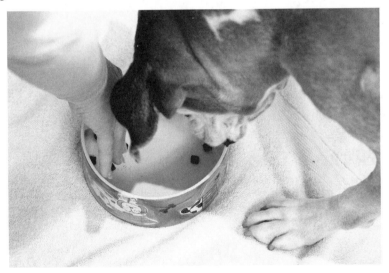

Ping was the first wholly clicker trained dog Mandy trained, and is now very casual about hands in or near her bowl. Notice how relaxed her ear set is.

Slick Clicks: Ping's Story
Mandy originally created the plan for this behavior when she got Ping, a five month old boxer, from the Humane Society of Silicon Valley. Her notes on the first day of getting this cute little hoodlum included "Charged Twister over water bowl—was on tie

down at the time." Day two—"Tested with Assessa-hand. Head in bowl, froze, stopped eating." Obviously, if this dog was going to join the household, something needed to be done immediately about her bowl issues around dogs and people (among many other issues that needed work!) Ping, by the way, was the first wholly clicker trained dog Mandy trained, and is now very casual about hands in or near her bowl. She's also a registered Delta Dog who works with children. The stories Mandy could tell about the things she learned with her! But that's a subject for another book.

Detailed Training Plan

1. Start someplace other than the feeding area if you've already had problems there. Put down an empty food bowl. The dog will investigate the bowl—click when the dog's head comes out of the bowl, and drop a piece of kibble on the floor a couple of feet away. (Kibble is a good option to use here, we don't want the food value to be too high.) Pick up the bowl and repeat. If you need to, you can have the dog on leash, and have someone step on the leash while you pick up the bowl, but don't work with the dog tied up. Continue at this step until the dog looks up immediately after seeing that the bowl is empty, anticipating a CT.

2. Put down an empty food bowl. Click when the dog's head comes out of the bowl, and drop a piece of kibble into the bowl. Repeat at least twenty times.

3. Decide how far away you want the dog to back up. Shape that, clicking and tossing the dog a treat when the dog is far enough away for that step, then putting a piece of kibble into the bowl for the dog to come forward again. Remember to shape this incrementally, and move on when the dog is successful 80% of the time at the distance you've decided on for that step. A foot or so away from the bowl is usually sufficient for the final distance.

Quick Clicks: Low criteria start

Most dogs will eat the kibble in the bowl then look at you expectantly at this step, while they figure out what will make you click again. Start with any movement, no matter how slight, away from the bowl.

4. Start with an empty bowl, and add several pieces of kibble after clicking the dog for backing off. Drop another piece of kibble in while the dog is eating (at whatever distance from the bowl that you need to be to remain safe). If the dog backs up as your hand comes toward the bowl, you are on the right track! Continue at this step until the dog is backing away from the bowl 100% of the time when your hand approaches the bowl, then do another set of ten for good measure.

5. Start with an empty bowl. Take several pieces of kibble in one hand and put that hand in the bowl. When the dog moves away from the bowl, click and drop a piece of

kibble into the bowl. Occasionally drop multiple pieces into the bowl, so that the dog is still chewing when your hand goes back into the bowl. At this point, the dog should back off quickly when your hand approaches the bowl.

Quick Clicks: Watch for clues

Pay attention to the dog's body language—is she eating as fast as possible, does she have a tense body posture, or has she stopped moving? Time to back off and repeat a few steps at a lower level or get help with this behavior. Since we're dealing here with a mostly finished behavior, it's okay to work at 100% for several sessions if you feel you need to, and in fact, it's a good idea for your safety.

6. Put the bowl down with a couple of piece of kibble in it, release the dog to eat, and put your empty hand in the bowl while she is eating. Click and toss a piece of ham or other tasty tidbit to the dog when the dog backs off. Build up the amount of kibble in the bowl, so that the dog has more remaining to eat when your hand goes into the bowl. Reward with a high-level treat *away* from the bowl when the dog backs off. It's important to Note: If the dog leaves kibble in the bowl when she backs away from it, that means you are making good progress. If she tries to eat it all first, continue at this step until she will back away with kibble still in the bowl 100% of the time.

7. Put the bowl down, release the dog to eat, and drop a mid level treat in the bowl. If the dog backs away from the bowl as your hand approaches, click and toss a super high value treat to the dog.

8. Change environments, working back to the feeding area if you didn't start there. Practice in multiple areas.

9. Pick up the bowl, add tasty bits and put it down again.

10. Work the same set of steps with high value items such as pig's ears or bully sticks.

11. Work the same set of steps with other dogs in the feeding area (you should put the other dog on leash and have someone hold it for safety.)

12. Lightly touch or bump the dog, CT-ing if the dog stops eating and backs away from the bowl.

CREATING AN INTEREST IN TOYS AND USING THEM EFFECTIVELY IN TRAINING

This behavior will help the dog learn to have fun with a toy that he was previously uninterested in. Once your dog is interested in playing with toys, you have those available as another form of reward besides food and petting. As the dog adds more toys to his repertoire, you can expand your definition of what a "reward" is. Mandy once used a leaf on the ground to reward a dog for going potty!

Suggested verbal cue: "Tug," "Let's Play," "Get It."

You will need: A tug toy—our favorites are the bungee type toys such as the "Scrungee Bungee." They are available online.

Quick Clicks: Toy envy

To start the game, you can create a really strong desire to have something by keeping it away from the dog in a drawer. Periodically take it out, look at it like it's incredibly interesting, toss it around a bit, drag it on the ground with an attached leash or string, and put it back in the drawer. Occasionally drop it on the floor and quickly grab it before the dog does. After a couple of weeks of this, "accidentally" let the dog get hold of it briefly. Pretty soon you will have the dog's instant attention as soon as you get close to the drawer. (Thanks to John Rogerson for this tip on creating "toy envy.")

Speed Steps

1. Show the dog the toy, CT when he looks at it.

2. CT if he sniffs it.

3. CT when he touches it.

4. CT when he opens his mouth to reach for it.

5. CT when his teeth touch the toy.

6. CT when the dog closes his mouth on the toy.

7. Build duration with his mouth closed on the toy.

8. Shape a strong Tug.

9. Add duration to the Tug.

10. Add a cue when it looks the way you want.

Generalize the behavior:

- Change locations.
- Add another toy to the dog's fun play, using the steps outlined above.
- Add non-toy items.

Keep in Mind

If the dog shows no interest in the toy, try pulling it along the ground, even attaching it to a string so you're not close to it. You can also find toys that are designed to have treats kept in a pocket inside (see Resources) or use an old sock with one end knotted.

Dogs will be more interested in sniffing, following and putting their teeth on these if you stuff them with smelly treats.

Troubleshooting

The dog doesn't show any interest in the toy.

- Try starting this behavior before you do something the dog finds exciting, like eating, going for a walk, getting in the car or visiting with a person or dog. Often, the dog will be a bit frustrated anticipating his fun activity, and you can use that to your advantage.

- You don't have to start with a toy. If you have something else the dog will grab onto (like a sock or a sleeve), you can start there. Pay special attention when you add the cue, as you want to be able to control this behavior so the dog doesn't randomly grab pieces of clothing (or body parts!).

Variations

Work on other dimensions of the Tug, such as a head shake, stronger tugging or adding play growling. Shape the dog to chase the toy or Get It when it is stationary on the ground.

Shape the dog returning to you with the toy. Shape the dog jumping on you so you can grab the toy and tug.

Quick Clicks: Take a break

Be sure to take frequent breaks with this behavior, especially if your dog is very shy or worried. Doing only one or two steps, then coming back to it later, will help keep the dog interested in the game.

Detailed Training Plan

1. Show the dog the toy, CT when he looks at it. Repeat three times, putting the toy behind your back in between each repetition. It's helpful if you "whisk" the toy away quickly, to help incite some chase behavior from the dog.

2. CT when he sniffs it. Repeat three times, hiding the toy between each repetition. Try not to stick the toy in the dog's face, which will make him avoid the toy. You'll have more success if you hold it out away from him.

3. CT when he touches it. Repeat three times, hiding the toy between each repetition.

4. CT when he opens his mouth close to the toy. Repeat three times, hiding the toy between each repetition. It's helpful to hold the toy a bit out of reach for this. You'll often see the dog reach up for it with an open mouth.

It's helpful to have the toy a bit out of reach to encourage the dog to open her mouth as she reaches up for it.

5. CT when his teeth touch the toy. Repeat three times, hiding the toy between each repetition. Try to whisk the toy away as soon as you click. This will help with Step 7, where we want the dog to close his mouth on the toy.

6. Change locations, and repeat Step 5.

7. CT when the dog closes his mouth on the toy. Be very careful to time your click with the mouth *closing*, not as it is *opening*. This is critical, or the dog will think he is getting clicked for an entirely different behavior than you want. This is generally where novice clicker trainers have the most difficulty. Repeat until the dog is 80% successful, hiding the toy between each repetition.

8. CT when the dog closes his mouth on the toy, and keeps it on for up to one second. Continue to add time, Bouncing Around (see Chapter 1) until the dog will put his mouth on the toy for at least three seconds and up to ten seconds. Repeat at each new average bounce at least one to ten times. You can wiggle the toy a bit at this step to encourage the dog to keep his mouth on it, but be sure to click while he has it in his mouth, not as he is letting go. You may want to have a helper pretend to be your dog, to practice your timing a bit before you work with the dog.

9. When the dog closes his mouth on the toy, pull slightly. CT the dog for holding on as you pull. Be *very* careful to click holding on —if you're too slow with your click, you'll be clicking for letting go!

10. Continue to build a stronger Pull, CT-ing the strongest Pulls.

Quick Clicks: Building a strong Pull

Building a strong Pull is another area of difficulty for many people. *If you work on duration (Step 9 above) first, you will often get a strong Pull as a side effect.* It will help to have the toy above the dog's head, so that you can time your click with the pulling behavior. You can use a tape measure or string taped to the wall to help you judge how far your hand is moved on each Pull. If the dog is able to pull your hand down a specified amount, he is clicked. This is also the advantage of using the bungee toy, so you can see how far it is stretched. Another way to get stronger Pulls is to use twofers. (See page 23 for more information.)

You can use a tape measure, yardstick or string taped to the wall to help you judge how far your hand is moved on each pull.

11. Build duration on the Tug, using the same technique as in Step 8. (Note: This step is not absolutely necessary, but will be helpful if you want to do other things with the behavior such as teach a Retrieve or add a Drop It to the sequence.)

12. Add a verbal cue when it looks the way you want. Be sure to practice adding the cue over the course of several days in different locations. You'll need at least fifty pairings of cue, behavior, reward before the dog starts grabbing the toy when cued. Don't forget to occasionally (about 10% of the time) NOT give the cue once you've paired the cue with the behavior. The dog should not grab the toy if he hasn't been cued to do it. This is an important part of teaching the dog to discriminate the verbal cue, and not just use the presence of the toy as a cue.

Generalize the behavior:

- Continue to change locations as you build this tugging behavior. Remember that sensitive dogs will need to have changes made very gradually to the environment. It's tough to concentrate on having fun if there are stressful things going on around you!

- Use the toy as a reward for holding on to the toy. To do this, click, then when the dog releases, do something exciting with the toy like run away with it or drag it on the ground.

- Add other toys to the dog's fun play, using the steps outlined above.

- Add non-toy items such as scary plastic bags, noisy plastic bottles, or other mild fear-inducing items, using the steps outlined above.

Quick Clicks: The feeling is mutual

Play needs to be mutual (both parties are enjoying it). Watch other people and dogs play with your dog and try to replicate what they are doing.

To get the dog engaged in play, you can try doing the same things another dog would do, like lowering your body.

Matching rewards to behavior

Another reason to teach your dog how to enjoy playing with toys is to have toys available as a powerful alternate reward to treats. In many cases, matching the type of reward to the end behavior can assist your training goals. For example, using food treats to generate speed on a behavior is somewhat difficult. Dogs just don't seem to be able to "walk and chew gum" at the same time very well, so it usually stops any forward movement as the dog eats the treat. On the other hand, if you reward with a toy that the dog has to chase, you can quickly generate a significant amount of speed in the performance of a behavior. There are advantages and disadvantages to all rewards, and you should understand them, both to be able to meet your training goals, and to prevent them from being derailed. We've noted some of them in the table below.

It's also useful to have a wide variety of reward types for your dog so that you can tailor your training to the task at hand and the dog's level of interest at that particular moment. You might find that in distracting environments, your dog will only work for food or his favorite toy. But in the quiet of your living room, you have a whole range of rewards at your disposal. The more you can vary rewards, the better your dog will respond to the training, and the more useful the training will be in the real world.

We consider life rewards to be things like the opportunity to greet a person or dog, or have access to a location, go for a walk, etc. Food treats include anything edible or drinkable. Toys are anything the dog is willing to play with, chase or chew.

	Advantages	Disadvantages
Toys	Can create speed and/or intensity in behaviors	May be difficult to use if you can't get it back
	Can prolong attention while you move from behavior to behavior	Dog can become easily tired or bored
	Medium time lag between repetitions	Dog may be uncontrollable and unable to work
		If dog is stressed, not generally useful
		Many dogs have to learn how to play with their owners
Food	Easy to dispense	Dog can get pudgy if used too much
	Creates stillness in behaviors (think Stays!)	Full dogs stop working or get sluggish
	Short time lag between repetitions	May have limitations on what can be fed for health reasons
Life	Can often be used as rewards for very difficult behaviors such as Attention around a distraction	Difficult to administer as rewards—have to be planned in advance
		Long time lapse between repetitions

How is it best to use them? We'll use an example to help you decide. If you want a dog to move speedily over a jump, you could click and hand the dog a treat or a toy. The dog would then learn to jump and come back to you. If you toss a treat or a toy, the dog will learn to jump and look for his reward in a particular spot (handy if you're trying to keep the dog's focus point forward). But think about how getting the reward ends the behavior. With a treat, the dog watches it land, goes to the treat, stops and eats it. If you are jumping one jump or in the early stages of teaching this behavior, it isn't such a big deal, but if you wanted the dog to charge over multiple jumps a thrown toy would be a better reward. Most dogs will scoop up the toy and keep running with it. You may have to teach the dog to bring it back to you, or may have to wait until the dog drops it, or you may have a crazy dog running all over the yard. All of those problems can be fixed with a little training.

Max (7 year old Golden Retriever mix) has been clicker trained since he was 2 years old and competes in agility.

Chapter 6

For Fun

Depending on where you live, there may be times when it is unappealing to go outside to exercise your dog. But your dog can become an annoying bother without appropriate daily exercise. (Trainers have a saying—"A tired dog is a good dog.") What is a conscientious dog owner to do? Many of these behaviors can help you burn off some of that canine energy in the warmth and comfort of your home. Learning itself is a challenging activity, so continuing to teach your dog new things can help keep your dog mentally active and happily worn out. And some of them (Touch using remote targets, Fetch, etc.) can get the dog or both of you up and moving even in a small home.

This chapter will cover:

- Touch (with nose).
- Paw Touch.
- Discrimination.
- Fetch.
- Sneezing/Barking/Growling on Cue.
- Bonus behavior—Tilt your head.

TOUCH WITH NOSE

The dog touches his nose, on a verbal cue, to either your palm or a touch stick. Either variation is taught the same way and uses the same cue. The dog can easily discriminate whether you are presenting your hand or a touch stick and respond appropriately. We will refer to both your hand and the touch stick as a target.

This is one of the best building block behaviors. You can use it to work on fear problems, for better heeling, to teach dance steps, to focus the dog for obedience exercises or stacking in conformation, to direct movement (such as a Spin, Bow, Crawl, or to Jump onto something) and to direct the dog to objects. It is an excellent behavior for helping a crossover dog to get excited about clicker training. The Nose Touch can even be used as a signal for an off-leash Recall. (We think so highly of both a Nose Touch and a Paw Touch that we wrote an entire book, *Right on Target*, using these and other body part touches to generate behaviors.)

Suggested verbal cue: "Touch," "Nose," "Target."

Suggested visual cue: Offer the target.

You will need: You can use your hand as a target to start, but if you want to teach both variations you'll want a touch stick. You can buy retractable or foldable varieties (see Resources) or you can make your own. Buy a quarter inch dowel about three feet in length. Paint the last two inches of one end to provide a more visible target for your dog, or wrap a rubber band several times around the end to make a sort of "button." Eventually, you may also want a shorter stick, depending on the behavior you are using it for. For example, if you have a larger dog and want to work on heeling, a long stick would be in the way, but a twelve to eighteen inch stick would be just right.

Speed Steps

1. Present the target. CT when the dog looks at the target. Remove the target between repetitions.

2. CT when the dog touches with his nose or paw.

3. CT when the dog touches with his nose anywhere on the target.

4. CT for touches gradually approaching the precise "correct" area of the target—the center of the palm of your hand, or the tip of your dowel or purchased touch stick.

5. Present your target in a different place relative to the dog, so he has to reach up, down or to either side for it. Change the location of the target each time you present it. Repeat until the dog will Touch no matter where or how the target is presented.

6. Add your cue.

Generalize the behavior:

- Practice so the dog will touch the stick when it is resting on the floor or the wall, in the palm of your hand or lying on a table or the floor.

- Wait until the dog touches multiple times before you CT.

- Have the dog follow a moving target, trying to touch the end of the stick or your palm.

Keep in Mind

Be careful—it's very easy to shape a bite rather than a Touch if you are consistently late with your click. It will be extra work to get rid of this problem. Better not to let it happen in the first place.

Practice with a friend if you need to, before you work with your dog.

If you're late with your clicking, the dog will end up biting the target.

Don't wave the stick or your hand around to get your dog's attention. Present it and hold it still. Let him figure out that he needs to interact with it. If he doesn't try to touch it, remove the target and re-present it.

A few dogs may not seem to notice the stick or your hand initially. For these individuals, put the stick on the ground or hold out your hand and click a few times for looking in the general direction of the stick or your hand. (The stick may be a better option at this point because it is different from what the dog sees every day.) Click a few times for looking *at* the stick. Then click a few times for touching anywhere on the stick with a nose or a foot. Next, click a few times for Nose Touches only. Now pick up the stick and proceed from Step 3.

Most dogs will be eagerly touching the stick by the end of the first training session, with some touches at the end.

Troubleshooting

How do I hold the clicker, touch stick and treats, or hold the clicker, treats and present my hand?

- Hold the clicker and stick in the same hand with your palm up and the clicker resting on top of the stick. Deliver treats with the other hand.

Hold the clicker and stick in the same hand, with your palm up and the clicker resting on top of the stick. Deliver treats with the other hand. Notice the treat is being given near the end of the target stick.

- Tape the clicker to the end of the target stick. Be sure you don't block the clicker mechanism with the tape.

- Purchase a click stick with the clicker already attached (see Resources).

- Put the treats in a bowl out of the dog's reach or in a bait bag and hold the clicker in one hand and the stick in the other, or hold the clicker in one hand and present the other. Reach for a treat as you need it. (Remember, the click marks the desired behavior, so it's okay if it takes you a second to get the treat to the dog, but try not to delay it too much.)

- Get a third hand. Have someone help you by dropping a treat on the floor or handing it to the dog each time you click. (Children generally *love* to help this way.)

- Hold the treats and clicker in the same hand, and deliver with the hand that is touched.

The dog is biting the stick rather than touching it with his nose.

- Click just *before* the dog touches the stick. Because the dog is getting the click before he actually makes contact, you can short circuit the biting behavior. If you are slow with your clicker and find it hard to get the click in before the dog makes contact, try moving the stick away while the dog tries to get to it—this will give you added time for getting the click before the bite. (But be sure and get that click in, so it doesn't become a game of "chase and bite the stick"!)

- Restart the training with the stick lying on the floor. Carefully reshape a Touch only.

- Click the dog for doing anything *but* biting the stick, such as touching it with his foot or not touching it at all.

- Practice your timing with a human helper first. They can try to grab the stick while you practice clicking before they get it. Don't forget to practice treat delivery too!

- Change to a metal stick. You might be able to find a telescoping pointer with an alligator clip on the end (makes a good target). Dogs are less likely to bite metal.

- Teach the Touch to your hand rather than the touch stick, and go back to the stick later.

The dog appears to be afraid of the stick, or reacts as if it bit him.

- Click just *before* the dog touches the stick.

- Modify the click sound so it's not so loud—hold the clicker in your pocket or put heavy tape on the metal part of the clicker. Or, use a retractable ballpoint pen as a clicker, or click with your tongue, or use a bridge word if necessary.

- Start with the touch stick on the ground and stay at this level for several sessions. Leave the stick out where the dog can investigate it at his leisure.

- Desensitize the dog to the stick. Start with a pencil and gently stroke him across the back with it while you give yummy treats. Do this for brief periods for several days. Gradually use longer and longer straight objects, such as an emery board, ruler, etc. Or, use dowels in progressively longer lengths if you have them available.

- Teach Touch your hand first instead of a touch stick.

Variations

If you've taught Touch using a target stick, now teach it using your hand. This is a target you always have with you! If you've used your hand, teach a touch stick. If you have a small dog, using a touch stick to help train your Heeling will save your back. Or, teach your dog to touch a Post-It Note—you can stick a note anywhere to direct the dog from a distance. Use the target to have the dog close a door with her nose. Teach the dog to do the Touch for an extended amount of time (a little tricky but a lot of fun to see).

You can use a nose target or a foot target to teach the dog to close doors and drawers.

Slick Clicks: Wolves can touch, too!

At Wolf Park in Indiana, Cheryl had the opportunity to clicker train a wolf to a touch stick. There were three wolves in the enclosure we were standing outside of. One was not interested in us, but the other two were right at the fence, eager to interact. We clicked and gave our chosen wolf, Apollo, a treat for about a dozen repetitions, then stuck the end of a touch stick through the fence. Wolves are curious animals, so Apollo immediately touched and got a CT. We did a half dozen or so repetitions with the stick right in front of him, then started presenting the stick so that he had to move to touch it. If Apollo wasn't quick enough, Karin, the other wolf paying close attention to what we were doing, beat him to the stick, even though she had not received any treats up to that point. Wolves are very good observational learners, and we got two wolves performing the Touch from working with only one! They are also quite forceful with biting the stick if you are a hair late with your click, and they hang on!

Detailed Training Plan

Note: We are writing the instructions for using the palm of your hand as the target. The steps are the same if you are using a touch stick. Just concentrate on getting the dog to the tip of the stick rather than the center of your palm.

1. Present your hand just in front of the dog's nose at his level. CT when the dog looks at your hand. Remove your hand between repetitions. Repeat three times.

2. Present your hand. CT when the dog touches your hand with his nose or paw or body, even if it's accidental. Repeat three times.

3. Present your hand. CT if the dog touches anywhere on your hand with his nose. Repeat five times, removing your hand after each CT.

4. Present your hand, and CT touches closer to the palm of your hand. Gradually shape the dog to touch only the palm of your hand. Decide before each set of ten repetitions how much closer the dog needs to be to the final contact point. Move on to the next closest point after the dog is hitting within the area you've designated at least 80% of the time, then move to the next closest point, and so on. Continue until the dog is reliably targeting the center of your palm with his Nose Touch.

Quick Clicks: Manage the target

If you are using your hand, present it flat, with your fingers together, palm facing the dog. Put it in position in front of your dog's nose, a few inches to a foot away, and hold it still until you click, then take it away.

If you are using a touch stick, present it so the stick is perpendicular to the dog rather than pointed at him, a few inches in front of his nose. (See photo on page 150.) Hold it still until you click and then take it away. Putting it behind your back is a good option. People have a tendency to leave the touch stick out in front of them rather than putting it behind their backs, but until you add a cue, the appearance of the touch stick is the only indication to the dog that he should touch. If you're not paying attention or not ready and he's touching the stick without being rewarded, you're stalling your training.

5. Change locations and repeat Step 4, clicking only for touches in the appropriate area. Stay at this step until the dog is 80% reliable.

6. Change locations and repeat Step 5.

7. Working in the same environment as Step 6, present your hand, but place it in a different location relative to the dog, so that he has to reach up, reach down, or move right or left to touch. Repeat ten times, changing the location of your hand each time.

8. In a new location, work until the dog will touch the center of your palm no matter where you are holding your hand or if it's your left or right hand.

9. Are you starting to be able to predict that the dog will touch the target correctly? Time to add your verbal cue. Present the target, say your cue, dog touches, CT, remove the target. Pair the cue with the behavior at least fifty more times, changing one

detail—where the target is held, how it is held, where you are working—every ten repetitions.

Quick Clicks: Target before cue

Since we want the dog to touch only when he hears the verbal cue, the target is presented first, then the verbal cue is given. If he touches without hearing the verbal cue first, he won't be clicked and treated. If you want the cues to be independent, you will say the verbal cue, then present the target (new cue then old cue) and CT every touch. If you want the cues paired together (so that the dog only does the behavior when he sees *and* hears a cue), say the verbal cue *at the same time* as you present the target.

Generalize the behavior:

- Dog touches your hand held on the floor or resting on a table.

- Dog touches the target multiple times before getting a click. This tends to introduce some variability into the Touch behavior, which is useful to build duration.

- Dog follows the target while it's moving, trying to touch the end of the stick or your palm. Remember to start by moving the target just a small amount initially (about an inch or so) then letting the dog touch it. Gradually build up to a greater distance, Bouncing Around as you go so that you are not just steadily increasing it every time.

 ## PAW TOUCH

The dog touches a horizontal, vertical or angled target with a front paw. Most dogs will show a preference for one paw over the other—that doesn't matter. You can use this to teach Shake, Wave, Ring a bell, Close the Door or a Drawer or Turn off the Lights. It's great for Flyball, and really useful for a lot of Agility obstacles.

Suggested verbal cue: "Punch," "Push," "Stomp," "Paw," "Launch."

You will need: A large target that can be oriented at any angle. This could be a small square of plywood or Plexiglas, a piece of carpet that can be taped where you need it or the plastic lids from detergent tubs or large margarine tubs. While you're training, it's best if your target won't move even if pushed hard. You don't want to spook your dog or train a light Touch. Once you're taught this, you can transfer it to other things, including objects you *do* want to move, such as a drawer.

Speed Steps

The steps for this behavior are not complex, so only a Detailed Training Plan is provided. You can just ignore the Quick Clicks boxes if you don't need them. The Keep in Mind, Troubleshooting and Variations sections follow the Detailed Training Plan.

Detailed Training Plan

1. Place your target on the floor, close to both you and your dog. Click for approaching the target. Repeat three times. Deliver the treat over the target every time until Step 8.

2. Click for looking at the target. Repeat three times.

3. Click for touching the target with any part of the body, nose or foot. Don't stay longer than three clicks at this level, or the dog may think it's the final picture. (If the dog has a very strong Nose Touch, do not click any contact with the target with the nose.)

4. Click for any touch with any foot. It doesn't matter if it's intentional or accidental. Repeat three times.

5. Place your target in a new location. Click for any touch with any foot, intentional or accidental. Repeat three times.

6. Click for any touch with either front foot anywhere on the target. Repeat five times.

7. Click for an intentional touch—the dog is looking at the target, not just tripping over it—with either front foot anywhere on the target. Repeat five times.

8. Generally the dog will favor one foot over the other. Decide which one you want him to use and CT touches only with that foot. Repeat one to ten times.

9. Shape a Touch to the center of the target. (See the Quick Clicks box below if you need help.)

Quick Clicks: Visualize a bulls-eye

Mentally divide the target into a bulls-eye. Decide before each ten-treat session where the dog needs to touch to get clicked. When the dog is touching that area *or closer* to the bulls-eye 80% of the time, move into the next ring of the bulls-eye for the next ten-treat session. If the dog doesn't succeed at eight out of ten, make your bulls-eye rings narrower so your steps are smaller each time.

10. Place your target in a new location and continue shaping center Touches until the dog is accurately hitting the center 80% of the time.

11. If your dog has been tentative, shape a harder Touch. (See Troubleshooting if you need help with this.)

12. When the Touch is as hard as you want and you can predict the dog will do it, time to add your cue. Say your cue, dog does the behavior, CT. Continue pairing the cue with the behavior for at least fifty repetitions, changing the location of your target every ten repetitions, and occasionally moving to another area to work.

13. Once the dog has started to do the behavior when cued, you will occasionally (about 10% of the time) not cue the behavior. The dog should not touch the target. This helps the dog discriminate that what you say is important.

14. Intersperse other cued behaviors with the Paw Touch cue.

Generalize the behavior:

- Reorient the target so it is vertical or at an angle. Make this change gradual, over several sessions.

- Put the target higher or lower.

- Send the dog to the target from a distance. Again, you are going to gradually increase the distance to the target, by one to two feet at a time, using Bouncing Around to add distance.

- Fade the target by making it gradually smaller, over the course of several sessions, until the dog can accurately hit a one-inch target placed anywhere.

- Introduce movement of the target, in preparation for closing a drawer or door.

Quick Clicks: Shutting a door
Attach the target to the front of a drawer or door. Open the drawer or door *slightly*, give your cue, and CT if the dog moves the target. Don't open the drawer or door very far at first—the dog needs to get comfortable with moving the target a small distance. Gradually increase the distance the dog has to push the target.

Keep in Mind
If your dog makes no attempt to touch the target at first, you can help by walking around it, encouraging the dog to move around in its vicinity. When the dog accidentally touches anywhere on the target with any foot, CT. Do this for *no more* than one session so your dog will not be dependent on your movement.

Some dogs may touch, but only lightly. Once the dog is Touching fairly consistently, shape a harder Touch. When the dog touches, don't click the first time. The dog will probably look at you expectantly ("Hey, you, aren't you paying attention? I put my foot on it!"), then touch the target a second time, harder, to be sure you notice. CT! If the second Touch isn't harder, wait for a third. If the dog stops responding or seems confused, stay at Step 9 until the dog is rapidly and accurately hitting the center. Then, try withholding the click again. Click the hardest five out of ten touches at each step until it's as hard as you want. You can also use twofers to get variation in your Paw Touch. (See page 23 for more information.) Remember to relax how accurate the dog must be—you can only work on one criterion at a time. Don't worry, you can work on accuracy in a different session.

Troubleshooting

The dog doesn't seem to notice the target

- If your dog knows how to Shake, use this cue to help you lure him into the behavior. Offer your hand over the target area, say your cue, but pull your hand away before he makes contact, so that he accidentally touches the target instead. CT.

- Move around the target as suggested in "Keep in Mind."

- Write down at least ten steps to shape from "not noticing" to "touching target." For example:

    1. Eye flick in direction of target.

    2. Head motion in direction of target. (And so on.)

- Pick the target up and put it down after each repetition. Stop doing this once the dog starts touching the target.

The dog doesn't seem to realize he should use his foot. He only tries to touch it with his nose.

- If your dog knows how to Shake, use it as a lure.

- Put a ball or a piece of food under the couch and click and treat the dog for reaching for it with his paw.

- If the Nose Touch is very strong, you may need to start with anything that is not a Nose Touch. For example, as the dog takes a step to touch it with his nose, CT the step forward. Give the treat to the dog away from the target, or put the target on the floor and deliver the treat over it, with the dog's head away from the target. Clicking earlier, instead of as the dog touches it with his nose, will help short circuit the Nose Touch. Be very careful not to accidentally click Nose Touches as you work on this behavior!

The dog touches the target, but only lightly.

- Maybe the dog is afraid the target will move. Make sure the target is completely secure and reshape the behavior from the beginning, using really good treats.

- Find things that your dog paws or scratches on his own—a cover on his bed, a certain patch of ground, whatever—and CT that behavior. Go back to the target and try again.

- Have someone watch and tell you if you're clicking too early and actually shaping a lighter Touch.

- Use twofers to get some variability in the behavior for one or two sessions, then CT the harder Touches.

The dog scratches the target rather than stomping it.

- You've probably been late with your clicks. Reshape the behavior from Step 5, *carefully* clicking just before the dog touches the target. It will help if you sit on a level where you can easily see the dog's paw approaching the target.

- Use what you've got, and teach the dog to turn off a light switch.

Variations

Teach the dog to Touch a touch stick with his paw, giving it a different cue than touching it with his nose.

Teach the dog to Touch a target with each of his paws, front and back. (You'll need four separate cues, either verbal or visual.) You could use this in stacking for Conformation, and it's also used for foundation work in Agility.

Teach the dog to Swipe the target, in preparation for turning off a light switch. Aim for just one gentle Swipe, or you may have to repair the area around your light switch frequently. You'll need to construct a dummy switch for the dog to use for practice (a piece of plywood and a light switch screwed into place will work—place it off center so it will be lower if you hold the plywood one way and higher if you hold it the other). Remember to gradually build up to the switch being at the actual height on the wall. Provide a chair if your dog is too short to reach it on his own.

Teach the dog to Push in order to close a door or a drawer.

Have the dog paint you some abstract art. Use water-based paints only. Put colors in bowls, have your dog dip a front paw, then target him to a piece of art paper taped to the bottom of a cookie sheet.

Have the dog paint you some abstract art. Jenni Dix and her Cocker Spaniel Gus demonstrate, above.

Teach the dog to use a flyball box. You need to load and launch the box a few times so the launch doesn't frighten your dog. Load the box with a favorite ball or treats. Hold the dog back a little, launch the box yourself, and let the dog catch the ball or treats. Repeat this until the dog appears excited when he hears the launch, and looks for the ball or treats. Now let him launch the box himself, helping with your own foot if necessary. As your dog's enthusiasm grows, he will hit the box harder and harder, or you can shape a harder Push on your original target.

Slick Clicks: Innovative animals

Kathy Sdao, proprietor of Bright Spot Dog Training and former marine mammal trainer says: "We used clicker training at the University of Hawaii to teach two bottlenosed dolphins to be creative (based on the pioneering work done by Karen Pryor and chronicled in *Lads Before the Wind*). One of the dolphins, Akeakamai ("lover of wisdom") grasped the concept better than we ever imagined possible. After a few weeks of training, she would respond to the gestural cue for "do a behavior I've never seen you do before"—basically an exaggerated shrug—with amazing feats of acrobatics and sheer silliness. We researchers got to the point where we had to abandon our attempts to record in words these behavioral creations because we couldn't keep up, and some were literally indescribable. I remember sitting beside the tank with my jaw dropped open, watching Ake leap, fling toys and swim backward. She truly understood that we wanted to see novel behaviors, and she seemed thrilled to demonstrate her skill."

DISCRIMINATION—BIG/LITTLE

The dog will make the correct choice, discriminating between relative directions or objects. You could teach Left/Right, High/Low, Squeaky/Fluffy, and so on. In the directions here, we're going to teach "Big/Little." The dog will learn the cue for each choice ("Big," "Little") and respond to it correctly.

Suggested verbal cue: Use the appropriate words for whatever you are teaching—in our case here, "Big/Little," "Large/Small," etc.

You will need: At least two sets of similar objects in at least two different sizes. (For example, a big and little plastic bin and a big and little block of wood would do.) If you wanted to stack cues (that is, tell the dog "Left, Big," meaning choose the big object from the group on the left side), you'll need two of the same sets of objects. To stack more cues ("Left, High, Big"), you'll need additional objects.

Speed Steps

1. Put your Little object on the floor between you and your dog. CT for any attention directed toward the object.

2. Continue gradually increasing your criteria until your dog actually touches the object with a paw.

3. Place the object in a different location when you present it—to the left or right, closer to you. CT for a Paw Touch.

4. Put out both your little and big objects, but so the dog is more likely to touch the little object.

Put out both your little and big objects, arranged so the dog is more likely to touch the little object. The objects should be placed between the dog and trainer.

5. Put out both objects, keeping the little object closer to the dog, but moving the big object so it is more visible. CT for a Paw Touch to the little object.

6. Put out the objects so the hot target is only slightly closer to the dog. (We refer to the object you want your dog to select as the "hot target.)

7. If your dog is touching the object reliably, time to add your cue.

8. Use your other set of objects. Go back a couple of steps if your dog is confused.

9. Now you want to teach your dog the opposite cue, "Big." Put your big object out alone. Be ready to CT the dog when he is near (or touches) the new hot target.

10. Work back up through Steps 2 through 8 with the Big object. You should have both Little and Big on cue.

11. Decide before each repetition which object you are going to cue. Put that object closer to the dog.

12. Gradually make the position of the objects more equal.

13. Work until you can place the object you *don't* want the dog to touch closer to the dog.

Keep in Mind

Realize that this can require considerable mental effort from the dog. Be sure to keep it upbeat and rewarding, and your sessions *short*. Never reprimand your dog for making the wrong choice.

Make sure the sizes of your objects are different enough to be easily discernible. If you use a set of four objects, you could start out using the biggest and smallest and then incorporate the other sizes to make the choice more difficult.

If you're teaching Left/Right discrimination, make sure *you* know your right from your left and you can tell which side the dog is choosing if he is facing you!

Quick Clicks: Be sturdy

Be sure your objects are sturdy enough to withstand some rough treatment. Cheryl started teaching this to her dog, Nestle, using sets of plastic bins that resembled mini laundry baskets. Nestle was very strong in his response and soon had put his foot through the bottom of several of them. Cheryl replaced the bins with blocks of wood cut to various sizes.

Troubleshooting

I can't put my objects on the floor before the dog is there, pawing at them at random.

- Have an assistant place and remove the objects while you control the dog.

- Put your dog on a Sit-Stay, place your objects, and release the dog.

- Toss the treat away from you, so the dog has to move away to get it, and reset the objects while the dog is occupied with getting the treat.

My dog isn't getting the idea. He just always goes to whatever object is on the left.

- Your dog is probably strongly left-pawed, so he favors that side. Put out *only* the Little object so that it is to the dog's right. Repeat this for several sessions so that your dog gets a good reward history for moving to his right. When you first start putting out two objects, put the little object to the right but closer to the dog.

- You're right-handed and you unconsciously favor that side, so your dog gets re-warded more often for moving to *his* left. Make a conscious effort to reward the dog to your left side often. You may also be putting the correct object on that side more often, without thinking about it. Make a diagram for each placement if you need to be more variable.

My dog got through "Little" fine, but when I try to work on "Big," the dog doesn't get a lot of rewards and loses interest.

- Set up your training to ensure that your dog has plenty of opportunity to earn rewards. Put out your big object and start over from the beginning—CT a look toward it, CT any movement toward it, CT moving a front paw toward it, etc.

When you put out both objects, put the big one to the dog's strong side and closer to the dog. If the dog makes a mistake and you take away the hot target (the big object), go back to only putting out the big object for another session or two.

- In one session, practice Little. Move to a different room and work on Big.

- Be sure that Little is firmly on cue, so that saying the cue versus being quiet has some meaning for the dog. Reward any tentative movement toward choosing Big—don't wait for a full-blown Paw Touch.

Variations
Teach your dog several discrimination choices and then combine the cues. You could ask the dog to indicate the Big-Squeaky, High-Big or Left-Little-Fuzzy. Take it as far as you care to go.

Detailed Training Steps
1. Sit in a chair or on the floor. Have the dog standing in front of you. Put your Little object on the floor between yourself and the dog. CT for any attention directed toward the object. Remove the object after each click. Repeat five times.

2. Using the same setup, wait for a better response from the dog. If you clicked for a look in Step 1, now CT for any movement toward the object. Repeat five times.

3. Continue gradually increasing your criteria until your dog actually touches the object with a paw. Continue to remove the object between repetitions. Do five repetitions where you place the object in the same place and the dog is touching it with a paw.

4. Now present the object in a different location when you present it—to the left or the right, closer to you, closer to the dog. CT for a Paw Touch and remove the object. Repeat five times.

5. Change locations and repeat Step 4.

6. Now put out both your Little and Big objects, but place them so the dog is more likely to touch the hot target, the Little object. Put the Little object toward the dog and the big object toward you, on the same line as the Little object. The dog would have to go around the Little object to get to the Big one, so is more likely to touch the easier object, the little one. Also, placing the big object first, so you are directing more attention toward the Little object, can help keep the dog focused on the hot target. CT for the dog touching the Little object. Remove the objects after each repetition. Repeat ten times.

Quick Clicks: Place and remove
You may want to practice placing and removing the objects without your dog around. Remember you'll also have to hold the

clicker in one of your hands and be able to get to your treats quickly. Practice so you can handle it all smoothly before you add your dog to the picture. The less you can be moving around or interacting with the objects when your dog touches, the better.

7. Put out both objects, keeping the hot target closer to the dog, but moving the big target to one side, so it is more visible. CT for a Paw Touch. Remove the objects after each repetition and place them in slightly different relation to one another each time. Repeat ten times.

8. Put out the objects so the hot target is only slightly closer to the dog. Be sure that sometimes it is to the left and sometimes to the right. Continue as in Step 7.

9. Change locations and repeat Step 8.

Quick Clicks: Don't click, don't react

If your dog touches the wrong object, don't CT, but don't react in any other way. Remove the objects and when you put them out again, make the hot target a little more obvious—move it closer to the dog or keep your hand on it longer. Losing the opportunity to get clicked is enough for many dogs to proceed more carefully with their next selection.

10. Is your dog readily touching the correct object at least 80% of the time? Time to add your cue. It's best if you can put the objects out, stand still, have the dog wait, say your cue Little, then release the dog to touch. But it will work if you have to say your cue before you present the objects—although it will require more repetitions. Continue varying the relative positions of the objects, sometimes having them equidistant from the dog. Do at least fifty repetitions, changing locations after every ten.

11. Use your other set of objects, still with the little object, the hot target. Back up a few steps if your dog seems confused.

Teaching "Big"

Now you need to teach your dog the opposite cue—"Big." If you stay any longer at rewarding Little at this point, it will be very hard to get the dog to target Big.

1. Put out your big object only. CT if your dog touches the object. Remove the object and repeat, ten times. Deliver your treats close to the new hot target each time. Now put out both objects, but with the big object closer to the dog and the little object nearer to you and in line, so it is harder for the dog to see and get to. CT if your dog looks at, moves toward or touches the big object.

Quick Clicks: Remove the hot target

If the dog touches the wrong target once or twice, ignore it and try to place your objects and time your click so you can be successful. But if your dog persists in touching the wrong object, *remove the hot target.* To repeat—remove the bigger object, the one you now want the dog to touch. Let the dog keep touching the little object without any reaction from you until he stops on his own. You are using extinction to get rid of (temporarily) touching the little object. Once the dog stops touching the wrong object, put out the hot target again and be ready to click even something as small as a look at it.

2. Work through Steps 2 through 11 of the initial Detailed Training Plan. Now you should have both Little and Big on cue, and can work on solidifying the behavior.

3. Decide before each repetition if you are going to cue "Big" or "Little." Place the objects so that whichever one you are going to cue is closer to the dog. Be sure to have the hot target sometimes to the left and sometimes to the right. CT when the dog's Paw Touches the correct target. Ignore it if he makes a mistake and make the next repetition easier. Repeat until the dog is successful at least 80% of the time.

4. Gradually make the position of the objects more equal. Be sure you are changing left/right sides and choosing which cue you will use at random.

Quick Clicks: A random tip
If you need help with being random, write Big on ten index cards and Little on ten index cards. Shuffle them and turn over a card before each repetition. It might also help to chart out where you are going to put the objects for each repetition.

Generalize the behavior:

- Work until you can place the object you *don't* want the dog to touch closer to the dog, making him go past it to touch the hot target.

- Use a completely different set of objects.

- Put out three objects.

FETCH

The dog waits until cued, then picks up a thrown object, brings it to the trainer and gives it up when told to. Or, if you just want to use this for play, the dog can run to Fetch as soon as you throw the item (so throwing is the cue) and bring the item back and drop it at your feet, rather than waiting for you to take it. If you want a formal Open obedience retrieve, the dog must start from a Sit and Sit in front of the handler on his return, holding the fetch item until cued to release the object.

Suggested verbal cue: "Fetch," "Go fetch," "Get it," "Bring it," "Retrieve."

You will need: An item that is safe and preferably pleasurable for your dog to fetch. Tennis balls are popular, as are floppy flying discs (hard plastic Frisbees can damage your dog's teeth if he's going to be catching the thrown object). For formal Obedience, you'll eventually need a wooden or plastic dumbbell, but you can start the training with something the dog is more likely to want to pick up. (Mandy likes to use a dumbbell or wooden dowel to start, because it is easy to hold the item between your knees. This leaves your hands free for CT-ing, and also allows you to judge how solid the dog's grab of the item is, leading to a stronger hold.)

Be sure your fetch object is sized correctly for your dog. The bar of a dumbbell should be just long enough that the bells (the flat, square pieces on either end) aren't tight against your dog's muzzle. The bells should be large enough to make it easy for the dog to scoop up the dumbbell, but not so big that they block his vision. Dogs with long noses may prefer a bit larger bell so they don't bonk their noses on the ground when they pick up the dumbbell. Balls should be big enough that they can't be swallowed.

The bells should be large enough to make it easy for the dog to scoop up the dumbbell but not so big that they block his vision.

Speed Steps

1. Hold your fetch object out in front of your dog. CT for looking at it, then for moving his head toward it, then for touching it.

2. Wait for the dog to approach the fetch object with an open mouth.

3. CT for the dog touching the object with an open mouth.

4. Wait for the dog to close his mouth on the object.

5. Work on the dog holding on to the object for a longer period of time.

6. Gradually lower the object to the floor, so that the dog is lifting it up each time.

7. While the dog has his mouth closed on the object, take your hand off of it for a second. Gradually work up to taking your hand off for a count of five, then Bounce Around varying times.

8. As the dog picks up the object, take a step backward, away from the dog. CT for movement toward you while carrying the object.

9. Gradually add to your number of steps backward.

10. Now throw the object a short distance. When he picks it up, walk backward a few steps, encouraging the dog to move toward you.

11. Gradually throw the object a little farther, continuing to move with the dog, until you are throwing it about six feet.

12. Throw the object and take a couple of steps with the dog, but then stop moving. Decrease your movement until you are standing still after throwing the object.

13. Add your "Fetch" cue.

14. Make some longer throws, some shorter throws, throws off to the side. Play in a variety of locations, with a variety of fetch objects.

15. Add your "Give" cue.

Keep in Mind

Some dogs are obviously more natural at this than others. If you have a retriever of some kind, you will probably just have to work on refining the hold and give—anything you throw will likely automatically come back to you via the dog. If you have a sighthound, on the other hand, the dog may chase the object with great glee, but lose interest as soon as it stops moving. Terriers may be prone to playing keep away rather than Fetch. You can work with any of them—you're just starting from a different point and you'll have to make a plan to work through the particular problem. Think about where you would CT to give the dog specific information on what you want him to do.

Just how formal you want to make this is up to you. If you just want to play Fetch for exercise and fun, then having the dog bring the thrown object back to drop at your feet could be fine. If you want to compete in obedience, then you'll need all the niceties of sitting and holding the object until cued to give. Or, you can choose anything in between.

Some dogs aren't as inclined to put things in their mouths. You don't have to start with the dumbbell if your dog doesn't like the dumbbell. Use something the dog will be more likely to take and hold like a stuffed toy or a chewy bone.

Be sure your fetch object is one that can be easily picked up from the floor. The bells of a dumbbell hold the bar up so the dog can get his bottom jaw under it. Balls and squeaky toys have sufficient bulk, but some flying disks may be hard to pick up.

If you desire a formal obedience retrieve, you would add steps here to work on the dog having a secure Hold and add the Sit in front. When you add the cue for "Give," you'll want to make sure that it is solidly on verbal cue, so the dog doesn't interpret leaning over or reaching for the dumbbell as a cue to release it.

Troubleshooting

My dog never makes any move toward taking the object.

- Are you sure you're not missing any little signs—a sniff, even a flexing forward of the whiskers? Have somebody else watch a session and see if they can point out something you haven't seen.

- Try using a different object. Maybe your dog would rather hold a plush toy than a wooden dumbbell. Or, make the dumbbell more enticing by rubbing a smelly treat on the bar.

- Play with the object by bouncing it on the ground to entice the dog, and then hold it slightly out of their reach to get the first grab.

As soon as I try to get the dog to move, he drops the fetch object.

- You may be asking for too much distance initially. Click just one foot moving forward and be ready to take the object from the dog. Relax your expectations about how long the dog will hold the object because you're adding difficulty in another area (movement).

- Try and keep the dog's head tilted up—he'll be less likely to spit out the object. Make some interesting sounds, or hold your hands high in front of you.

My dog runs and picks up the object, but doesn't bring it back.

- Back up a few training steps and build up a lot of reward history for picking up the object and just turning to give it to you.

- Have a second object so you can throw it as soon as the dog brings the first one to your vicinity. Don't insist on niceties like sitting or dropping the object into your hand. Make it exciting for the dog to bring it back by immediately allowing him to chase again.

My dog brings the object back, but won't give it to me.

- Is this a case of resource guarding? (See Chapter 5 for instructions on how to deal with it, and correct that before worrying about Fetch.)

- Is your dog trying to get you to play Tug? Have a tug toy at hand and offer it to your dog and have a quick game of Tug. Review the rules of Tug with your dog (see the Quick Clicks box on page 137) and work on enforcing them if necessary.

- Have super tasty treats that your dog can't resist to trade for the retrieve object.

I want to work on a formal retrieve and my dog won't stay when the object is thrown.

- Work on your Sit-Stay separately, with a variety of distractions.

- Make a throwing motion, but don't actually throw anything. If your dog breaks the Stay, shorten up the amount of your throw and gradually work up to a more normal motion. Make sure to reward the dog for not moving forward by immediately giving a treat.

- Drop the item directly in front of you and reward for not moving. Gradually extend the distance thrown.

- Throw the object, count to one, and release your dog. Extend the count very gradually, using Bouncing Around to add duration.

Variations

Rather than having the dog wait at your side, have him catch the object you throw and bring it back. Be sure the object is safe for your dog to catch.

Combine Find and Fetch, so you can send the dog to find your keys *and* bring them back to you. (Note: Many dogs don't like to pick up metal, so you may need to have a leather fob on your keys and teach your dog to grab that.)

Add a jump to the whole sequence, as you would encounter in open obedience. Start with the jump low so your dog can learn to hold onto the object while jumping.

Quick Clicks: Where is the clicker?
We're going to **back chain** this behavior. That just means we start at the end of a more complicated behavior and work back to the beginning. Because the end portion of the behavior gets rewarded the most, it tends to become very strong. The dog will be more likely to bring the object back and give it to you.

Quick Clicks: Watch how you hold
Be aware of where you are holding the clicker. Hold the object in one hand and the clicker in the other or hold the clicker by your side, not next to the dog's face. You don't want to click right in the dog's ear.

Detailed Training Plan

1. Hold your fetch object out in front of your dog, slightly above his head. Do NOT push it into the dog's face. CT for the dog looking at it or better. Remove the object after each repetition. Repeat five times.

2. Now wait for the dog to move his head toward the object before you CT. Repeat five times.

3. CT when the dog touches the object with his nose or mouth. Repeat five times.

Quick Clicks: Easy on reps
We don't want to do too many repetitions at the early steps, or you will have a hard time getting an open mouth bite. Especially if the dog is really good at Nose Touches! Remember when we were working on the Nose Touch, we warned that clicking late sometimes caused the dog to bite the target? You can use that to your advantage here by not clicking when the dog touches with his nose.

4. Now you want the dog to approach or even touch the object with an open mouth. Don't click for a closed mouth Touch. When the dog doesn't receive the click, he should try something different. Watch for any open mouth movement, and CT it. Repeat at least five times (up to ten times if the dog has a strong Nose Touch).

5. Wait for the dog to touch the object with an open mouth, CT. Repeat five times.

Quick Clicks: Spitting out
Don't worry if the dog immediately spits out the item to take the treat. We'll build a longer hold next as a separate step.

6. Hold the object at the same level and wait for the dog to close his mouth on the object. Keep your hand on the object so it doesn't drop when you CT and the dog lets go. Build up to a longer time with the mouth closed, using Bouncing Around to increase the duration to at least five seconds. It can help to have the item slightly over the dog's head so he has to reach to grab it, and he pulls it down a short distance. Repeat until the dog will hold the item for at least five seconds at least 80% of your repetitions.

Quick Clicks: No telegraphing
Be sure you don't telegraph "treat coming" at this step. We don't want the dog to spit out the item until he has been clicked. Have someone observe you if you're having difficulty building time on the hold.

7. Move the object slightly more toward the floor. Vary how long you have the dog hold each time before you CT. Repeat at each level closer to the floor until the dog is at 80% success, then move a few inches closer to the floor. When you get to the floor, the dog should be picking it up, although you will still have your hand on the item.

8. Now you are going to work on taking your hand away from the object. At first, keep your hand close so it is still in the picture. Remember to get a grab and hold for a varying number of seconds each time. Move to the next step when the dog is successful 80% of the time.

9. Gradually move your hand farther from the object, a few inches at a time. Continue until you can stand up straight after placing or dropping the object. At each level of change in your position, work to 80% success before moving on.

10. As the dog picks up the object, take one step backward, away from the dog. CT the dog for moving toward you while still carrying the object.

Quick Clicks: A sticky spot
Getting the dog to move with the object in his mouth is another sticky place in this behavior. Be sure to work slowly as you increase the distance.

11. Gradually add to the distance the dog must carry the object toward you. Once the dog is moving at least one foot toward you while you back up, start Bouncing Around different distances, adding one to two feet to your average each time you increase it. Stay at each new average distance until the dog is successful 80% of the time.

12. Now we're going to work on the actual fetching part of the behavior. Have the dog next to you and throw your fetch object a short distance (no more than a few feet) in front of you. Run with the dog to the object and, when he picks it up, move backward to your starting point before you CT and take the object. Repeat five times. (If you will do a formal obedience retrieve with this behavior, put your hand on the object before clicking to prevent the dog from spitting it out prematurely. You may have to shape this over several steps.)

13. Gradually throw the object a little farther, continuing to move with the dog, until you are throwing it about six feet. Stay at each new distance until the dog is successfully carrying the item back to you at least 80% of the time.

14. Now wean the dog off your forward movement. Throw the object and take a couple of steps forward with the dog, but then stop moving about one step away from the object. If the dog stops when you stop, or goes to the object, but doesn't pick it up, repeat a couple of sessions longer at Step 13, then try this step. Repeat three to five times, then stop two steps short of the object. Continue to stop gradually farther from the object until you can throw it and stand still.

Quick Clicks: Sticky spot #2
The history of reinforcement up to this point is what keeps the dog moving forward to grab the item and return to you. Picking it up has been rewarded so many times that most dogs don't pay a lot of attention to the fact that you aren't right there next to them anymore. But, if you're struggling with this criteria change, don't hesitate to back up a few steps and re-teach it more slowly. Having an observer can also help pinpoint where the problem is.

15. Change locations and repeat Step 14.

16. Is your dog successfully retrieving 80% of the time, as fast as you want, at the distance you want? Time to add the "Fetch" cue. Say it just before you throw, then let the dog get the item. Pair the cue with the behavior over several days in several different locations.

Quick Clicks: Stay and then go

If you desire a more formal Fetch, this is where you would start to work on having the dog stay, for only a second at first, before you say your Fetch cue. Don't have the dog stay every time, as it can kill his enthusiasm for getting the dumbbell. Build up the duration of remaining next to you slowly. Add the automatic Sit in front of you, and the release to your hand as a separate cue if you want the full competition Retrieve.

17. Make some longer throws, some shorter throws, some throws a bit off to one side or the other.

18. Is the dog holding the object and bringing it to you for most of the repetitions? Time to add your Give cue. Say "Give" before you CT each time. Be ready to take the object. Repeat pairing the cue with the behavior at least fifty times, changing locations after each ten repetitions.

Generalize the behavior:

- Play Fetch in a variety of locations

- Play Fetch with a variety of objects.

- Vary how you play—sometimes just throw and let the dog retrieve, sometimes throw and race the dog to the object, sometimes play Tug when the dog brings the object back.

Sneeze/Bark/Growl on Cue

The dog makes the desired sound on cue, and repeats it as requested. As this is a natural behavior, obviously sometimes the dog will make these sounds on his own, without your cue, even after the behavior is "on cue." While you are training, the more you can reward any spontaneous offering of the behavior, the better your training results will be.

We will work on Sneeze for these instructions, but the process for the other sounds is much the same. The steps for this behavior are so short that we're only going to provide the speed set of instructions. If you've worked on other behaviors in this book, you should be able to select out the noises you want once the dog starts vocalizing. If you aren't getting anything, start observing when your dog makes noises in the course of his day, so that you can be ready to capture one.

Suggested verbal cue: Suit your cue to the sound you are training. For sneezing, "Bless you" or "Gesundheit;" for growling, "Guard" or "Watch 'em" or "Sssss;" for barking, "Speak" or "Talk."

Quick Clicks: Be selective

Simple tricks can be enhanced by carefully selecting your cues. For example, Mandy initially used, "Is Timmy in the well?" as a cue for her Golden Retriever, Perretta, to bark. She then generalized the cue so that any question asked is answered with a bark, since a question asked in English always goes up in pitch at the end. Now, it appears as if her very smart dog is directly answering her questions.

Suggested visual cue: For Sneeze, wrinkle your nose and pretend you're going to sneeze yourself; for Growl, if you want to use your dog as a reassuring presence, touch the top of your dog's head; for Bark, hold up an index finger (lends itself well to "counting").

Speed Steps

If there are circumstances when you know your dog is likely to sneeze, have your clicker and treats ready and set up those circumstances. CT any sound. Or just have your clicker and treats ready to do an "innovation" training session. Remember the Warm-Up Exercises from Chapter 1, where you clicked a behavior once, then clicked a different behavior? You're going to use that technique to get things started. CT for movement if you have to in order to get the dog started working, but be alert for any sound you can CT to get this behavior started.

Quick Clicks: Capturing

Capturing a behavior like a sneeze can sometimes take a long time (several weeks). You might only get one repetition of the behavior before the dog gets focused on the treat. As you and the dog get more clicker-savvy, you'll find capturing will go much more quickly since the dog will attempt to repeat what he just did that got clicked.

1. If your dog is mostly barking, CT a whine or a growl or a snort, or anything that's not a bark, or even a lesser bark than what he normally does, to start. The barking should decrease as other sounds are clicked and treated, so you have a greater variety of sounds to work with.

2. When you get the clicker out, your dog should start offering a variety of vocalizations. Choose the ones closer to your goal to CT. A Sneeze might start with a huff of air out of the dog's nose or mouth.

3. Continue to refine the sounds the dog is making until it's a recognizable sneeze.

4. Change locations, relax your criteria a little, and build back up to the Sneeze you were getting in the previous location.

5. Try to identify some movement or expression that lets you know your dog is about to make the sound. This will be helpful when you add your cue. If you can't see anything, don't worry—you can still add the cue, it just may take longer.

Quick Clicks: Lick Your Lips

Because Nestle already knows Sneeze and Bark on cue, Cheryl decided to teach another natural doggie behavior, Lick Your Lips. She quickly observed that if given the right kind of treat, Nestle would usually do a Lip Lick after eating a piece. She could give one treat for free, then be ready to click the subsequent Lip Lick, give another treat, get another Lip Lick and so on. It also meant she knew that she could say the cue after giving a treat and expect the Lip Lick behavior to follow.

6. When the sound is how you want it, time to add your cue. If you've been able to identify a precursor, say your cue when you see the precursor. Otherwise, start a session, CT the sneeze a couple of times, then say your cue. The Sneeze should follow just because that's what you've been working on. Repeat pairing the cue with the Sneeze at least fifty times, changing locations after every ten repetitions.

Quick Clicks: Rewards aid predictions

You can use this strategy (rewarding a behavior a couple of times, then saying the cue predicting that the behavior will happen again) with a variety of behaviors. It's especially helpful for natural behaviors that you are capturing, and those that aren't triggered by environmental cues from the training.

Generalize the behavior:

- Cue the Sneeze when you aren't engaged in a training session, so the dog isn't expecting the cue.

- Work in a variety of locations.

- Combine the Sneeze with other behaviors, so your dog will Sneeze while Spinning in Circles or Sitting Up.

Keep in Mind

Your choices for getting sneezing are limited. You can capture it, waiting for the dog to offer it spontaneously and clicking (or using a bridge word) when it happens. You can try mimicking it and see if that will encourage your dog to mirror it back to you. Or, you can try and set up situations where the behavior is more likely to happen. Some dogs sneeze when they are excited, so you want to be ready with your clicker in any circumstances that will generate excitement. Some dogs will sneeze if you blow at their face, but be careful—some dogs will snap instead. You don't have to wait for a full-blown sneeze at the beginning. CT any snort, sniff, or other approximation that could lead to a sneeze.

In this behavior, you'll get some experience with capturing behaviors that the dog already does. Think about other cute behaviors your dog does (rolling on his back, putting his chin on his paws) that you could capture and put on cue.

Quick Clicks: Capturing a Sneeze

Mandy's dog, Ping, sneezes when she is excited, so Mandy can trigger it by putting on her sneakers and getting out the leash. She's also prone to sneezing after she rolls on her back. See if you have any situations where you've seen your dog react by sneezing and be prepared for them.

Troubleshooting

My dog doesn't offer a lot of sneezes.

- Then you don't have much to work with. Start with some of the other sounds your dog does make and work on that first. Not only can it give your dog the idea that making sounds during training sessions can pay off, once you start getting sounds, you can choose those closer to what you want by using twofers to vary the behavior. (For barking, one obvious trigger is ringing the doorbell or knocking on the door. Many dogs will growl when they play so you can capture the sound by playing with them. Sneezing can be triggered by excitement, or by sniffing a new scent.)

I keep forgetting to carry my clicker, and I miss those excited sneezes.

- Use your bridge word rather than miss the opportunity. It isn't as precise, but should be good enough to get started.

- Get one of those coiled plastic bracelets, hook your clicker onto it, and wear it so you have your clicker with you at all times. Or, attach the clicker to your pant's belt loop. Practice grabbing the clicker so you won't have a big delay when you really want to use it.

When I get out the clicker, my dog does all kinds of silly things, but he doesn't sneeze.

- Hooray, you have a clicker-savvy dog! He understands that experimenting with behaviors can lead to rewards. CT any sound that he makes and he'll start to offer more sounds. Then you can start choosing the ones closer to what you want.

Variations

Make a whole performance out of Sneeze by combining it with Fetch. Teach your dog to Sneeze and then go pull a tissue out of a box. (Caution: If you teach your dog to Fetch tissues, keep all tissue boxes out of reach when you're not training or performing, or you may find your home carpeted in tissues.)

If you teach Barking on cue, train a stop cue as well as a start cue and you can have your dog Bark out the answers to arithmetic problems. Make your cues as subtle as possible if you really want to wow an audience.

BONUS BEHAVIOR—TILT YOUR HEAD

The dog tilts his head either to the right or the left, creating a cute, quizzical attitude. You need to trigger the behavior with a sound that makes the dog tilt his head. (See Keep in Mind below, for more ideas.)

Suggested verbal cue: "Cute," "Huh?" "Confused?"

Speed Steps

Because the steps are so few and so straightforward, there is no Detailed Training Plan.

1. Sit your dog. Make your sound (if you've found one that works), or just wait for any head movement, and CT. Repeat five times.

2. Repeat Step 1, but look for a head movement slightly closer to what you want as your final behavior. Repeat five times.

3. Continue to gradually raise your criteria until you have something that looks reasonably like a Head Tilt. Stay at each level for about five repetitions.

4. Change locations and repeat Step 3.

5. Does your dog perform an acceptable Head Tilt at least 80% of the time when you make your sound? Time to add your cue. Say your cue, make the sound, get the Head Tilt, CT. Repeat at least fifty times, changing locations every ten repetitions.

6. If the dog tilts his head when he hears the cue, you can eliminate the sound trigger.

7. Mix the Head Tilt cue up with other cues.

Keep in Mind

This is a behavior that you can either free shape or lure. The "lure" can be food, if you can find a way to move it to get the effect you want. Or, you can try using sound. Sometimes a quiet high-pitched squeak or a lip smacking sound or some other unusual sound you can generate will get that quizzical Head Tilt you're after. Try a kazoo, an electronic sound from a game, an animal noise, saying "Cookie!" or using an unusual sound that your dog hasn't heard before. Experiment and see what might work for you.

Know what you want the behavior to look like so you'll know what you're aiming for. Does the direction of the Head Tilt matter or could the dog go in either direction? (If you choose a specific direction, be aware that you may be fighting the dog's natural tendencies.) Does the position of the ears matter? Should the mouth be open or closed? Do you want a tilt first in one direction then in the other? These are all things you could work on as you go.

Troubleshooting

I can't find a sound that makes my dog tilt his head.

- Try different squeaky toys, bird calls, blow ticklers, a kazoo, anything you can find that might get a reaction.

- Be sure you aren't missing even the tiniest head movement. It may not be a full Head Tilt at first, so don't expect that. You only need something that you can build on.

- Just get out your clicker and click any head movement.

When I get out the clicker, my dog dances around and jumps and does all kinds of silly things. I can't tell if his head is moving—everything is moving!

- Put your dog in a Sit so that he doesn't have much to move other than his head and front feet. You can even put him in a Down. Be aware that once you are getting a reasonable Head Tilt, you'll need to work on getting it with the dog in other positions.

Variations

Use these behaviors to tell a story. For example, if you've taught Bark on cue, give your dog a really hard arithmetic problem and have him tilt his head rather than answering. Give him a hint or remind him "Carry the one" or whatever applies, and then have him answer.

Deenie (3 year old Border Collie mix) has been clicker trained since her owner rescued her at 4 months of age, and is preparing for a career in agility.

Chapter 7
FOR FITNESS

If you have a rowdy new puppy or roly-poly old dog, physical conditioning is important for your dog's (and your own) health and mental well-being. There are a number of fun games and exercises you can train with your clicker. In this chapter, we'll introduce some behaviors that may require a bit more real estate and some specialized equipment, but all of them are guaranteed to improve your dog's physical fitness or work on conditioning.

We'll cover:

- Skateboarding.
- Balance Work (elephant on the box).
- Swimming.
- Pace Work
- Jumping into Your Arms.
- Back Up.
- Bonus behavior—Hiho Silver! (Sit Up/Stand Up).

SKATEBOARDING
The dog puts both front feet and one rear foot on the skateboard, and pushes with the other rear foot. Large dogs may only be able to fit both front or one front and one rear foot on the board. This is a fun behavior to wow an audience, works on balance, and uses the muscles in the rear leg well. It's also great for a dog who's a little nervous, if you work through the steps slowly and carefully. Mandy teaches it to her dogs to help them get used to movement for the teeter in agility.

Suggested verbal cue: "Board," "Ride," "Dude!" "Go."

You will need: A skateboard—it doesn't have to be expensive, there are small models designed for young children that suit smaller dogs well, and a set of phone books.

Quick Clicks: Choose your method
You could use a touch stick to teach this, or a paw target (see Chapter 6) or a food lure. We'll show you how to shape it here, but feel free to try another method if you prefer or if you get stuck.

Speed Steps
1. Put the skateboard between you and the dog and secure it. CT for looking at the board.

2. CT touching the skateboard with any part of his body.

3. CT touching the skateboard with either front leg or a front foot.

4. CT touching with a front foot.

5. CT either front foot on the board. Deliver the treat while he is still on the skateboard.

6. CT duration with one front foot on the skateboard.

7. CT the second front foot on the board at the same time as the first.

8. CT duration with both front feet on the skateboard.

9. CT moving either back foot with both front feet on the board.

10. CT one rear foot and both front feet on the board.

11. Build duration with all three feet on the board.

12. Unblock the wheels so that the skateboard can move a couple of inches forward or backward. CT any forward movement when any foot is already on the skateboard.

13. Build to all three feet on the skateboard, with the rear foot moving the board forward.

14. Increase the rolling distance.

15. Add your cue.

Generalize the behavior:
- Working in different rooms and on different surfaces.
- Working indoors and out.

- Vary where you are in relation to the dog.
- Try it on a different skateboard.

Keep in Mind

Insecure dogs may be unwilling to approach or step on the skateboard. Leave it out in the room where you and your dog spend most of your time and allow the dog to become used to its presence. Practice some behaviors the dog knows a short distance from the skateboard, gradually moving closer. Keep the skateboard wheels blocked to keep it from moving until you are sure the dog is perfectly happy working on the skateboard.

Quick Clicks: Wobble board

You can teach the dog, as a separate exercise, to stand on moving surfaces by making or buying a wobble board (a three-foot square plywood board with a hole in the middle large enough to rest on a tennis ball). Sprinkle the top with sand when you paint it, so it's not too slick. Start on a carpeted surface and shape the dog for putting first one, then two, then three, then all four feet on. CT when the board moves and the dog doesn't shy away, and deliver the treat on the board. Move to a more rigid surface as the dog becomes more comfortable with the noise and movement. It can help if you restrict the movement a bit by stepping on the board initially.

Troubleshooting

The dog won't keep his feet on the skateboard.

- Make sure the skateboard wheels are blocked so it can't move. Some boards also shift sideways on the wheels, so having something beneath the board, almost enough to lift it off the ground, will keep it still in the beginning.
- Once the dog gets on the skateboard, delay the click for one second, then add more time to the delay.
- Deliver the treat so that the dog stays on the board while he eats it.
- Work on Feet Up on a variety of other objects as well. Use your Hand Touch (Chapter 6) to target the dog's front Feet Up onto a picnic bench, tree stump, or your thigh.

The dog jumps over the skateboard without touching it.

- Spend more time working other fun behaviors around the skateboard at the beginning.
- CT for touching any part of his body to the skateboard, even if it's accidental.
- Work more slowly and quietly, reinforcing calm behavior. Hand the dog the treat slowly instead of throwing it, to reduce movement. Deliver the treat right over top of the board.

- Have the dog Sit close to the skateboard, facing it, and ask him to "Wave." CT if his foot touches the board.

The dog does fine until I let the skateboard move, then he jumps off or won't get back on.

- Are you asking for too much too quickly? Only let the wheels move half a revolution or less at first, and increase the distance very gradually. Use blocks of wood on both sides of the wheels, only an inch or two from the wheels, so the skateboard contacts the wood after rolling a very short distance and stops.

- Work with the skateboard on a rug rather than a smooth surface so it doesn't move easily.

- Teach the dog to push the skateboard with his nose or foot before he gets on it, rewarding movement. The dog controls the movement, so it's not as scary for him.

- Make a wobble board and get the dog comfortable with moving objects first.

Variations

You could use the same general training plan to teach the dog to "roll out the barrel" or roll a ball with his front feet. Have the dog stand with all four feet on the board while you pull it. Teach the dog to ski or surf!

Quick Clicks: Skipping steps

If you're working with a clicker savvy dog, shaping can go a lot faster than our step-by-step instructions. If your dog puts both front feet on the skateboard as soon as you put it on the floor several times in a row, CT and rejoice. You can skip a lot of the instructions and just start where he wants to. That's why you need to have the final picture and the steps you'll follow in mind before you start. Otherwise, you'd have to stop and figure out where to go. If the dog puts both front feet on the skateboard initially, but then just stares at it after that, start at Step 1. Don't stand around waiting for the dog to repeat it. In other words, one or two repetitions are not a pattern—remember your 80% rule to move to the next criteria step! Also, if you've carefully shaped the dog at the beginning of a behavior, and you decide to jump a few steps, you'll find that the dog will repeat the last thing he was clicked for when he is confused. That's your clue that you need to back up a bit.

Detailed Training Plan

1. Put the skateboard between you and the dog and secure it with phone books so that it doesn't move forward or backward. When the dog looks at the board, CT. Repeat five times. Deliver your treat directly over the skateboard each time, to increase the chance that he will touch it. (If the dog seems frightened of the skateboard, see the earlier Troubleshooting section.)

2. CT when the dog touches the skateboard with any part of his body. Repeat three to five times.

3. CT when the dog touches the skateboard with either a front leg or a front foot. Repeat three to five times. If the dog places a front foot on the board each time, skip to Step 6.

Quick Clicks: Easy on the reps

We don't want to do too many repetitions in the early stages of this behavior, before the dog gets a foot on the board. That's why you're only repeating three to five times at each step before moving on to a higher level of criteria.

4. CT when the dog touches anywhere on the skateboard with either front foot. Repeat three to five times.

5. CT when the dog lifts his foot over the board. Repeat three to five times, delivering the treat each time so that the dog places his foot on the board as he shifts his weight to get the treat.

6. CT when the dog puts either front foot on top of the board. Deliver the treat while he is still on the skateboard, a little forward of where his foot is. Give a second treat (you don't need to click) if he remains on the board. Repeat five times.

Deliver the treat while she is still on the skateboard, a little forward of where her front feet are. Notice the trainer is using her foot to block movement of the skateboard for this step.

7. Build a short duration with one foot on the skateboard. To do this, count "one-one-thousand" when he puts his foot on it, then click and give the treat. Repeat five times.

8. Increase the count to two seconds before you CT. Repeat five times.

9. Now work on adding a second foot to the skateboard. When the dog puts his first foot on the board, wait for the dog to shift his weight so that his other foot lifts slightly. CT and repeat five times.

Quick Clicks: Shifty

There are several ways to encourage the dog to shift his weight. If you deliver the treat slightly to the side, he'll lean to get it, lifting the foot on the floor. You can CT that motion as well. You can also CT twofers when he puts his first foot on the board (so that the dog puts his foot on twice before getting clicked). (See page 23 for more information on twofers.) Or, you can be patient and wait for him to figure out what he needs to do.

10. When the dog brings his second foot closer to the board, CT. Repeat five times.

11. When the dog touches the skateboard with his second foot while the first foot remains on the board, CT. Repeat five times. Continue until the dog is putting both feet on the skateboard at least 80% of the time.

12. Build a short duration with both front feet on the board, as in Step 7 and 8. Repeat five times.

13. CT moving either back foot when both front feet are on the board. Continue working to add a rear foot on, starting with a weight shift forward and the movement of a rear foot, then proceeding as in Steps 9-11. Stay at each step for one to ten repetitions. You'll move to the next criteria step when the dog is successful 80% of the time. Be sure to build a short duration into the "three feet on" criteria. (This step is optional for large dogs—just continue with Step 14 with the two front feet on the board.)

Quick Clicks: Watch the feet

If you have trouble seeing what the dog's feet are doing, it may help for you to sit on the floor so you are nearer the action.

14. Once the dog is putting three feet on, you are going to have him do it as quickly as possible. When we start to work on board movement, this step will help get the initial movement. To do this, click three feet on, then toss the treat forward and tell the dog to get it. The dog should eat the treat, and quickly turn around to get on the board again. CT all three feet on, and toss the treat forward. Continue at this step until the dog gets on the board with no hesitation 80% of the time.

15. Unblock the wheels so that the skateboard can move a couple of inches forward or backward (about one rotation of the wheels). When the dog jumps on the board, the skateboard will move forward slightly. CT any forward movement when any foot is already on the skateboard. Deliver the treat slightly forward of the board.

Quick Clicks: Drop the criteria

We're dropping our criteria a bit here as we introduce board movement, so we won't look for all three feet on the board initially.

16. Build to all three feet on the skateboard with forward movement, as quickly as you can. Use 80% to decide when to raise your criteria. It will help if you start the dog a short distance away from the board each time, so that he moves it forward when he hits it, and if you then deliver the treat just slightly in front of the dog. Don't toss it on the ground at this step, as the dog will tend to get off the board to get it.

17. Now we will increase the rolling distance. As you do this, the dog will have to start to push with his rear foot. This is the trickiest part of the behavior to get. If you've shaped it carefully to this point and the dog is excited about the opportunity to get on the board, you'll be halfway there. Move your phone books so that the board can roll about six-eight inches farther in both directions. You will be CT-ing for all three feet on, with the foot on the floor moving forward in a pushing motion. Concentrate on the foot on the floor, and gradually build up the distance pushed by Bouncing Around.

18. When the behavior looks the way you want it to, and the dog is ready to jump on when he sees the skateboard, add your verbal cue. You will cue the dog to Wait, place the board down, say your cue, then CT when the dog jumps on and pushes the distance you've decided in advance. Continue to pair the cue with the behavior over the course of several days, about fifty to sixty times. Don't forget to change locations occasionally.

Generalize the behavior:

- Work in different rooms and on different surfaces. Be aware that different surfaces will affect how the board moves. The dog will have to push harder on rough surfaces.

- Work indoors and out.

- Vary where you are in relation to the dog.

- Try it on a different skateboard.

- Have the dog push with either rear leg (not as easy as it might seem, since dogs generally show a preference for one or the other side) as a variation.

BALANCE WORK (ELEPHANT ON THE BOX)

Here is one exercise designed to teach your dog about body movement that strengthens the rear leg muscles. For more physical conditioning behaviors, check out *Pilates for Pooches* (see Resources on page 231 for more information). This DVD shows several other ways to get this behavior, as well as many other outstanding conditioning exercises and is a must-have for anyone who does competition level sports with their dog. In this behavior, we'll have the dog put his front feet on top of a box or stool, then have him move his rear end around in a circle. Kind of like what the elephants do in the circus but trained in a much better way! This is a great way to start a dog on

Side-Stepping, which is a different physical movement for most dogs and common in Freestyle (doggie dancing). This behavior is great for teaching the dog to move the rear legs without moving the front end.

Suggested verbal cue: "Orbit," "Circus," "Round," "Rotate," "Close/Away."

You will need: A stool appropriate for the size of your dog (large enough that he could comfortably have two front feet on it), a sturdy box or a couple of phone books duct taped together. Start with a stool that is less than elbow height for your dog. Cover the surface with rubber or duct tape to give the dog some purchase.

Speed Steps
1. CT one paw on the stool.

2. CT both paws on the stool.

3. Build duration with both front paws on the stool.

4. Deliver treats so that the dog takes a side step with the rear legs in order to get the treat (or use a Hand Touch, see Chapter 6).

5. Increase the distance the dog side steps until the dog will go all the way around the stool.

6. Add a cue for one direction.

7. Reverse the direction.

8. Add a cue for the reverse direction (optional).

Generalize the behavior:
- Work with different items or step heights.
- Work in multiple locations, both inside and out.
- Add a costume and a crowd to make this a fun trick!

Keep in Mind
The behavior of keeping both front feet on the stool needs to be solid before you start moving the dog's rear end around, but shouldn't be at 100%. Otherwise the dog will think that there isn't any more to the behavior. Remember the rule of 80%.

Put away your tools (the stool or box) when you aren't working so the dog doesn't try to interact with the item when you aren't there to click it. Leaving it out so that the dog doesn't get paid for working with it is one way to ensure that he won't be interested in the item the next time.

It's important that you don't drill this behavior multiple times, both as you are training, and once the behavior is on cue. Like any new physical activity, you need to build up the dog's muscles. Once the dog is moving his rear feet around the box, two to three repetitions at each session is plenty to start.

Troubleshooting

The dog won't start stepping with her rear legs.

- Use your body or hand to move the dog sideways (usually just the movement is sufficient; you don't need to push the dog). Remember to wean off the "help" quickly if you don't want it to be part of the behavior. Move your hand or body toward the dog rather than pulling the dog to you.

- Try working on side stepping on the ground first.

- Use a familiar behavior such as Close if the dog already knows that on the ground.

- CT even the smallest movement with a rear leg (such as a weight shift) to start the behavior. Gradually increase your criteria from there.

Variations

Have the dog put all four feet on the stool and spin in a circle (teach both directions). Use a Balance Dome (www.cleanrun.com) to work on balance adjustments and core strengthening in preparation for agility competition or other dog sports. Teach the dog to put his rear legs on the stool and move the front end around (this is typically a much harder variation).

Detailed Training Plan

1. Start with the stool between you and the dog. CT if the dog moves toward the stool. Repeat three times.

2. CT if the dog touches the stool with either front paw. Repeat three times.

3. CT if the dog picks up one paw. Deliver the treat over the stool, so that the dog's foot is in position over the stool. Repeat three times.

4. CT when the dog puts one front foot on the stool. Repeat at this step until the dog immediately puts one foot on at least 80% of the time. Deliver about half of your treats to the dog while he is on the stool, and about half on the ground a short distance away.

Quick Clicks: Treat delivery

Delivering some treats while the dog remains in place allows you to really focus on the idea of being up on the stool, and may help you get the next step more easily. Delivering treats away from the stool allows the dog an opportunity to redo the behavior and makes it easy to tell when he's met the criteria for that step.

Unless you have a specific reason for doing one or the other, you can alternate randomly. (You could also tell the dog to get off and reward that separately, but it adds significantly to the training time.) Sometimes it will be important where (and how) you deliver the reward (such as in Step 5), so you should always plan for it in your shaping steps.

5. CT when the dog shifts his weight so that the paw on the floor is lifted while the other paw is on the stool. Each time you click, deliver the treat so that he is more likely to put the second paw on the stool. Repeat three times.

6. Wait for the second foot to get incrementally closer, and deliver the treat over the stool when you click. Repeat three times.

7. CT both paws evenly on the stool. Repeat at this step until the dog immediately puts both feet on the stool at least 80% of the time.

Quick Clicks: Skipping steps

Many dogs will skip the first six steps and go right to Step 7. If you've been working on other behaviors in the book, the dog will often start immediately interacting with the stool in the most obvious way. Another lovely side effect of clicker training! Be ready to move forward from wherever the dog starts, but also realize that one repetition of "Feet On" is not necessarily your starting point. The dog has to be doing it at least 80% of the time to meet the criteria to move to the next step.

8. Build duration with both front paws on the stool. To do this, start by delaying your CT for one second once the dog has put his feet on the stool. Gradually increase the count until the dog will wait at least three seconds before getting clicked and treated. You can then work on Bouncing Around to increase duration even more, if you like. For our purposes with this particular behavior, a three second duration is sufficient.

Quick Clicks: This may go quickly if...

If you've worked on duration on other behaviors, this step will go very quickly, because the dog "knows the drill."

9. Now we will start the rear end motion. CT the dog for putting two feet on the stool. Deliver the treat so that the dog takes a side step with the rear legs in order to get the treat (or use a Hand Touch, see Chapter 6). You will hold the treat off to the side of the dog's head in the opposite direction you want the dog to move. CT again if the dog takes a step sideways. Try to time this click with the movement of the rear foot as it is *lifting* rather than coming down. The first rear foot to move will most likely be the one farthest from you. Deliver the treats to the side, to continue with the stepping motion. Stay at this step until the dog is immediately taking a step once his front feet are on the stool at least 80% of the time.

Hold the treat off to the side of the dog's head in the opposite direction you want the dog to move.

Quick Clicks: Get the dog moving

It may help to move toward the dog to get the movement started, but remember, you will need to eliminate it if you don't want your movement to be part of the behavior. Think about how you are going to use this behavior. If it's just for conditioning the dog, your movement doesn't really matter. If you don't want it to be part of the cue, don't rely on it for more than five repetitions.

10. Continue to build additional steps around the stool, one step at a time, using 80% as your goal. After you have the dog taking at least three steps for one CT, move to Bouncing Around to get the dog gradually moving all the way around the stool.

11. If the dog will readily get on the stool and start moving around it, add a cue. Time your cue just before you can predict the dog will do the behavior. Repeat the pairing of cue-behavior at least fifty times, in a variety of locations, over the course of several days.

Quick Clicks: A cue for each direction?

If you don't want each direction to have its own cue, you can do Step 12 first, then add your cue. We do find that dogs tend to prefer one side over the other, though, so we recommend separate cues or at least some human body language to help the dog discriminate.

12. Reverse the direction, following Steps 10-11 above. The dog will be a little resistant to changing direction at first, so it's important that you introduce the opposite direction as soon as you have a cue for the first direction (or when the behavior is at 80%, if you aren't going to cue it separately). Otherwise, you and the dog will really struggle with changing direction. You can use body movement or treat delivery to get the dog started in the new direction. Remember to get rid of the body movement after just a few repetitions if you don't want it as part of the behavior.

13. Add a different cue for the reverse direction if you like, following the instructions in Step 11.

Generalize the behavior:

- Work with different items or step heights. Higher steps require more physical work for the dog and also involve some stretching of the rear legs, so limit the number of repetitions in the early stages, until the dog is in good condition.

- Work in multiple locations, both inside and out.

- Add a costume and a crowd to make this a fun trick! With a few other behaviors under your belt and a cute elephant headdress, you can really wow your audience. For inspiration, look at some video of circus elephant performances.

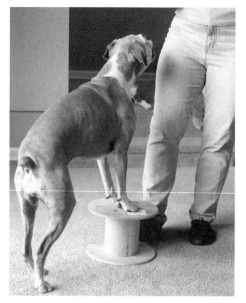

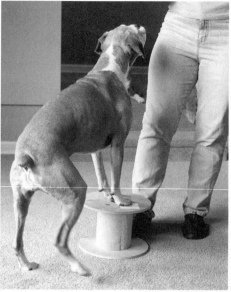

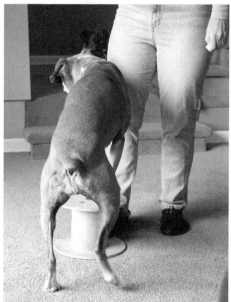

Notice the weight shift to the left leg (upper left photo) in preparation for moving the right leg (upper right photo). In the last photo, Ping is naturally turning her head as she moves counterclockwise.

 ## WATER PLAY/SWIMMING

Swimming is one of the best ways to condition dogs of any age. But not all dogs like to be in the water, so you may need to actually train them to get in. Even dogs that like the water may have trouble staying afloat. For this behavior, we'll give instructions for introducing the dog to water in a fun way and building on that to actually having the dog swim with you (with a few rules). In our experience, some dogs can take a very long time to get used to water (several of Mandy's Boxers have taken two seasons to really learn to get in the water and swim). But all of them can get more comfortable with Water Play. Generally this behavior goes much faster if the dog has a toy that she is thrilled to chase (see Chapter 5). Plan on taking a lot longer if you only have treats as an option. If you have a dog who already swims, skip to the end of the Detailed Training Plan for suggestions for in pool behaviors.

Suggested verbal cue: You won't need a special cue for this behavior, but for safety, you should teach the dog that she can't get in the water without permission first ("Okay" or "Release" is fine for this purpose).

You will need: A child's plastic wading pool, and your dog's favorite toy to start (ideally not cloth!). With tiny dogs you may have to cut a space from the side of the pool so that they can get into the pool easily, or you can start with a giant plastic dog bowl (don't use metal or ceramic for this as the noise can frighten the dog). When the dog is ready to swim, you'll need a swimming area (pool or pond), plus a life jacket for the dog (for both safety and to progress the behavior). Our favorite is sold by Ruff Wear (www.ruffwear.com) and includes a handle on the top to control the dog's movement.

Quick Clicks: Safety

The life jacket isn't optional—a panicked dog could seriously injure herself or *you* in the water, or even drown. You should observe the usual safety rules when swimming with your dog— don't swim alone (always have a second person in case things go awry), use appropriate and well-fitted life jackets, and have emergency tools such as a life ring buoy and telephone handy. Don't leave filled wading pools around—they are unsafe for dogs and children, and attract mosquitoes!

This dog is just learning how to swim, so he wears a life jacket for confidence and safety.

Speed Steps (Water Play)

1. Start with an *empty* wading pool. Use treats to introduce the dog to the pool, and switch to a toy when indicated below. CT when the dog puts a foot over the edge or into the pool. Drop the treat outside the pool.

2. CT the second foot inside the pool.

3. CT lifting a rear foot into the pool (this is a difficult step for many dogs).

4. CT the second rear foot in the pool.

5. Play with the toy in the pool.

6. Add one inch of water to the pool and repeat the above steps. Deliver the reward (whether it's a treat or play with the toy) outside the pool until you get all four feet in.

7. Gradually increase the height of the water. Continue at this step until the dog jumps eagerly into the pool.

Speed Steps (Swimming)

8. Acclimate the dog to the life jacket, if needed.

9. Get in the pool or pond, facing the dog. CT one foot, then the second, and so on, until the dog is standing in the water.

10. Use the toy to lure the dog further into the water. Allow the dog to grab the toy and get out if she wants. (See detailed steps for additional considerations in pool play.)

11. Wean the dog off of the life jacket (an optional step). Start by working in a shallow zone with your hand supporting the dog's chest.

Keep in Mind

You may not get your dog to Step 10. It depends on how easily your dog can get into the water and how motivating the toy is for her. Patience and a long term view are often rewarded by a dog that swims the following season, or the season after that. It sometimes helps if another dog is playing in the water, or your dog may be intimidated by the splashing of another dog (or a child), so take those considerations into account.

Mandy's dogs do not swim when there are children in the pool, period. There are too many things that could go wrong with that scenario, in so many ways. Keep safety at the forefront and remember to supervise your dog at all times in the pool. Pay attention to whether the dog is tiring (the head is lower in the water, or the dog is not swimming as quickly or as strongly) and give your dog a rest break. A few laps are sufficient to start, and no dog should swim more than ten minutes without a break, if only to practice stopping when told and waiting for permission to return to the pool.

Troubleshooting

My dog won't get in the water, no matter what I do.

- Teach the dog to chase a special toy that she only sees for Water Play.

- Many short-coated breeds don't like to be cold. A heated pool, or practicing on a really hot day, may be enough to convince your dog how much fun swimming is.

- Have someone else observe you (always a good tool) to see if you are making it fun or frightening the dog.

Variations

Many enthusiastic dogs will jump into the pool after you or to chase a toy. Search the web for Dock Diving to find out more about a competition sport for diving dogs.

Some dogs are even willing to dive under water—try holding the toy under and see what your dog does! Cheryl's Springer mix, Spirit, was an ace at retrieving a rock from the bottom of a stream or pond. And her Newfoundland mix, Serling, passed a Level 1 water test easily on his first try. Another sport you could try!

Detailed Training Plan (Water Play)

1. Start with an empty wading pool. (You may have to place it in a corner, so it doesn't move around while you work this first stage. This is especially important if your dog is worried.) Use treats to introduce the dog to the pool, and switch to a toy when indicated below. CT when the dog puts a foot near the pool, and gradually build to one foot in the pool. If you need help, review the earlier instructions for Balance Work or the starting instructions for Skateboarding. Drop the treat outside the pool each time.

Quick Clicks: Drop it out

Dropping the treat outside the pool allows you to get many repetitions of the behavior quickly and also helps if the dog is frightened of the wading pool. You are, in effect, rewarding the dog for getting in by letting her get out.

2. CT both front feet inside the pool. Deliver the treat outside of the pool. Continue at this step until the dog quickly puts both front feet in at least 80% of the time.

3. CT lifting a rear foot into the pool (this is a difficult step for many dogs). You may have to shape this more carefully than the front feet, and break your steps much smaller. You could, for example, start with a weight shift forward, build to a foot lift, then a movement forward, and so on. Repeat one to ten times at each level of criteria.

4. CT the second rear foot in the pool, using as much criteria breakout as you need for this step. It generally does not take as long as Step 3, however. Deliver the treat outside the pool each time. Continue at this step until the dog readily hops into the pool 80% of the time.

5. Switch to a toy, but make sure it is one that the dog *really* likes! (See Chapter 5 if you need to build the dog's interest in a toy.) Once the dog jumps in, click and play with the toy in the pool for a few seconds, and toss it outside so the dog gets out of the pool. Repeat ten times.

Quick Clicks: Toy instead of treat

If your dog is looking for a treat after the click instead of playing with the toy, skip the click. At this point, we don't need the precision of the clicker as a tool. Later on, make sure you work on clicking paired with other types of rewards, so they can be used for behaviors.

6. Add one inch of water to the pool and repeat Steps 1-5. It should go much more quickly than the first time you worked through those steps. Deliver the reward (whether it's a treat or play with the toy) outside the pool until you get all four feet in, then play in the pool with the toy a bit. Stay at this step until the dog is responding readily 80% of the time, and will play enthusiastically with the toy once all four feet are in the pool. If your dog does zoomies and jumps in and out of the pool, you're on the right track.

7. Gradually increase the height of the water, adding about an inch at a time, until you get the water as high as you'd like it. For small dogs, the wading pool is a good option for swimming (as long as they can't touch the bottom). Continue at this step until the dog jumps eagerly into the pool when given permission. You could also add a verbal cue here to get in the pool ("Get In"). Spend several weeks at this step, playing with the toy enthusiastically while the dog is in the pool, and stopping play when the dog gets out. Many dogs also like to chase splashing water if you kick the sides of the pool, or make a whirlpool using a hose.

Detailed Training Plan (Swimming)

8. Acclimate the dog to the life jacket, if needed. Mandy puts the jacket on as soon as the dog is outside, so it's not associated just with getting into the pool. For dogs that don't yet swim, it's also extra insurance in case they get knocked into the pool by another dog. The life jacket has the secondary advantage of increasing the dog's body heat, making her much more likely to want to get in the cooling waters.

Quick Clicks: Doggie dress up

You can use the clicker to get the dog quickly used to hats, sunglasses or other clothing. Just put the item on, CT, then immediately take it off. Repeat until the dog isn't resisting (pulling away or trying to rub it off), then build duration by Bouncing Around. We've used this many times to get photos for a last minute shoot, to introduce the dog to a costume for a pet visit, or to get the dog used to something he needs to wear for medical reasons.

9. Get in the pool or pond, facing the dog. CT one foot, then the second, and so on, following Steps 1-5 above, until the dog is standing in the water. Deliver each treat a little in front of the dog, so she has to reach a bit forward to get it. Let her get out as often as she wants to. Each time the dog gets in the pool, remember that you are clicking and treating for meeting or exceeding your current criteria. So you won't, for example, be CT-ing one foot in the water when you are past that step of the behavior.

10. Use the toy to lure the dog further into the water. You can splash it around, toss it or make it disappear under the water. When the dog comes forward a little bit, allow her to grab the toy and get out if she wants. This is important so that the dog learns that she can get out of the pool at any time, and also learns *how* and *where* to get out. Get the toy back from the dog, and repeat until the dog is readily getting into the water. The only time you will play with the toy is in the pool—there is no fun to be had with the toy outside of the pool. You will gradually shape the dog to go further into the water, using 80% to decide when to try and move to a higher level of criteria (i.e., the dog getting more of her body into the water). Completion of this step may take anywhere from a couple of weeks, to several months, of work.

Pool safety and related behaviors

Caution: Before training the behavior, please be sure you have reviewed the Wait, Leave It and Touch behaviors with your dog and she is reliably doing them.

11. Once the dog is readily entering the water, you can begin teaching the dog directions. Use a Hand Touch to direct the dog to either side of you and prevent her from swimming into you. You can also use a Hand Touch to have her swim in a circle, working on rear leg muscles. Some great physical games include swimming in a circle, holding on to the handle on the life vest to encourage strong swimming with the front legs, pushing the dog away from you, and retrieving in the water. Teach the dog to come to you in the water when called, as well.

12. Teach the dog to play with specific toys and keep her mouth off of chlorine dispensers, thermometers and inflatable toys. If you have multiple dogs, designate a pool toy for each dog to prevent conflict in the water. (See Leave It in Chapter 4.)

13. Make sure the dog knows exactly where and how to get out. Repeat, repeat, repeat every season.

14. Don't let the dog get into the pool without permission. Use the Wait behavior to practice getting in, and hanging out around, the pool without letting the dog jump in. You can gradually build up to rolling a toy into the pool or more enticing distractions, rewarding the dog with something better poolside. These skills are important to practice for the safety of the dogs and any humans using the pool.

15. When you feel ready to wean the dog off the life jacket, start in a shallow area and hold your hand lightly under the dog's chest to support her in the water. This

allows the dog to move all four limbs freely. You can let the dog do the work, and gauge whether she is able to keep her rear end up before you eliminate the life jacket completely. Some dogs may always need to wear the life jacket. It's not a bad idea to keep it on the dog.

16. Be careful that you don't tire a dog, even a good swimmer, past the point that they are able to work at. Look for a sinking head, body lowered in the water, or a slower return to you as indicators that they may be tiring. Build up to more laps or longer play over the course of the swim season. Eager swimmers especially need to be monitored so that they don't overtire.

17. Don't leave dogs unattended around a pool, ever. Even good swimmers can tire and panic trying to get out.

 ## PACE WORK

This behavior uses a set of children's step hurdles to teach the dog to separate his legs and move evenly over the hurdles. This is a great exercise for building strength in the rear and front, for getting the dog to move smoothly over the hurdles without a lot of bouncing, to condition the dog for jumping, and to prepare the dog to learn to change his pace. The idea for this exercise is based on Kay Laurence's *Teaching Flexibility: Cavaletti* DVD, available from www.dogwise.com or directly from Kay Laurence at www.learningaboutdogs.com.

Suggested verbal cue: "Fast," "Quick," "Trot," "Speed," "Go," "Slow," "Walk," "Pace" (for pace changes), none needed for the hurdles since they already provide a visual cue.

You will need: Multi-Height Hurdle Cones—buy the twelve inch height. You need at least four to start with, and eight (or more) is better if you have the room to use and store them. You can also build your own set from PVC if you are handy.

Speed Steps

1. Place one hurdle out and CT one front leg, then the other front leg, then a rear, then the other rear leg stepping over the bar (at least four separate criteria steps).

2. Place all four hurdles in a square pattern and repeat Step 1 with all four legs. Increase the height of the hurdles and repeat.

3. Vary the height of the hurdle square, and CT each rear leg stepping over a bar.

4. CT when the dog moves smoothly over one corner (two bars) or across the square, splitting his rear legs.

5. Set up the hurdles in a straight line. Measure the dog from the back of the front foot to the front of the back foot to get the initial placement of the hurdles. The dog should be able to split walk over all four bars comfortably.

6. Start at the lowest height. Build distance first, tossing the treat beyond the last hurdle, until the dog navigates all hurdles smoothly.

7. Build speed. Alter the distance between the hurdles as needed so that the dog moves smoothly, with one foot between each of the hurdles.

8. Increase the height and decrease the distance between the hurdles until the dog works at the full height (eight and a half inches) of the hurdles. Repeat to 80% proficiency and move to the next step if you want to work on speed variations.

9. To speed the dog up, increase the spread distance and lower the height. Add a cue for this if you like.

10. To slow the dog down, put the hurdles high and close together and CT duration with each foot lift. Deliver the treat directly in front of the dog. Add your cue.

Keep in Mind

Do not do more than ten reps in any training session (five times up, five times back). This is very tiring for the dog, especially in the early stages—try stepping over the hurdles back and forth over and over if you don't believe us! If the dog is ticking the hurdle with his toes, it means he is tiring. As the dog becomes more conditioned, you can increase the repetitions.

Troubleshooting

My small dog is struggling with getting over the bar, even at its lowest.

- Put the hurdle bar on the ground to start, and work on getting the split step (especially the rear legs) as your focus. Adjust each height accordingly to meet the needs of your dog. If you are using the purchased hurdles, it's likely you won't be more than a couple of inches off the ground to work on speed in this behavior.

My dog is too nervous to step over the bar.

- Put the bar on the ground to start. Use a line of string to start if you need to, then a yardstick, then a small dowel, and plan on adjusting the heights as needed for each step. Leave a hurdle out for the dog to explore. Put the hurdle across a hallway and toss a favorite toy on the other side.

Variations

Wean the dog off of the hurdles and practice pace changes walking next to you (you do not change pace, just the dog). This is a great variation for agility, rally and conformation competitions.

Detailed Training Plan

1. Place one hurdle out with the bar at the lowest point (two and a half inches high) and CT one front leg, then the other front leg, then a rear, then the other rear leg stepping over the bar. These are at least four separate criteria steps. You will CT each leg until the dog is stepping over the hurdle 80% of the time with that leg. Choose another leg to CT and work to 80% and so on, until the dog has been CT'd for each leg stepping over the hurdle. Expect to spend longer to get the dog to step over the hurdle with each rear leg individually than it took for the front legs. Most dogs will want to hop over with both rear legs initially, so you may have to break this step down more with the rear legs.

Quick Clicks: Fear of the new

If you have a dog who is easily frightened by new things, you may have to break Step 1 down very finely, including looking at, CT-ing a foot movement, then a foot lift, then a higher lift, then movement forward, then movement over the bar. If this is your dog, you will also have a tougher time getting the rear legs to split, so write out a plan for your incremental changes for the rear legs. Also, plan on an extra session (ten treats) or two at each level even after the dog has reached 80% success at that level.

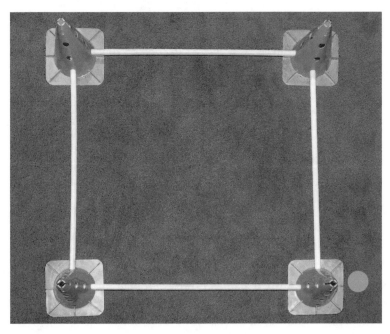

2. Place all four hurdles in a square pattern with all four bars at the lowest point, and repeat Step 1. If you have a dog who is nervous about the hurdles, repeat a few sessions at each level before moving on.

Quick Clicks: Over, not around

The reason for having the hurdles in a box pattern initially is to prevent the dog from going around the hurdles. Once the dog gets in the box, he has another opportunity to get a CT with a second bar. You are also more likely to get the dog moving each rear leg separately over a hurdle when the dog is already in the box, since he is slowed down by navigating the box.

3. Increase the height of the hurdles to the midpoint (five and a half inches high). CT each rear leg stepping over the hurdle bar. This is at least two separate steps, as you work with each rear leg to 80% proficiency. (At this point, you won't bother any longer with clicking the front legs unless the dog has a tendency to hop the bar with his front legs as well.)

4. Increase the height of the hurdles to the top slot (eight and a half inhes high) and repeat Step 3.

5. Vary the height of each bar while the hurdles are still set in a square, and CT the rear legs splitting to step over a bar (not each individual step, but the separation of the rear legs, essentially CT-ing a step over with the first rear leg only). Reward in front of the dog so that he brings his body out of the box to get his treat. Let the dog choose which bar he will go over each time, but use your treat delivery to vary which bar he happens to be standing in front of for the next pass. Tossing the treat such that the dog is approaching the hurdle box at a different angle each time will help him increase the variety of his approach. The dog needs to be comfortable stepping over each height with each rear leg separately.

6. CT when the dog moves smoothly over one corner (two bars) or across the square, splitting his rear legs. Your focus is on the split of the rear legs. You can CT each bar if you like or only the second one, delivering the treat in front of the dog to keep forward momentum.

7. Set up the hurdles in a straight line. Measure the dog from the back of the front foot to the front of the back foot to get the initial placement of the hurdles, but you may need a slight adjustment in distance. Set the hurdles at their lowest point (or on the ground for a small dog). The dog should be able to split walk over all four bars comfortably, putting just one foot in between the bars. CT the rear leg split over each bar. The treat is given in front of the dog to encourage continuing forward, and to give him an opportunity to step over the next bar and get clicked and treated again. Do not repeat more than ten passes (five in each direction) at a session to prevent tiring the dog.

The dog should be able to split walk comfortably over all four bars. Here, Jenga is running a 24" spread between the hurdles. Notice her attention is forward. At this height the hurdles should be spread out a little more, to straighten her topline.

8. Build distance until the dog navigates all the hurdles smoothly. To do this, you will CT one split step with the rear legs over the first bar, and toss the treat a distance away from the last hurdle. Do not worry about what the dog does over the remaining hurdles. Continue until the dog is splitting the rear legs over the first hurdle at least 80% of the time. Then CT a split step over the second hurdle to 80% and so on. Usually the dog will maintain the split step over the initial hurdles as you build distance, but if not, go back a step and work on whichever hurdle he is hopping. You may also need to adjust the distance between hurdles an inch or two (the dog will hop if they are too close together or too far apart, because it's less work than stepping).

Jenga is hopping with her rear legs in this photo—be sure not to click that behavior!

Quick Clicks: Mats for targets

Kay Laurence teaches a mat target at both ends of the set of hurdles, or uses two people calling the dog back and forth, to get the dog moving swiftly and smoothly over the hurdles. This isn't completely necessary if your treat delivery is good and you are only using four hurdles, although there are certainly plenty of advantages to using either of her options. The DVD explains how to do both variations.

9. Build speed. Alter the distance between the hurdles as needed so that the dog moves smoothly, with one foot between each of the hurdles. They will need to be spread farther apart as the dog increases speed. Watch the rear end—the dog should bounce one foot between each hurdle, splitting all four legs over the bars. If he's hopping, you need to refine what you are marking with the clicker, or modify the distance between the hurdles. CT the dog for quickly starting the set of hurdles first (until the dog is getting into the set as fast as you like at least 80% of the time). Then work on quick completion by following the Quick Clicks tip below. Pay attention to what you are clicking—you don't want to accidentally CT hopping while you work to increase speed.

Quick Clicks: Speeding up behavior
Speed in a behavior is one of the behavior variables that beginners often struggle with. An easy way to monitor it is to do three repetitions of the behavior and count out how long it takes the dog to complete each repetition. We use "one-ba-na-na" because each syllable is more or less equal to ¼ second. Average the three repetitions, then only click and treat repetitions that are faster than your average. When the dog is faster than average 80% of the time, set a new, lower average. In Step 9, you will set your average based on counting from the time the dog enters the hurdle set, until he exits it. Another way to get speed in a behavior is to have your dogs compete against each other. Only the fastest dog in the group to do a Down or Come, for instance, receives the treat. (You do have to be careful with this if you have dogs with resource issues.)

10. Increase the height to the next level and decrease the distance an inch or two between the hurdles. Continue at this step until the dog completes the hurdles with good speed at each height 80% of the time. You can stop here if conditioning is what you're after, or complete Steps 11-12 if you want to work on pacing speed variations.

11. To speed the dog up, spread the hurdles farther apart and lower the height to the mid or low point. When you feel like the dog is moving as fast as he is physically able to, add a cue for speed if you like. The cue needs to be paired with the behavior at least fifty to sixty times over several sessions. Initially, you will say the cue just as the dog moves into the hurdles (as he is picking up speed.) As you work to add the cue, you will say it earlier and earlier in the process. You'll know that the dog understands the cue when he picks up speed when you say it. A toy thrown as a reward will also help to generate more speed.

12. To slow the dog down, put the hurdles high and close together and CT duration on each foot lift. Deliver the treat directly in front of the dog's nose. This stops the forward movement so that you can CT the next foot lift. Add your cue when the behavior is to your liking 80% of the time.

Keep in Mind

You'll need to get the speedy performance on cue before working on slowing the dog down. Otherwise, he'll be confused as to what is expected when he enters the hurdles. Add the Slow Down cue as quickly as you can once you have the behavior, then alternate which behavior you ask for in the hurdles. The dog will be a bit confused at first, but will quickly learn that what you say before he enters the hurdles has an impact on whether he is clicked and treated. Modifying the spread and height of the hurdles, and how you deliver your reward, will also help him discriminate in the beginning.

There isn't an accepted procedure for teaching two directions (such as spinning left and spinning right) or different variations (such as fast and slow) to a dog. We've done interchanging practice where you work on both directions in alternating sessions, and tried teaching one first and then the other, and found that either way you end up with both behaviors *as long as* you don't practice one over, and over, and over to perfection before teaching the other. But even if you do, it is still possible to change it (although it takes a lot more work). We've done it with both chickens and dogs successfully.

For smaller dogs, you will want to adjust the height accordingly while practicing. The maximum height should be *no more than half* the overall height of the dog at the withers. For Mandy's twenty one inch tall dogs, eight and a half inches is a good maximum height for high stepping practice (Step 12). They work at five and a half inches high when training for speed (Step 11), with a spread of between twenty-one and twenty-eight inches. If the dog is struggling with not moving evenly over the bars, or ticking the bars, you are working the dog at a height too high for the speed you are trying to get, or they need to take a break.

JUMPING INTO YOUR ARMS

Yeah, we know you've spent months teaching your dog *not* to jump, but this fun behavior is a can't-miss crowd pleaser. Teach your dog to Jump into Your Arms (on cue!). Make sure you are strong enough to catch the dog first. This is a great behavior for building muscle in the rear legs. It's easiest to teach the dog to use your leg to get up into your arms, but some talented and athletic dogs can jump straight from the floor—adjust your steps accordingly if the dog doesn't need a "leg up." There are variations you can teach to work within you and your dog's physical abilities if you aren't able to catch him. For dogs too large to jump, teach a "Hug" instead and have them stretch up to put their paws on your shoulders (see Bonus Behavior—Hiho Silver for tips). The first part of the instructions require the dog to balance on your lap once he jumps, another great physical activity. This is a pretty straightforward behavior, so only the Speed Steps have been included below. If you need help breaking the behavior down, take the opportunity to write out a ten-step plan, then add at least one level in between each of those steps. You can use the Speed Steps as a starting point. Obviously, Step 2 will have to be broken down into multiple steps!

You can see Fia is using the bent leg to jump up, and her trainer is prepared to catch her.

Suggested verbal cue: "Hup!" "Up!" (a strong verbal cue association is critical for the safety of the dog and visitors!).

Suggested visual cue: Not recommended.

Slick Clicks: The problem with common cues
Mandy's dog, Tonka, was a master at this behavior. Her visual cue was Mandy patting her chest. Unfortunately, it's a common behavior for a lot of humans when they are talking. Tonka was standing in front of a woman who accidentally cued it, and both Tonka and the woman were surprised when Tonka jumped up and the woman didn't catch her. After that, Mandy added a verbal cue to the hand signal.

You will need: A chair for a large dog, a stool for a smaller dog or one who has difficulty jumping.

Speed Steps

1. Sit on the stool or chair. Hold the treat forward a bit over your lap and lure the dog to jump into your lap. The lower your lap, the easier this will be (see Keep in Mind). For many dogs, this is the most difficult part of the exercise, and it may help if you pat your lap or make kissy sounds the first few times. The dog can face you or be at your side, whichever is most comfortable for you to catch. For large dogs, it will be easier to have them come from the side.

> ### Quick Clicks: Lose the lure
> Remember that you will need to get rid of your lure quickly if you don't want it to become part of your cue. Try luring three or four times, then see if the dog will try it on his own. You can then CT him for jumping into your lap. Give the treat while he is still on your lap. Then use this as an opportunity to work on Off and also reward that with a treat (no click needed)!

2. Using a wall to brace yourself, gradually stand up, working the dog to 80% at each change in lap elevation. Take your time building up to a full stand (great for your own thighs!).

3. Move away from the wall, working to 80% at each distance change of a few feet.

4. Add the verbal cue when the behavior is completed and the dog is doing it 80% of the time. Don't work past 80%, as the dog is likely looking at body cues as a signal to do the behavior. We don't want visual cues to elicit the behavior.

Generalize the behavior:

- Practice in a variety of locations—both indoors and outdoors.
- Work around different people.
- Have other people catch your dog (make sure they are willing and able, first!).

Keep in Mind

If your dog is resistant to jumping into your lap initially, it may be because he is worried, or it may be because he is physically unable. Many dogs will not jump onto a surface they can't see, so it may help for you to lower your lap by sitting on a stool or even starting on the floor if you need to. Don't worry if you have to start by sitting on the floor. You can quickly shape the behavior to full height as long as you can get a starting point. If the dog has physical difficulty, he will gradually build up the muscles needed as you increase the height.

Variations

Have the dog Jump on your back, or use your back as a springboard to Jump into someone else's arms or catch a flying disc. These variations require that the dog be in excellent physical condition, and are used for Freestyle and Frisbee competitive events.

BACK UP

This behavior is used in a lot of ways, including daily in our houses. You never know when you'll need to move the dog out of the way in a small space where they can't turn around. Mandy uses it at the front door so that her dogs don't crowd the door when someone rings the doorbell, and also when she enters the house from the garage with an armful of groceries. The behavior is great for physical conditioning and body awareness. We work here on moving the dog back in a straight line, but, in Freestyle, dogs are often taught to back up between the handler's legs in a serpentine movement, or sometimes even in a circle.

Quick Clicks: Verbal and visual alternatives

We'll discuss how to eliminate extra body language and add a visual cue so that you can use both verbal and visual cues separately in this behavior. The process is the same for any other behavior you might want to do this with.

Suggested verbal cue: "Back," "Beep Beep," "Get back," "Toes!"

Suggested visual cue: A waving motion with your hand (similar to what you would use to signal a driver to back up).

You will need: A chute set up, such as the area between the couch and coffee table or a couple of chairs lined up next to a wall.

Left photo is the beginning of the Back Up behavior using a chute. On the right the trainer is working without the chute, but still using forward body movement.

Speed Steps

1. Draw the dog forward into the chute several times. (You will be backing up while the dog moves forward.)

2. Lead the dog into the chute. Take a step toward him. CT any movement of the back feet. Release the dog forward.

3. Build to the dog taking one step, then several steps backward, as you move toward him.

4. Continue until the dog will take at least five steps backward, then use Bouncing Around to increase the distance.

5. Begin to eliminate the chute prop by gradually opening it up at one end into a "v" pattern. Continue until the dog is not relying on the chute any longer, but is still backing straight.

6. Add the verbal cue.

7. Wean the dog off of your forward movement.

8. Add a visual cue.

9. Generalize the behavior.

Keep in Mind

Expect to take a little extra time with a worried dog who doesn't want to be in the chute, and set your chute up so you don't accidentally bang against it. Release the dog after every repetition so he can leave the chute moving forward and come back into it while walking forward. As he builds confidence in the chute, you won't need to release your dog from the chute every time.

Variations

Teach the dog to Back Up and go under your legs, circling your leg in reverse. The easiest way to start this variation is to have the dog Back Up around a cone, then transfer the behavior to around each leg.

An alternate way to teach the behavior is to have the dog at your side and Back Up with him next to you. Can you design a plan to teach it this way? What would be the advantages or disadvantages of doing it this way?

Detailed Training Plan

1. When you set up your chute, make sure you have enough room for your rear end so you don't spook the dog by banging into a chair as you back up. Draw the dog forward into the chute several times with a treat, taking him through the entire chute. (You will be backing up while the dog moves forward into the chute.) Spend additional time at this step if your dog seems anxious about the chute.

2. Face the dog and lead him into the chute with a treat, which you will give him. Take a step toward him, keeping your hands low. (If your hands are held up, most dogs will want to sit.) CT any movement of the back feet. Release the dog forward and repeat five times. (You can let him come forward out of the chute if he is nervous, or just let him take a few steps forward if he seems comfortable with the chute.)

3. Build to one step, then several steps backward. (You can choose just one foot to focus on or select either rear foot to click.) At each level, repeat at least ten times, or until the dog does the behavior at least 80% of the time during your session. Once you've reached 80%, do another set of ten repetitions at each step if the dog is still unsure of the chute. Continue until the dog will take at least five steps backward as you move toward him, then use Bouncing Around to increase the distance to as many steps as you need. Five to ten steps backward is a good goal for most everyday uses for this behavior. For Freestyle, you may want a lot more.

4. Begin to eliminate the chute by gradually opening it up at one end into a "v" pattern. Repeat ten times at each change in the chute opening. If the dog begins to curve to one side as he backs up, go back to your previous step. You want the dog to be taking several steps straight backward for at least 80% of your repetitions before changing the chute. Continue until the dog is not relying on the chute any longer, but is still backing straight. In other words, your chute is opened up enough that it isn't a big part of the behavior.

5. Does the behavior look the way you want it to? Time to add the verbal cue: say the cue, step toward the dog, the dog backs up, CT, release the dog forward. Repeat at least fifty times over the course of several days, in several different locations.

6. Once the behavior is on cue, you can wean the dog off of your forward movement. To do this, say your cue and pause. If the dog takes a short step back, CT and release forward. Repeat, quickly building up the distance the dog backs up. If the dog does not do anything when you say your cue, repeat Step 5, making sure that you separate your verbal cue from your physical movement each time.

7. Add a visual cue by pairing it with the verbal cue. The process is: visual cue, verbal cue, dog backs up, CT, release. Repeat fifty to sixty times over several sessions.

8. Generalize the behavior by working in a variety of environments.

Quick Clicks: Using both visual and verbal cues
If you are going to use both the visual and verbal cue together, you can do them at the same time. If you want them to each work independently, make sure you give the visual (or new) cue first, then the verbal (or old) cue. An easy way to remember this is New-Old or NO or alphabetically! When the dog starts to anticipate the new cue, you can eliminate the old cue. You use the same process to change a verbal cue to a different verbal cue. Say the new cue first, then the old cue. It's also how we get

rid of the dog's reliance on your body language (a visual cue). The dog's goal is to do the behavior so he can get a CT. The faster he figures out what you're looking for, the faster he gets his reward. It's in his best interests to pay attention to anything that predicts a reward is coming. In each case, we are using the dog's anticipation of the next cue in the sequence to add a new cue. Ever have a dog who gets excited when you put your walking shoes on? That dog has learned that shoes are the first step in the sequence that leads to a walk.

Bonus Behavior—HiHo Silver! (Sit Up and Stand Up)

This is an easy behavior to lure using a treat or a Hand Touch. You only need to worry about getting rid of the lure if you don't want to use it as part of your hand signal. Teach the dog to do a Sit Up using the same basic directions, by adjusting where your hand is. Sit Up uses a lot of muscles in the dog's back, and is a terrific conditioning behavior. Stand Up uses multiple muscles in the dog's rear. Teach them both, then have the dog go from a Sit Up to a Stand Up by adjusting your hand up and down. If you are going to teach both Sit Up and Stand Up, we recommend that you teach Sit Up first to the dog, get it on cue, then work on Stand Up. Generally, Stand Up is easier for the dog physically and they will want to do that anyway, so teach the harder one first.

Suggested verbal cue: "Sit Up," "Sit Pretty," "Beg," "HiHo," "Dance."

Suggested visual cue: Using one or both hands, with palms facing down, fingers together, moving fingers from horizontal to vertical position.

Speed Steps

1. Using a Hand Touch, or with a treat in your hand, put your hand over the dog's head. For the Sit Up, you want the hand just a little over the dog's head and behind it a bit (see picture). For Stand Up, you will hold your hand up high. You may need to cue Touch or tell the dog to get the treat initially. CT when the dog touches, and give the treat while the dog is vertical. Continue until the dog is tilting his head back readily to Touch 80% of the time while still remaining either seated or standing (depending on which variation you are working on). If you are using a treat to lure it, get rid of the treat after a couple of tries and use just your hand motion (even if you don't have a Hand Touch).

The hand is held low and behind the head for the Sit Up (left) and even with the dog's head to get a Stand Up (below). Notice in the Sit Up that Perretta's rear legs are wide for balance, and her front legs are pulling into her body.

2. Do a session or two of twofers to get some variability in how long the dog remains vertical.

3. CT only the position holds that are quarter-second or longer. When the dog is doing a quarter-second hold at least 80% of the time, increase to a half-second hold. Continue until the dog is holding one to two seconds, then use Bouncing Around to increase to five to ten seconds (or longer, if you want). Generally, dogs have a much easier time standing on their hind legs for the longer time period than sitting up. It may take some time for your dog to build up the muscle strength to hold the Sit Up for an extended period.

Quick Clicks: Reintroduce a lure

It may be helpful to reintroduce a treat lure in your hand when the dog is learning to balance. You have to be careful about the treat delivery, so that the dog does not start snapping at your fingers after the click. Make sure you put the treat into the dog's mouth, rather than dropping it from above. This helps maintain the balanced position. Bring in a lure for three to four times, then work without it for a few repetitions, so that the dog doesn't become dependent on the treat in your fingers.

4. Add your verbal cue, if you like. You can also use the hand motion as a visual cue instead of or in addition to the verbal cue.

5. Eliminate the hand motion if you don't want to use it as a cue.

6. Generalize the behavior by working in a variety of environments and around different people.

7. After teaching Sit Up, teach Stand Up using the same instructions and adjusting your hand motion accordingly. Use a different cue for Stand Up.

8. Have the dog go from a Sit Up to a Stand Up. You can start the dog in Sit Up, then cue "Stand Up," or just use a hand motion to pull the dog from a Sit Up to a Stand Up. Remember that this movement takes some physical conditioning, so you will need to work up to multiple repetitions gradually.

Variations

Teach the dog to hop and walk on both rear legs, both forward and backward.

Can you teach the dog to have both right legs up, opposing legs up or both rear legs up (see the Silvia Trkman videos referenced in the Resources on page 232 for a great visual demo of these variations).

Bernie (11 year old Beagle) has been clicker trained since he was 5 years old, has his championship in CPE agility and still competes regularly.

Chapter 8

BEYOND THE CLICKER

As wonderful as the clicker is, you'll still want to get rid of it once a behavior is trained, and it isn't always helpful or needed for every behavior. This chapter delves into when *not* to use a clicker, when and how to drop it once you've trained a behavior with it, plus a few other useful things such as how to combine behaviors into chains.

When not to use a clicker to teach a behavior

Remember that a clicker is most useful for marking pieces of behavior so you can build on them to create a finished behavior—the process of shaping. But some behaviors occur in complete or nearly complete form right from the beginning. You could use a clicker, but it wouldn't have any great benefit and might even get in the way.

Also, some behaviors not only occur in complete form, they are inherently rewarding to the dog. A CT might even prove distracting from what the dog is already doing.

Finally, in behaviors such as Scentwork and Tracking, not only are the behaviors self-rewarding, but when they are put into actual practice, the dog has the advantage! The human doesn't know where the scent article is or where the track lies, so how can the human accurately mark what the dog is doing correctly?

In all of these circumstances, the clicker is unnecessary. Bob Bailey refers to a clicker as a scalpel, and to throwing food at the dog as using a butter knife. When you don't need a scalpel, you don't need to use a clicker. We are providing instructions for two behaviors here—Find Me and Scentwork—that *do not* use a clicker. This will help you get a better idea of when a clicker might not be necessary and how best to work without it.

FIND ME

The dog waits in one place until told to play the game, then locates a hiding person (or a hidden object).

Suggested verbal cue: "Find (person's or object's name)", "Where's (fill in the name)", "Seek," "Search."

You will need: A rock-solid Stay or an assistant to hold the dog while you hide (generally a helper is good at the beginning of the behavior, even if your dog has an excellent Stay).

Why you don't need a clicker: This behavior is mostly complete the first time it occurs—the dog finds you (even though it's close by, to start). For your dog, finding you should be a rewarding behavior, plus, you can offer a food treat or play with a toy when the dog makes the Find. You could click when the dog Finds you, but it wouldn't really have any meaning for the dog, since it technically comes after the reward, which is locating you. (In other words, the clicker isn't salient for the behavior.) Also, when you get to advanced versions of this game (hiding in tough places), the dog will be using his nose to track you down, and dogs live to sniff!

Speed Steps

1. Leave the dog in a Sit-Stay and duck around a corner or behind a door. Say your release word and the dog should zoom straight to you. Praise and treat.

2. Repeat, making your hiding place a little farther away or a little harder.

3. Start saying your cue before you say your release.

4. Don't let the dog see you hide.

5. Start with the dog in a different location.

6. Find opportunities to hide without having the dog Sit-Stay—duck behind a tree while out for a walk. Just wait for the dog to find you.

7. Work up to harder hiding places.

Generalize the behavior:

- Have the dog find a different person.
- Transfer the Find concept to objects rather than people, using a touch stick.
- Sometimes have the dog Find you, sometimes the keys, sometimes another person.
- Make the game progressively harder by using really tough hiding places.

Keep in Mind

You want the dog to be successful early, so be sure that finding you is very easy in the beginning. If the dog doesn't come to find you at all, think about the history for the dog. Does coming to you mean having his nails clipped or having a bath or the end of a fun romp? You'll have to work on making coming to you a rewarding behavior. Have the dog come to you for a game of Tug or a really great massage or for fun clicker sessions. Make yourself a fun person for your dog to be around.

If the dog sometimes comes to find you, but sometimes doesn't, the distractions in the environment may be too high or your reward may not be motivating enough. Switch to a more boring environment and make sure you have a treat or a toy your dog really likes. Make a big fuss over the dog when he does find you. Don't make him wait more than a few seconds before being released to find you.

Troubleshooting

I'm working on my own and the dog doesn't stay where I left him.

- Go back and work on Stay (see Chapter 2) until it's solid.

- Make the dog's wait time as short as possible—Sit the dog only a couple of feet from where you can duck around a corner or behind a door and release the dog as soon as you're out of sight.

- Practice leaving and immediately coming back and rewarding the dog for staying. Only release the dog to Find you every fifth or sixth time so he can't anticipate.

- Get another human to hold the dog so you can play the game.

The dog does something other than coming to find me when released.

- Practice Come in the house, being sure to make it upbeat and pleasurable for the dog (see Chapter 2). Not all dogs think coming to their owner in the house is a good thing.

- Make yourself more interesting—really get excited when the dog finds you, have a celebration (but don't go too far and scare your dog). Use your best treats and/or a favorite toy.

- Play in a really boring environment such as a long hallway, where there really isn't anything else for the dog to do.

The dog can't seem to find me once I make my hiding places more difficult.

- You may have made too big a jump in difficulty. Go back to easier hiding places and work up again. Plan your hiding places beforehand so you can be sure you're increasing difficulty gradually.

- Some physical problem could be impairing your dog's sense of hearing or smell. Have you noticed any other indications of something being amiss? If you think something physical may be going on, consult your veterinarian. Also, be aware that some medications can impact your dog's sense of smell.

• If your dog is new to clicker training and you skipped ahead to this chapter, he may not yet have the confidence to think for himself and problem solve. It will come over time. Go back and work on clicker training other behaviors to get the dog used to working through problems.

Variations

Use individual names when you cue the dog to search and you can have the dog searching for specific people. You can have a group of people hide and have the dog find you one after the other—teach the dog to lead each found person back to the starting point, then send him to Find the next person. This is particularly great for rounding up kids or even other dogs in the household!

Teach the dog the names of a variety of objects—the car keys, the remote control, your glasses—so you can ask him to Find any of them.

Slick Clicks: Finding keys—A useful trick

Thank you to Turid Rugaas, author of *On Talking Terms with Dogs,* for this wisdom. Turid has group classes in her native Norway, in a field surrounded by woods. At one class, a woman declined to take part, saying she didn't believe dogs could be trained by positive methods and would just observe for herself. She walked her large dog around the perimeter and in the woods the whole time the class was progressing. When class was over and people were leaving, the woman was still wandering around the woods. Turid finally asked what she was doing, and the woman was forced to admit that she had dropped her keys and couldn't find them. Turid called over one of her positively trained dogs, told the dog to "Find Keys," and the dog set off around the woods, tail wagging, and in less than a minute had found the missing keys. The woman, in a less than gracious response, shoved her dog into her car and drove off. But, Turid knew she'd demonstrated that dogs could indeed be positively trained to do quite useful things.

Detailed Training Plan

1. Put the dog in a Sit and tell him to "Stay" (or have your assistant hold him). Show him you have a treat, then let him watch while you duck around a corner or behind a door. Say your release word (or have the assistant let go). The dog should zoom straight to you as soon as he's released. Praise and treat when he finds you. Repeat five times.

2. Repeat, making your hiding place a little farther away or a little harder (around two corners or in a closet with the door partially closed). Praise and treat each time the dog finds you. Repeat three to five times.

3. If the dog is rushing to find you each time, start saying "Find (your name)" before you say your release word. If you are working with an assistant, have the assistant say "Find (your name)" just before releasing the dog.

Quick Clicks: Early cue addition

You may be wondering why we're adding a cue so early here. If the dog has come to find you the first few times, the odds are very good that he'll continue coming to find you. The 80% or better reliability is already there. Also, the behavior is complete right from the start—the dog finds you—so we can add the cue.

4. Now, don't let the dog watch you hide, so he isn't getting as much visual information. If you're working with another human, she can have the dog face away from you, or actually hide the dog's eyes. If you're working alone with the dog, you'll have to use visual barriers such as sitting the dog behind a couch, so you can move away without being seen. (Be aware that this can cause the dog to break the Stay cue. If this becomes a problem for you, end this session and work on strengthening the Stay cue before continuing with this behavior.) Say "Find (name)" and Release to your dog and wait to be found, or have your assistant say the same and release your dog. Praise and treat when the dog finds you. Repeat three to five times.

5. Start in a different location—have places in mind where you're going to hide. Put the dog in the place where you will leave him, tell him to "Stay," go out of sight, and, being as quiet as you can, go hide. Try to keep it the same level of difficulty—how long it takes you to hide, distance from the dog, and how distracting the environment is—as in Step 4. If working with an assistant, have her cover the dog's eyes before you depart. Say your cue and release, or have your assistant do so, and praise and treat when the dog finds you. Repeat three to five times.

6. To keep this from being the same static situation all the time—the game only happens if you leave the dog in a Stay—find times when you are out of sight of the dog, hide, and simply wait for the dog to find you. This is terrific for improving the dog's attention, because he learns that you'll try to run off if he's not watching you carefully. This is especially good to practice with puppies. It's a great game to play in the woods, where you can duck behind a tree while the dog is sniffing something (in a safe area, of course). But, you can also play it in the house by slipping behind doors or into closets while the dog is around a corner. You will probably only be able to do this one trial at a time, because the dog will stay with you once he's found you, anticipating more fun. Find times to do this whenever you can. Note: Dogs with separation anxiety problems may get worse if you randomly disappear on them.

Quick Clicks: Mix in Stay

Also, mix in some practice on the Stay cue by telling the dog to Stay, then coming back and releasing him instead of having him find you, so he doesn't get the idea to automatically run to look for you any time you leave him. (In this case, you want to reward the dog with a treat before you release him, so waiting for you to come back also provides a payoff.)

7. Gradually work up to harder hiding places. Plan your hiding places in advance, so you can rate their difficulty and know where you're going to hide each time.

8. Take the game outdoors. Be sure you're in a safe fenced environment. You're likely to have a lot more distractions in the great outdoors, so you may have to take less time hiding in a place closer to your dog so you don't lose him to distractions. If he doesn't come to find you when you say your cue and release, go back indoors and practice some more. Start back at Step 1 when you move back outdoors. Repeat three to five times at each level.

9. Work up to the same level of difficulty you achieved indoors.

10. If you have only been having the dog find you, switch to having another person hide. You might want to make the hiding place a little easier at first. Repeat three to five times.

11. Work back up to your previous level of difficulty with the new person.

Slick Clicks: The herding instinct

Cheryl's dog, Nestle, is part herding dog, so it was clear from the beginning that he liked having his friends, both human and canine, all in one place. It was only natural that on a nice short loop trail around a picnic area in the woods, when Cheryl took Nestle in one direction and her friend Judy took her dog, Diamond, in the other direction, Nestle would eagerly go Find the other person and dog. Then, he could be sent back to Find Cheryl. And so on, all the way around the walk. It was not only terrific training, it helped run Nestle much farther than the short distance of the path, burning off some of his abundant adolescent energy.

12. Transfer the Find concept to objects rather than people. Hold your touch stick next to the object—perhaps your car keys—say "Find Keys" as the dog goes to Touch, and CT when he touches the object. Repeat five times.

Quick Clicks: Explain the behavior

For the "Find an object" variation, you have to do a little more "explaining" to the dog of the behavior you want. Now, using a clicker (and a touch stick) can work in your favor. The behavior isn't complete right from the beginning—you have to get the dog to understand that finding otherwise boring objects can lead to rewards. If you understand this distinction, you'll be able to work out other times when you might not need to use a clicker.

13. Place the keys slightly farther from the dog, place the touch stick next to the keys, say "Find Keys" as the dog goes to touch, CT. Repeat five times.

14. Continue placing the keys in different positions, placing the touch stick next to them, saying "Find Keys," and CT when the dog goes to touch. Repeat for at least fifty more repetitions, changing locations every ten repetitions. Fade the touch stick at the same time, by holding it farther away form the keys every three to five repetitions.

15. Place the keys down close to the dog, without the touch stick. Say "Find Keys" and CT when the dog touches them. Repeat five times.

16. Gradually place the keys farther from the dog. Say "Find Keys," CT when the dog touches the keys. Repeat three to five times at each distance.

Generalize the behavior:

- Changing locations each time, have the dog Find you sometimes, the other person sometimes and the keys sometimes.

- If you have only been using food as a reward, play with a toy when the dog finds you instead. Vary your rewards. Include petting and praise.

- Gradually make the game more difficult. Add twists and turns to your path away from the dog. Go to a hiding place you've used before, but then go from there to a different hiding place. Hide the keys in tougher places. Be inventive.

 ## SCENTWORK/THREE BOWL MONTE

There are all sorts of variations of Scentwork. Every dog already knows how to use his nose. The trick is to teach the dog what you want him to look for. In Scentwork, the dog has to find a specific target scent amid a variety of choices. This behavior, and its variations, lends itself to a number of fun tricks and outlets for excess energy!

The instructions here are for a fun, easy-to-manage variant, based on Three Card Monte (or Find the Lady), a street corner betting game where three face-down playing cards are moved on a table and the bettor has to choose the "lady," the queen. For the dog, it becomes Three Bowl Monte, with the scent object taped inside one bowl and the bowls placed on the floor. The dog indicates, by pawing at, focusing on, or sitting in front of, the correct bowl. Have fun!

Sequim police officer Mike Hill and his K9 partner Titus (a rescue from the King County animal shelter) practice a find.

Suggested verbal cue: "Find it," "Sniff," "Seek," "Where Is It?"

You will need: Three bowls of the same material and size. A set of unbreakable cereal bowls would work well. A treat that can be taped to the inside of the bowl (so the bowl can be moved without dragging the treat across the floor). A solid Stay or an assistant to move the bowls.

Speed Steps

Because this is such a quick behavior to teach, and the instructions aren't very complex, we are only providing the following Speed Steps:

1. Tape a treat to the inside of one of your bowls. Put the bowl on the floor a few feet from the dog, let the dog approach the bowl, and when he sniffs or paws at the bowl, give him a treat. Repeat three times.

2. Put two bowls on the floor, one with the treat and one without, about two feet apart. Let the dog approach and when he sniffs or paws at the bowl with the treat, give him a treat. Repeat five times.

3. Now put all three bowls on the floor and repeat Step 2. Repeat five times, changing the position of the bowls each time.

Place all three bowls on the floor in front of you and the dog.

4. If you want a particular behavior that indicates the dog has found the scent such as a stand or a bark (called an "Alert"), work on adding it in this step. (The dog will need to have the Alert behavior on cue already.) When your dog paws or sniffs the correct bowl, cue the Alert that you want, and give the dog a treat when he complies. Repeat one to ten times, changing the position of the bowls each time.

Quick Clicks: A clicker would work here
You could use the clicker here to mark the completion of the Alert behavior.

5. Wait for the dog to offer the Alert signal you want. If he does, reward him quickly. If he doesn't, work at Step 4 for another session.

6. Gradually move the bowls closer together until they are each about a foot from one another.

7. Is your dog reliably indicating the bowl with the treat taped to it? Time to add your cue. Say your cue before you release your dog to sniff the bowls. Repeat approximately fifty times, moving the bowls every time and changing locations every ten times.

8. Have an assistant move the bowls around while you and the dog watch, so it really looks like you're playing the doggie equivalent of Three Card Monte.

Quick Clicks: Confusing scents

Be aware that, if your treat is placed on the floor underneath the bowl rather than taped into the bowl, its scent will linger. You will have to change locations for each repetition initially to make it easy for the dog. Many dogs can learn to find the stronger scent as they gain experience.

Generalize the behavior:

- Take it outside, where the environment is more distracting.

- Use a variety of treats, and let the dog have a whiff of the treat before you hide it so he knows what he's looking for.

Keep in Mind

You may try to follow the movement of the bowls by sight, but the dog is working on scent. It will help make it easier in the beginning if you keep the bowls separate by a foot or more.

Be sure you reward the dog with a treat at least as desirable as the one taped to the bowl, and keep your reward treats a good distance from the bowls, to prevent contaminating the scent area for the dog.

Troubleshooting

My dog doesn't find the bowl with the treat.

- It's possible his sense of smell is being impacted by some medical condition or medication he is taking. Check with your veterinarian.

- Maybe the dog isn't attracted to the treat you've taped into the bowl. Use something you know the dog will want to get at.

My dog attacks the bowl hiding the treat.

- Maybe your treat is a little too good! Switch to something a little less enticing.

- Cue the dog to Sit as soon as he starts his attack on the bowl, and give him his treat while he is sitting. After some number of repetitions, the dog will realize that he has to Sit to get what he wants, and the Sit will become his Find signal.

My dog isn't interested in the bowls.

- Play the game when your dog is hungry.

- Start out with the bowls on the floor, place a treat under one, run your dog to the bowls, turn over the one with the treat, and let your dog take the treat. Repeat this a few times, then try again with the treat taped in the bowl.

- Tape a treat under each of the bowls, so the dog is successful no matter what choice he makes. Then put a treat under only two bowls, then only under one.

Variations

You could do the same thing with a line of boxes with a favorite toy placed in one of them. The boxes help focus the dog on where to sniff, as well as help pool the scent. The very act of sniffing is rewarding to most dogs, so they'll be interested in checking out the boxes, and then are rewarded with treats and/or play when they find the toy. This is the basis for the K9 Nosework training mentioned below.

Tracking is a different application of Scentwork, but you could use Find Me and the Three Bowl Monte to get you started on your dog having the idea to look for you, and to indicate when he finds an appropriate scent. These are the two essential starting behaviors of Tracking.

Use the same theory to have your dog find the ace of spades (which is scented) from a deck of cards spread on the floor. Or, teach your dog to "read" by writing words like "Ham," "Swiss," "Bacon" on index cards and scenting them appropriately by placing them in a sealed bag with whatever food they name.

Slick Clicks: Nosework games

K9 Nosework is a new avenue to explore with your dog that is just gaining ground in California. It's based on the work that drug detection dogs do to find a particular scent. The training is appropriate for dogs of all ages (dogs from six months to eleven years old participated in the seminars that Mandy attended recently). The dogs are *thrilled* to participate—eight year old Ping was bouncing like a puppy every time she got a chance to do a Find! Since the dogs are worked individually in both the training and in competition, it's a terrific avenue for a less-able or older dog, or a dog that has issues with people or other dogs. (Check out http://www.k9nosework.com/ and http://www.nacsw.net/ for more information on training and competition events in your area. We encourage you to try this new sport if you have the chance.)

Combining behaviors and making chains

Just as we created complicated behaviors by CT-ing parts of the behavior and slowly building on them to the finished behavior, you can combine a series of finished behaviors into a behavior chain. For Fetch, we worked on the dog taking the object, holding it, going after it when it was thrown, and giving it up, and they all came together to form the behavior we call Fetch. You could do the same sort of thing by combining Sneeze, Down, Sneeze, Scentwork, Fetch, and Skateboard into a story line. Here's how it would look.

Your dog sneezes a couple of times, lies down, and sneezes some more. You say something like "Oh, you're not feeling well? Go and get your cold medicine." The dog goes to a number of bags, each labeled, and selects and brings back the one labeled "cold medicine." You take a "pill" (treat) out of the bag and give it to the dog, wait a second and ask "Feeling better?" and the dog responds by jumping on a skateboard and riding off.

Once the act is put together and the dog practices the combination sufficiently, you will not have to cue each separate behavior. The environment (the line of labeled bags and the skateboard) will tell the dog you are going to do the act, and once you cue the Sneeze, he'll continue on his own. Your patter becomes a cue of sorts, as you want the dog to Wait before proceeding to the next behavior, but you aren't cueing "Sneeze," "Sneeze," "Down," "Sneeze," "Sneeze," "Wait," "Find it," "Fetch," "Wait," "Board."

A more pure form of chaining (without the intervening human conversation) occurs in chicken camp (which were mentioned in Chapter 1). There's actually a level called Chaining. It uses an apparatus with a ladder leading up to a platform, then a balance beam to another platform, then a ladder leading down. The campers have to teach a chicken to walk up the ladder, perform a behavior on the first platform, walk across the balance beam, perform a behavior on the second platform, and walk down the ladder. Once the chicken learns what to do at each place, the apparatus and props provide the cues. The trainer has to put the chicken on the table and then have no more interaction until the chicken finishes walking down the final ladder. It's up to the campers in what order they want to train the separate behaviors and what behaviors the chicken will perform on the platforms, but they all have to end up with one continuous chain with only one reward at the end.

The campers have to teach a chicken to walk up the ladder and perform a series of behaviors in a chain. This chicken is just learning to navigate the apparatus.

Let's say that you want to compete in dog sports. How might chains benefit you?
The behaviors in AKC Novice Obedience are performed in the same order every time. The entire performance is actually one big behavior chain. You can still give all the cues you are permitted, but if your dog knows that for novice-level obedience, you always do Heel on Leash, then Heel Off Leash, then Stand for Examination, then Re-call, and you've practiced that way, and made it all rewarding, then he'll know what's coming next and be ready to perform. For higher levels of AKC obedience (and in rally) the order of the exercises changes, but each exercise is the same from start to finish. For example, in Retrieve Over a Jump, the dog sits next to you, the dumbbell is thrown, the dog is cued to get it, he jumps the jump, picks it up, returns over the jump, sits in front of you, and is cued to release the dumbbell. This is one long chain of behaviors that can be put together effectively.

In agility, the obstacles are put together in a different order each time. But each obstacle is performed in the same way every time, and there are some common transitions (such as a serpentine of jumps) that the dog will see many times in his career. It would be worthwhile to spend the time to create a chain of behavior for the specific patterns that the dog will see on courses.

Freestyle is a dog sport just made for chaining. The handler devises a routine for handler and dog choreographed to music. The handler can verbally cue each move, but inevitably the dog is more reliable on some moves than on others. You can use not just chaining, but the Premack Principle as well, to make it more likely that your dog will perform the shaky behavior.

Spin is a behavior that frequently seems to fail in the freestyle ballroom. Take Spin and put a behavior after it your dog really loves to do, maybe put his front Feet Up on your hip. Remember Grandma's Rule—you have to eat your vegetables to get dessert. Now your dog has to Spin before he can do the Paws Up move. The repeated pairing of the not-as-well-liked behavior with the highly favored behavior will make the less liked behavior more rewarding and more likely to occur on cue.

To put this into practice, cue Spin, and as soon as the dog does however many spins you require, cue Paws Up. Then reward. Spin gets doubly rewarded by being at the beginning of the chain. Of course, you can't bring any food or toys into the freestyle ring (or most other competition venues). But the Premack Principle will still work to strengthen the Spin behavior.

The emphasis in working with chains should be in the links between pairs of behaviors. In an A-B-C-D chain, it's the pattern of going from A-B, from B-C, and from C-D that you should build. It's not necessary to build a chain A-B, then A-B-C, then A-B-C-D (called forward chaining) or even C-D, then B-C-D, then A-B-C-D (called backward chaining). It doesn't really matter where you start, as long as the connection between each pair of behaviors is strong (the links). This also means that if any part of the behavior falls apart, you can take just that piece out and strengthen it separately, then put it back in the chain. Going back to our Fetch example, if the dog won't hold onto the object while he is walking toward you, you can work on just that piece, then put it back into the Fetch sequence when it's perfect.

You can chain many behaviors together. Just give some thought to where to start and stop a chain. And don't worry that you won't be able to change the behavior order—you can always break the chain and make a new one. You'll just build new links between behaviors.

When/How to get rid of the clicker for a behavior

You don't need to carry a clicker around with you for the rest of your life (though it's not a bad idea, especially if you want to capture behavior). Remember, the utility of the clicker is its ability to precisely mark a behavior or piece of behavior so you can reward it and increase its likelihood of occurrence. Once you have a behavior the way you want it and on cue, you can dispense with the clicker. You can go cold turkey and just stop using the clicker, you can substitute a bridge word or you can just give a treat. We don't find that most dogs notice when the clicker is gone, although many of them are more focused when the clicker is being used. Some dogs actually find the clicker motivating, so you'll want to experiment with how your dog reacts to the absence of it.

If the dog seems to be foundering without the clicker, you can gradually wean him off of it. Start on a generalization step. About every three repetitions, don't click. Just treat and release if the circumstances require it or if the behavior is one that ends naturally, just give a treat. When you have done several repetitions without the click, stop and assess how your dog responds. Most dogs will not be at all bothered, but if your dog seems confused over the lack of a click, substitute your bridge word. Gradually make a greater percentage of repetitions without a click, until you are no longer using it at all.

Once the behavior is on cue and you are no longer using the clicker, you will still be reinforcing the behavior, but you'll want to vary the types of rewards you offer. Using a variety of rewards keeps the dog playing the game, just like getting a variety of rewards (money, fame, recognition, good feelings) at work keeps you at your desk.

Some trainers insist that you should also vary how often you give a reward. But we've found that humans are fairly casual (and random) in delivering rewards once they have a behavior, so you won't really need to focus on that. You'll already be doing it. For more information on random reinforcement, see the next section.

Reinforcement schedules

We've talked a bit about rate of reinforcement (how many times and how fast the dog gets rewarded) at the beginning of the book. Your rate must be high or you risk losing your dog's interest while they are learning. Learning requires a lot of effort and must be abundantly rewarded. We also want to address schedules of reinforcement, or which behaviors get reinforced.

One of the complaints often lodged against clicker training is that the dog won't perform if the handler doesn't have a treat available. If that happens, it's the fault of the handler, not the training method. Continuous and variable schedules of reinforcement affect how a behavior is maintained.

While you are teaching a behavior you use a continuous schedule of reward—every time the dog performs the desired behavior, you click and give a reward. Once a behavior is established and on cue, you probably want to change to a variable schedule of reward. That means that the dog is not rewarded every time he does the behavior. It's important that you have the behavior solidly to the level that you want, because introducing variable reinforcement can also introduce variability into the behavior (remember our twofers!) You should switch to variable reinforcement only after a behavior is fluent—it looks the way you want it to, as fast as you want it, in every environment you want it in.

Staying on a continuous schedule of reinforcement once a behavior is established can mean that if, all of a sudden, the behavior is not being rewarded every time, the dog stops offering the behavior (called extinction). Think of it this way: If you put a dollar in a soda machine, you expect a soda to come out. If that didn't happen, you'd probably stop putting dollars in that machine. If it started happening with other soda machines, you probably wouldn't use them at all.

With a variable schedule of reinforcement, sometimes three behaviors in a row are rewarded, but sometimes five behaviors might be necessary before a reward is forthcoming. Getting a payoff from a slot machine and catching a fish are both examples of variable reinforcement for humans. And think how obsessed people can become with pulling that lever or casting that line. Variable schedules of reinforcement encourage the player, be they fisherman or dog, to keep trying. Behavior becomes very resistant to extinction.

One of the ways that beginners can move easily to variable reinforcement is to vary the TYPE of rewards given. We've discussed them earlier as life rewards. The dog will have a preference for some rewards over others. Once you have the behavior named, looking the way you want it to, and generalized, it's a great idea to start to vary the types of rewards, and to occasionally "forget" to give a reward (a pretty easy task for the average human). This helps keep the behavior strong, and resistant to extinction when you can't reinforce every instance.

Here are some ways you can use primary reinforcers other than food:

- Reward attention by letting your dog visit another person or dog.
- Reward coming when called by letting your dog run loose (under safe conditions, of course).
- Reward sitting quietly with rambunctious play.
- Reward walking beside you with moving forward.

- Reward any behavior with access to a distraction.

- Reward waiting (to get out of the car or into the water) with movement (getting out of the car or into the water).

Give the dog a few moments to enjoy the reward, then lead or call the dog back to you. Ask for another behavior, and again release the dog to the reward. You are conditioning the dog to understand that he must wait for permission to get the reward (sometimes called a life reward), which will improve his attention around distractions. Start with the dog on leash, if you have to, so he can't help himself to the reward until you release him.

You can also pair things like clapping, whistling, throwing your arms up, or other cues with a your dog's primary reinforcers, to make them secondary reinforcers. This would be valuable if you have a competition dog, because your ability to use treats or toys while competing is limited.

For more details on reinforcement schedules and how they impact training, see the excellent book *Excel-erated Learning* by Pamela Reid, PhD.

We hope you enjoy clicker training as much as we have enjoyed bringing it to you and teaching it to our own dogs! Good luck with your training, and remember, it's supposed to be fun!

Nestle is an 11-year-old Kelpie mix who has earned titles in agility and freestyle, and sometimes works as a ranch dog with sheep. He is a Canine Good Citizen and registered therapy dog. He has been clicker trained since Cheryl adopted him at about 5 months old.

GLOSSARY

Back chaining—training a behavior or series of steps by starting with the end piece and working backwards. For example, a formal retrieve involves the following steps: dog sits, dumbbell is thrown, dog is sent to pick up, dog returns with dumbbell, dog sits in front of owner, owner takes dumbbell. In back-chaining, the first behavior taught would be the last behavior in the sequence, giving up the dumbbell. Then the dog would be taught to Sit in front and give up the dumbbell, and so on. The idea is that you are always training into familiar territory.

Behavior—Anything an animal does.

Bouncing Around an average—a technique used to increase distance or duration on a behavior. It involves choosing an average count to vary around (rather than counting the same amount every time). The average count is gradually increased although the actual count is different every time.

Bridge—Anything that functions as a predictor of a reward or a punishment for the animal. The bridge can be sound, touch, taste, smell or visual. Bridges can be intentional (such as pairing a sound with a treat) or unintentional (such as pairing getting the clippers out with toenail clipping). Also called a marker.

Capturing behavior—Taking advantage of something the dog does naturally (such as stretch or yawn) by marking and rewarding when it happens so that it happens more frequently.

Criteria—A principle or standard by which something is judged. A piece of the behavior that is shaped in a particular step.

Crossover dog/crossover trainer—A dog or trainer who has learned or taught behaviors using methods such as food luring or collar corrections, and who now switches to clicker training.

Cue—Anything that provides information to the animal about what behavior they should do (cues can be intentionally added or may just be observed as a precursor by the animal).

Duration—Increasing distance or time performed on a behavior. One of the more difficult aspects of a behavior to modify.

Extinction—Eliminating a behavior by ignoring it or not rewarding it.

Fluency—The ability to do the behavior accurately in many different environments.

Generalization—Practicing under a variety of different circumstances so that the animal understands the behavior is always the same regardless of the environment. One of the ways to get fluency in a behavior.

Hot object—The designated target object. The object the animal is being rewarded for touching.

Jackpot—Giving a high value reward for a large effort, or giving multiple rewards for one effort. Jackpots have not been shown scientifically to have an impact on learning, except in very specific circumstances.

Life reward—Something that the animal likes to do, and would seek out and find rewarding, such as water, social contact, chasing or the opportunity to do something. As a human, you have control of a lot of the dog's life rewards.

Limited hold—The "open bar" concept is also called a limited hold. It means that the opportunity to earn treats is only available for a certain amount of time. It tends to speed the dog's response time.

Lumping—Trying to take steps too big, too quickly or trying to combine steps.

Luring—Using a treat, a toy, a target or another behavior to get the dog to do a behavior. Luring is not in itself a bad thing. It can be very useful in getting the behavior, but it's important to understand how to use it in a way that helps your training.

Mark, marker—A generic term for anything used to indicate to the animal that the behavior was correct. Markers are paired with a reward. Ex: A clicker or bridge word.

Meeting criteria—Generally defined as doing the behavior in the way specified in a particular step. If the dog "meets (or exceeds) criteria" 80% of the time, it is time to move on to the next step.

On cue—Doing a behavior when indicated. If the dog sits when told, "Sit," the Sit is said to be on cue.

Premack Principle—Using a high probability behavior (something the dog gets a lot of reinforcement for or intrinsically enjoys) to reinforce low probability behaviors (something that isn't reinforced often, or that the dog doesn't particularly care about). Many trainers call it "Grandma's Rule," otherwise stated as, "you have to eat dinner before you get dessert."

Primary reinforcer—Something the animal naturally finds reinforcing and will work to get or keep. Commonly identified as food, water, sleep. Some researchers also add play, social contact , etc. Other primary reinforcers might include freedom or physical contact.

Rate of reinforcement—How often or fast the reward is being delivered (usually referring to the speed of clicks and treats delivered).

Repetition—One CT pairing.

Reversal—Changing the hot target or changing the directionality of the behavior to the opposite.

Secondary reinforcer—Something that becomes reinforcing by being paired with a primary reinforcer. It gains value by being associated with a primary reinforcer. When you click and then treat, or smile and then pet your dog, you are "conditioning" the click or the smile to be a secondary reinforcer.

Session—One set of repetitions (typically ten clicks and treats).

Shaping—Creating behavior by breaking it into a series of steps that approximate the final desired behavior and rewarding each step multiple times. Being able to work in small steps is one of the major advantages of clicker training.

Splitting—Breaking behaviors down into a series of finely differentiated steps.

Stacking cues—Adding one cue to another. Used in discrimination behaviors such as left and right, up and down, or big and little. Combining cues in sequence such as having the dog select the "right, big" item.

Step—One set of criteria in a shaping plan.

Timing—Being able to accurately mark (click or use a bridge word) and deliver a reward when the dog has met criteria.

Topography—What the behavior looks like or the dimensions of a behavior such as duration, intensity, repetitiveness and accuracy.

RESOURCES

Websites

http://www.agilityinmotion.com/—agility fitness and training DVDs

http://www.alphadogtoys.com/scrungee_bungee_plush_dog_toys_squeaker_rattle.
html—one site for the Scrungee Bungee mentioned in Chapter 6, also search the web
www.apdt.org—finding a trainer who uses positive, treat-based training

http://www.behavior1.com/—Bob and Marian Bailey's site on behavior

www.cleanrun.com—treats, toys, supplies, balance domes and pods

www.clickandtreat.com—Gary Wilkes' site for books, videos, supplies including targets

http://www.clickersolutions.com/—articles, website and mailing list, run by Melissa Alexander

www.clickertraining.com—Karen Pryor's site for books, videos, supplies, and articles

www.doggonegood.com—treats and supplies for clicker training

www.dogwelfarecampaign.org/index.php—current research in dog training

www.dogwise.com—books, videos, toys. Search "clicker" to find a number of great books, DVDs and tools for clicker training. Dogwise is a source for the *Cavaletti* DVD on flexibility and the *Pilates for Pooches* DVD.

http://www.jjdog.com/—dumbbells and formal obedience tools, basic supplies

http://www.k9nosework.com/—K9 Nosework training information website

www.learningaboutdogs.com—Kay Laurence's training website, including books and DVDs

www.legacycanine.com—conferences and seminars on dogs, touch sticks, host of chicken camps

http://www.nacsw.net/—National Association of Canine Scentwork competition website

www.nosetouch.com—some fun electronic training tools and targets

http://www.premierflyballbox.com/—flyball box or search the web for "flyball box" for plans to make one

www.ruffwear.com—canine life jackets

http://www.shirleychong.com/keepers/nailfile.html—information on nail filing behavior

www.silvia.trkman.net—videos of a variety of tricks from a talented trainer

http://www.tawzerdogvideos.com/—videos of a multitude of great trainers on different topics

http://www.wolverinesports.com/—hurdle cones and balance domes (this is a difficult site to navigate, try searching for "hurdle cones" to find the Multi-HEIGHT Hurdle Cones specified in Chapter 7)

www.writedog.com—Cheryl's website

YouTube

You can find lots of great clicker training videos for a wide variety of species on YouTube, and also some not-so-great ones. Below are some of our favorites.

www.youtube.com/user/pamelamaxsen—variety of fun videos of clicker training in action

www.youtube.com/user/kikopup—variety of videos of clicker principles such as adding a cue

http://www.youtube.com/user/twoTAWZERDOGVIDEOS—clips from videos available for sale

Recommended Reading

Animal Training: Successful Animal Management through Positive Reinforcement, Ken Ramirez—clicker training a variety of species

Behavior Modification, What It Is and How to Do It, Garry Martin and Joseph Pear—all the scientific details in an easy to understand book

Choose to Heel, Dawn Jecs—training easily accommodates using a clicker

Click for Joy, Melissa Alexander—answering common clicker training questions

Click to Calm, Emma Parsons—specifically for fearful and aggressive dogs

Clicker Journal—order at www.clickertrain.com—includes articles on training other species

Control Unleashed, Leslie McDevitt—working with reactive dogs

Culture Clash, Jean Donaldson—behavior problems, general dog behavior, desensitization and counter-conditioning programs

Don't Shoot the Dog, Karen Pryor—The "bible" of clicker training

Excel-erated Learning, Pamela Reid, PhD—reinforcement schedules and how they impact training.

Right on Target, Mandy Book and Cheryl Smith—detailed training using target sticks

The Thinking Dog, Gail Fisher—how to crossover to clicker training

Anything by John Rogerson—his most current book is *The Dog Vinci Code*

INDEX OF BEHAVIORS

Hold still	Ch. 3 (Relax for Vet Exam)	Dog lies quietly on his side while someone examines his body
Hup	Ch. 6 (Jump into Arms)	Dog jumps into arms
Jump into arms	Ch. 6	Dog jumps into arms
Launch	Ch. 5 (Paw Touch)	Dog touches target with paw
Leave It	Ch. 4	Dog removes his nose/teeth/paws from whatever he is touching
Let me see	Ch. 5 (Possession Problems)	Dog willingly gives up whatever he has
Lick lips	Ch. 5 (Sneeze)	Dog licks lips on cue
Look	Ch. 2 (Attention)	Dog looks at you when requested

Matching rewards to behavior Ch. 5

Mine	Ch. 5 (Possession Problems)	Dog willingly gives up whatever he has
Mother may I?	Ch. 5 (Focus)	Dog looks first to you for permission if he wants something
Moving wait	Ch. 2	Dog stops forward movement
Nice	Ch. 2 (Take a Treat Gently)	Dog takes treat from fingertips without injuring you, using his tongue
Nose	Ch. 5 (Touch)	Dog touches target with nose
Nosework	Ch. 7 (Scentwork)	Dog finds a scented item among a number of choices
Off	Ch. 4 (Leave It)	Dog removes his nose/teeth/paws from whatever he is touching
Offer Paw	Ch. 3	Dog lifts his paw
Orbit	Ch. 6 (Balance Work)	Dog puts front Feet Up on stool and circles around on his back feet
Pace work	Ch. 6	Dog single steps through hurdles
Park it	Ch. 2 (Sit)	Dog puts rear on ground

Paw TouCh.	Ch. 5	Dog touCh.es target with paw
Paint	Ch. 5 (Paw Touch)	Dog swipes with paw to create painting
Play dead	Ch.3 (Relax for Vet Exam)	Dog lies flat on side
Playing with toys	Ch. 5	Adding value to a toy so the dog wants it
Play's Over, Go Play	Ch. 4	Dog stops what he is doing to go with handler, then is released to play again
Pose	Ch. 3 (Freeze)	Dog freezes in place
Possession Problems	Ch. 5	Dog willingly gives up anything he has
Problem barking	Ch. 5	Dog comes to check in when someone walks by your front window
Punch	Ch. 5 (Paw Touch)	Dog touches target with paw
Push	Ch. 5 (Paw Touch)	Dog touches target with paw
Recall	Ch. 2 (Come)	Dog comes directly to you when requested
Relax for veterinary exams	Ch. 3	Dog lies quietly on his side while someone examines his body
Resource guarding	Ch. 4 (Possession Problems)	Dog willingly gives up anything he has
Retrieve	Ch. 5 (Fetch)	Dog runs to pick up throw object, brings it back and gives it to handler
Ride	Ch. 6 (Skateboard)	Dog rides a skateboard
Roll a ball	Ch. 6 (Skateboard)	Dog rolls ball with front feet
Roll a barrel	Ch. 6 (Skateboard)	Dog rolls barrel with front feet
Rotate	Ch. 6 (Balance Work)	Dog puts front feet on stool and circles around with his back feet
Scentwork	Ch. 7	Dog finds scented item among choices

Search	Ch. 7 (Find Me)	Dog waits until told to find person
Seek	Ch. 7 (Find Me)	Dog waits until told to find person
Settle	Ch. 3 (Relax for Vet Exam)	Dog lies quietly on his side while someone examines his body
Shake	Ch. 3 (Offer Paw)	Dog puts paw in your hand
Sit	Ch. 2	Dog puts rear on ground
Sit at a Distance	Ch. 2 (Wait)	Dog puts rear on ground at a distance
Sit-Stay	Ch. 4	Dog sits while you let someone into the house or greet someone on the street
Sit Up	Ch. 6 (Jump into Arms)	Dog sits up on haunches
Skateboard	Ch. 6	Dog rides a skateboard
Sneeze	Ch. 5	Dog sneezes on cue
Standing still for grooming	Ch. 3	Dog stands quietly while you bathe or groom him
Stand Up	Ch. 6 (Jump into Arms)	Dog stands up on hind legs
Stay	Ch. 3 (Stand Still for Grooming)	Dog stands quietly while you bathe or groom him
Stomp	Ch. 5 (Paw Touch)	Dog touches target with paw
Swimming	Ch. 6	Dog swims with or without a life jacket
Take a Treat Gently	Ch. 2	Dog takes treat from fingertips without injuring you, using his tongue
Three bowl monte	Ch. 7 (Scentwork)	Dog indicates the bowl that hides a treat
Tilt your head	Ch. 5	Dog tilts his head in either direction
Toenail clipping	Ch. 3	Dog allows you to clip his nails
Touch (nose)	Ch. 6	Dog touches target with nose
Tug	Ch. 5	Dog plays tug by the rules

INDEX

From Dogwise Publishing
www.dogwise.com   1-800-776-2665

BEHAVIOR & TRAINING

ABC's of Behavior Shaping. Proactive Behavior Mgmt, DVD set. Ted Turner

Aggression In Dogs. Practical Mgmt, Prevention, & Behaviour Modification. Brenda Aloff

Am I Safe? DVD. Sarah Kalnajs

Barking. The Sound of a Language. Turid Rugaas

Behavior Problems in Dogs, 3rd ed. William Campbell

Brenda Aloff's Fundamentals: Foundation Training for Every Dog, DVD. Brenda Aloff

Bringing Light to Shadow. A Dog Trainer's Diary. Pam Dennison

Canine Body Language. A Photographic Guide to the Native Language of Dogs. Brenda Aloff

Changing People Changing Dogs. Positive Solutions for Difficult Dogs. Rev. Dee Ganley

Chill Out Fido! How to Calm Your Dog. Nan Arthur

Clicked Retriever. Lana Mitchell

Do Over Dogs. Give Your Dog a Second Chance for a First Class Life. Pat Miller

Dog Behavior Problems. The Counselor's Handbook. William Campbell

Dog Friendly Gardens, Garden Friendly Dogs. Cheryl Smith

Dog Language, An Encyclopedia of Canine Behavior. Roger Abrantes

Dogs are from Neptune. Jean Donaldson

Evolution of Canine Social Behavior, 2nd ed. Roger Abrantes

From Hoofbeats to Dogsteps. A Life of Listening to and Learning from Animals. Rachel Page Elliott

Get Connected With Your Dog, book with DVD. Brenda Aloff

Give Them a Scalpel and They Will Dissect a Kiss, DVD. Ian Dunbar

Guide to Professional Dog Walking And Home Boarding. Dianne Eibner

Language of Dogs, DVD. Sarah Kalnajs

Mastering Variable Surface Tracking, Component Tracking (2 bk set). Ed Presnall

My Dog Pulls. What Do I Do? Turid Rugaas

New Knowledge of Dog Behavior (reprint). Clarence Pfaffenberger

Oh Behave! Dogs from Pavlov to Premack to Pinker. Jean Donaldson

On Talking Terms with Dogs. Calming Signals, 2nd edition. Turid Rugaas

On Talking Terms with Dogs. What Your Dog Tells You, DVD. Turid Rugaas

Play With Your Dog. Pat Miller

Positive Perspectives. Love Your Dog, Train Your Dog. Pat Miller

Positive Perspectives 2. Know Your Dog, Train Your Dog. Pat Miller

Predation and Family Dogs, DVD. Jean Donaldson

Quick Clicks, 2nd Edition. Mandy Book and Cheryl Smith

Really Reliable Recall. Train Your Dog to Come When Called, DVD. Leslie Nelson

Right on Target. Taking Dog Training to a New Level. Mandy Book & Cheryl Smith

Stress in Dogs. Martina Scholz & Clarissa von Reinhardt

Tales of Two Species. Essays on Loving and Living With Dogs. Patricia McConnell

The Dog Trainer's Resource. The APDT Chronicle of the Dog Collection. Mychelle Blake (*ed*)

The Dog Trainer's Resource 2. The APDT Chronicle of the Dog Collection. Mychelle Blake (*ed*)

The Thinking Dog. Crossover to Clicker Training. Gail Fisher

Therapy Dogs. Training Your Dog To Reach Others. Kathy Diamond Davis

Training Dogs. A Manual (reprint). Konrad Most

Training the Disaster Search Dog. Shirley Hammond

Try Tracking. The Puppy Tracking Primer. Carolyn Krause

Visiting the Dog Park, Having Fun, and Staying Safe. Cheryl S. Smith

When Pigs Fly. Train Your Impossible Dog. Jane Killion

Winning Team. A Guidebook for Junior Showmanship. Gail Haynes

Working Dogs (reprint). Elliot Humphrey & Lucien Warner

HEALTH & ANATOMY, SHOWING

Advanced Canine Reproduction and Whelping. Sylvia Smart

An Eye for a Dog. Illustrated Guide to Judging Purebred Dogs. Robert Cole

Annie On Dogs! Ann Rogers Clark

Another Piece of the Puzzle. Pat Hastings

Canine Cineradiography DVD. Rachel Page Elliott

Canine Massage. A Complete Reference Manual. Jean-Pierre Hourdebaigt

Canine Terminology (reprint). Harold Spira

Breeders Professional Secrets. Ethical Breeding Practices. Sylvia Smart

Dog In Action (reprint). Macdowell Lyon

Dog Show Judging. The Good, the Bad, and the Ugly. Chris Walkowicz

Dogsteps DVD. Rachel Page Elliott

The Healthy Way to Stretch Your Dog. A Physical Theraphy Approach. Sasha Foster and Ashley Foster

The History and Management of the Mastiff. Elizabeth Baxter & Pat Hoffman

Performance Dog Nutrition. Optimize Performance With Nutrition. Jocelynn Jacobs

Positive Training for Show Dogs. Building a Relationship for Success Vicki Ronchette

Puppy Intensive Care. A Breeder's Guide To Care Of Newborn Puppies. Myra Savant Harris

Raw Dog Food. Make It Easy for You and Your Dog. Carina MacDonald

Raw Meaty Bones. Tom Lonsdale

Shock to the System. The Facts About Animal Vaccination... Catherine O'Driscoll

Tricks of the Trade. From Best of Intentions to Best in Show, Rev. Ed. Pat Hastings

Work Wonders. Feed Your Dog Raw Meaty Bones. Tom Lonsdale

Whelping Healthy Puppies, DVD. Sylvia Smart

Phone in your Order! 1.800.776.2665 8am-4pm PST / 11am-7pm EST

Sign in | View Cart

Search Dogwise

Everything ▼

GO

Browse Dogwise

Books & Products
* By Subject
* Dogwise Picks
* Best Sellers
* Best New Titles

Book Reviews
* Find Out How

Resources & Info
* Dogwise Forums
* Dogwise Newsletters
* Dogwise Email List
* Customer Reading Lists
* Dog Show Schedule
* Let Us Know About Your Book or DVD
* Become an Affiliate
* APDT, CPDT
* IAABC
* CAPPDT

Help & Contacts
* About Us
* Contact Us
* Shipping Policy

Employee Picks!
See which books the Dogwise staff members love to read.
* Click Here!

Dog Show Supplies from The 3C's
* Visit the 3C's Website
* View our selection of 3c products.

Save up to 80% on Bargain Books! Click here for Sale, Clearance and hard to find Out of Print titles!
* Click Here!

Prefer to order by phone? Call Us!
1-800-776-2665
8AM - 4PM M-F Pacific Time

Be the First to Hear the News!
Have New Product and Promotion Announcements Emailed to You.
Click Here To Sign Up!

Free Shipping for Orders over $75 - click here for more information!

Win a $25 Dogwise credit - click here to find out how!

Featured New Titles

STRESS IN DOGS - LEARN HOW DOGS SHOW STRESS AND WHAT YOU CAN DO TO HELP, by Martina Scholz & Clarissa von Reinhardt
Item: DTB909
Is stress causing your dog's behavior problems? Research shows that as with humans, many behavioral problems in dogs are stress-related. Learn how to recognize when your dog is stressed, what factors cause stress in dogs, and strategies you can utilize in training and in your daily life with your dog to reduce stress.
Price: $14.95 more information...
DIG IN

SUCCESS IS IN THE PROOFING - A GUIDE FOR CREATIVE AND EFFECTIVE TRAINING, by Debby Quigley & Judy Ramsey
Item: DTO230
The success is indeed in the proofing! Proofing is an essential part of training, but one that is often overlooked or not worked on enough. We all know the story of the dog who can perform a variety of behaviors perfectly in the backyard but falls apart in the obedience ring. This book is full of great ideas and strategies to help your dog do his best no matter what the distractions or conditions may be. Whether competing in Rally or Obedience, trainers everywhere will find this very portable and user friendly book an indispensable addition to their tool box.
Price: $19.95 more information...
DIG IN

REALLY RELIABLE RECALL DVD, by Leslie Nelson
Item: DTB810P
From well-known trainer Leslie Nelson! Easy to follow steps to train your dog to come when it really counts, in an emergency. Extra chapters for difficult to train breeds and training class instructors.
Price: $29.95 more information...
DIG IN

THE DOG TRAINERS RESOURCE - APDT CHRONICLE OF THE DOG COLLECTION, by Mychelle Blake, Editor
Item: DTB880
The modern professional dog trainer needs to develop expertise in a wide variety of fields: learning theory, training techniques, classroom strategies, marketing, community relations, and business development and management. This collection of articles from APDT's Chronicle of the Dog will prove a valuable resource for trainers and would-be trainers.
Price: $24.95 more information...
DIG IN

SHAPING SUCCESS - THE EDUCATION OF AN UNLIKELY CHAMPION, by Susan Garrett
Item: DTA260
Written by one of the world's best dog trainers. Shaping Success gives an excellent explanation of the theory behind animal learning as Susan Garrett trains a high-energy Border Collie puppy to be an agility champion. Buzzy's story both entertains and demonstrates how to apply some of the most up-to-date dog training methods in the real world. Clicker training!
Price: $24.95 more information...
DIG IN

FOR THE LOVE OF A DOG - UNDERSTANDING EMOTION IN YOU AND YOUR BEST FRIEND, by Patricia McConnell
Item: DTB890
Sure to be another bestseller, Trish McConnell's latest book takes a look at canine emotions and body language. Like all her books, this one is written in a way that the average dog owner can follow but brings the latest scientific information that trainers and dog enthusiasts can use.
Price: $24.95 more information...
DIG IN

HELP FOR YOUR FEARFUL DOG: A STEP-BY-STEP GUIDE TO HELPING YOUR DOG CONQUER HIS FEARS, by Nicole Wilde
Item: DTB878
From popular author and trainer Nicole Wilde! A comprehensive guide to the treatment of canine anxiety, fears, and phobias. Chock full of photographs and illustrations and written in a down-to-earth, humorous style.
Price: $24.95 more information...
DIG IN

FAMILY FRIENDLY DOG TRAINING - A SIX WEEK PROGRAM FOR YOU AND YOUR DOG, by Patricia McConnell & Aimee Moore
Item: DTB917
A six-week program to get people and dogs off on the right paw! Includes trouble-shooting tips for what to do when your dog doesn't respond as expected. This is a book that many trainers will want their students to read.
Price: $11.95 more information...
DIG IN

THE LANGUAGE OF DOGS - UNDERSTANDING CANINE BODY LANGUAGE AND OTHER COMMUNICATION SIGNALS DVD SET, by Sarah Kalnajs
Item: DTB875P
Features a presentation and extensive footage of a variety of breeds showing hundreds of examples of canine behavior and body language. Perfect for dog owners or anyone who handles dogs or encounters them regularly while on the job.
Price: $39.95 more information...
DIG IN

THE FAMILY IN DOG BEHAVIOR CONSULTING, by Lynn Hoover
Item: DTB887
Sometimes, no matter how good a trainer or behavior consultant you are, there are issues going on within a human family that you need to be aware of to solve behavior or training problems with dogs. For animal behavior consultants, this text opens up new vistas of challenge and opportunity, dealing with the intense and sometimes complicated nature of relationships between families and dogs.
Price: $24.95 more information...
DIG IN

MORE FROM Dogwise Publishing

WHELPING HEALTHY PUPPIES DVD - Sylvia Smart

AGGRESSION IN DOGS: PRACTICAL MANAGEMENT, PREVENTION & BEHAVIOUR MODIFICATION - Brenda Aloff

PUPPY INTENSIVE CARE: A BREEDER'S GUIDE TO CARE OF NEWBORN PUPPIES - Myra Savant-Harris

TRAINING THE DISASTER SEARCH DOG - Shirley Hammond

GIVE THEM A SCALPEL AND THEY WILL DISSECT A KISS: DOG TRAINING PAST, PRESENT, AND FUTURE DVD - Ian Dunbar

PERFORMANCE DOG NUTRITION: OPTIMIZE PERFORMANCE WITH NUTRITION - Jocelynn Jacobs

PREDATION IN FAMILY DOGS: PREDATION, PREDATORY DRIFT AND PREPAREDNESS SEMINAR DVD - Jean Donaldson

CANINE REPRODUCTION AND WHELPING - A DOG BREEDER'S GUIDE - Myra Savant-Harris

RAW MEATY BONES - Tom Lonsdale

CANINE MASSAGE: A COMPLETE REFERENCE MANUAL - Jean-Pierre Hourdebaigt

DOG LANGUAGE: AN ENCYCLOPEDIA OF CANINE BEHAVIOR - Roger Abrantes

MASTERING VARIABLE SURFACE TRACKING BOOK AND WORKBOOK - Ed Presnall

SHOCK TO THE SYSTEM - THE FACTS ABOUT ANIMAL VACCINATION, PET FOOD AND HOW TO KEEP YOUR PETS HEALTHY - Catherine O'Driscoll

THERAPY DOGS: TRAINING YOUR DOG TO REACH OTHERS - Kathy Diamond Davis

TRY TRACKING! THE PUPPY TRACKING PRIMER - Carolyn Krause

WORK WONDERS, FEED YOUR DOG RAW MEATY BONES - Tom Lonsdale

Find out what professional dog trainers from APDT recommend to read and watch!

Click Here for CPDT Reference Books Carried by Dogwise